Guitar Player

THE INSIDE STORY OF THE FIRST TWO DECADES OF
THE MOST SUCCESSFUL GUITAR MAGAZINE EVER

Guitar Player

THE INSIDE STORY OF THE FIRST TWO DECADES OF
THE MOST SUCCESSFUL GUITAR MAGAZINE EVER

EDITED BY
JIM CROCKETT

WITH
DARA CROCKETT

**Backbeat
Books**

An Imprint of Hal Leonard Corporation

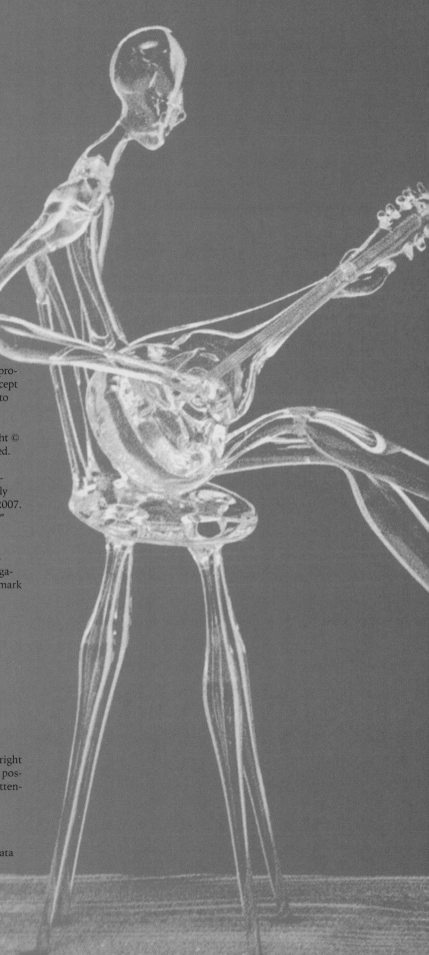

Previous spread: GPI jam in 1981 with B.B. King and Dennis Fullerton, Jim Crockett, Tom Wheeler, Cordell Crockett, and David Grisman (Jon Sievert)

This spread: A 1975 *Guitar Player* magazine Readers Poll Award (Jon Sievert)

Published in cooperation with Music Player Network, NewBay Media, LLC, and *Guitar Player* magazine. *Guitar Player* magazine is a registered trademark of NewBay Media, LLC.

Published in 2015 by Backbeat Books
An Imprint of Hal Leonard Corporation
7777 West Bluemound Road
Milwaukee, WI 53213

Trade Book Division Editorial Offices
33 Plymouth St., Montclair, NJ 07042

Printed in the United States of America

While every effort has been made to trace copyright holders and obtain permission, this has not been possible in all cases; any omissions brought to our attention will be remedied in future editions.

Book design by Damien Castaneda

Library of Congress Cataloging-in-Publication Data is available upon request.

ISBN 978-1-4803-9792-7

www.backbeatbooks.com

Contents

Jas Obrecht (Saroyan Humphrey)

NEW SERIES: HIGH-TECH GUITAR

POSTER ART

JIMI HENDRIX

15.1.69   **EXPERIENCE**

Guitar Player®

FEB. '88

Rock's Outer Limits:

JOE SATRIANI

FREE RECORD INSIDE

RISING
BLUESMEN

EUGENE
CHADBOURNE:
HE'S SO
UNUSUAL

WORKSHOPS:

HOT GUITAR
BACK TO BASICS
HOME RECORDING
& MANY MORE!

02   U.S.
$2.95
Can. $3.95
U.K. £2.35
Display
until 2/20

73874   0 262935 3

February '88 (Cover photo by Ray Olson)

Foreword

The first time
I discovered
GP magazine I
was stunned,
overjoyed.

I started to play guitar in 1970. Jimi Hendrix had just passed away, and although the news of his death destroyed me, it also awakened in me a burning desire to make some guitar music myself. It required a leap of faith and fantasy for me, just a kid from Long Island on a quest to keep the flame that Jimi ignited burning bright.

Back in the day a fourteen-year-old former drummer was hard-pressed to find someone to teach him how to play like Jimi. No Internet, no instructional DVDs, not even credible rock guitar teachers were around to help get my feet off the ground.

So I relied on books, magazines, and friends. They were my teachers in the beginning. There was always a friend around the block or across town who was a few steps ahead of me and could show me a few new chords or riffs. There were the Mel Bay and Mickey Baker books that had all kinds of info in them too, but they all seemed so "square," not cool, or up-to-date with what the new generation of players were creating.

The magazines, on the other hand, were fun and up-to-date. They catered to my older siblings' generation, which made them seem that much more cool to me. *Rolling Stone, Circus, Creem*—they covered the fantasy part of my rock 'n' roll dream, but not the knowledge part, the "how to" part, or the "tools of the trade" part. I would stare at the pictures and wonder where the real story was, the guitarist's story.

Then there was *Guitar Player*. The first time I discovered *GP* magazine I was stunned, overjoyed. Here was a publication that not only featured the artists making guitar music, but left no stone unturned when it came to the inspiration, the "how to," and the tools that they used. Month after month it contained well-written, much-needed information and cool photos of past, present, and soon-to-be superstar guitarists.

It was dedicated to exactly what I was interested in. No gossip, just exciting, useful stuff about guitars, gear, artists, their music, and their approach to playing.

Joe Satriani and Jas Obrecht
in 1987 (Jon Sievert)

One day, I thought to myself, *I'm going to be on the cover of that magazine.*

Year after year *GP* was my go-to publication for in-depth guitar news and insight. It was the one magazine you could trust because of the quality of the writing and the wonderful absence of trendy sensationalism. As a teenage musician I took it all in, read every rock rag I could lay my hands on, read them once, but never again. *Guitar Player* could be read, saved, reread, and savored, time and time again.

One day, I thought to myself, *I'm going to be on the cover of that magazine.*

Little did I know how right I was, but I didn't get on the cover right off the bat; something more important happened: they reviewed my first solo EP. It was bass player extraordinaire Bobby Vega who brought Dan

Forte's review to my attention at a doomed band's rehearsal, deep in a cramped basement in San Francisco's Mission District. As I read the short, somewhat positive review, I realized right then and there that I was now officially "Joe Satriani, solo artist." Bobby said, "Hey, you're famous!" Hardly. I was still broke and obscure. However, that review in *GP* made "feel" legitimate all at once. I never looked back after that day.

A few years later I *was* on the cover! What that cover story did for my career was amazing, and long-lasting. It was the right kind of introduction for the kind of solo artist I had evolved into, and for my new record, *Surfing with the Alien*. The legitimacy of *Guitar Player* had a kind of anointing effect on how I was received by the readers, and by the press as well. The cover shot and feature photos inside had a good amount of humor to them too, which I loved. The issue also had a Soundpage that contained a new track of mine, "The Crush of Love," which *GP* had asked for, and in doing so helped me create what went on to become a real radio hit for me.

The month that issue came out, Mick Jagger saw it and brought me in to audition for his solo band. I got the gig and, in that same week of January 1988, signed with manager Bill Graham. The people at *Guitar Player* had their finger on the pulse of guitar-driven music, and that insight had a direct and positive effect on my career, again!

They've never stopped supporting me, but, more importantly, they've never stopped entertaining me, informing me, challenging me.

It's 2014 as I write this, and *GP* is still an institution of enormous proportions. The magazine's glory years were in fact glorious for me too. My development as a musician, then as a solo artist, seems to have coincided with, and benefited from, *GP*'s rise. Our fates have been intertwined ever since.

I think all the years of its publication have been glorious, but the stories in this book are unique, fun, and enlightening, and they shine a brilliant light on a very special moment in time, a time when guitar players ruled the world of music. *Guitar Player* magazine was there to document it for us as no one else could.

Joe Satriani
San Francisco, 2014

> It's 2014 as I write this, and *GP* is still an institution of enormous proportions.

Preface

Decades have passed since the Eastmans and my father sold GPI Publications in 1989, and yet to this day, he has been recognized and approached by musicians while out and about living his daily life, who've made it known to him how much they still value the early days of *Guitar Player* magazine. They talk about how they continue to keep, and refer to, those early issues and how much it all meant—and still means—to them. Certainly, time has gone on, and there have been many awesome advances in the music magazine publishing field, and yet there just is something so special about that early era, when the magazine was independent, and the first of its kind, that remains in the hearts and souls of those who love music in general, and the guitar and guitarists in particular.

Dara and Jim in 1986 at CNN, where Dara worked and ran camera for his live interview (Jeffrey Mayer)

"Dad, have you thought any more about writing a book about your days at the helm of *Guitar Player* magazine?"

"Well, yes . . . I've thought about it many times, and I've saved so much in my archives . . . but really, there are just so many memories, so many details, so many people involved, that I just get overwhelmed by it all and figure I'll leave it for some young writer to deal with after I'm gone."

BINGO.

I'm a writer, having followed in my father's footsteps in that area. I may not be all that young anymore, but I figured I could do this— and while he's still here! I made the offer to work collaboratively with him to create a retrospective of a period in music history that, to this day, means so much to so many. I knew that the story had to be told, and if he would allow me to take on the lion's share of the footwork, I thought we could have something here.

He agreed. And, thankfully, so did the Hal Leonard Performing Arts Publishing Group.

We knew that the magic of *Guitar Player* magazine came about by virtue of Bud Eastman's initial vision, and owing to the talent and passion of all of the staff, freelancers, artists, advertisers, and readers, who gave their heart and soul to each and every issue. If this book was going to be a complete reflection of what made *GP* the quality publication that it was during the early years, we decided that it would have to include these individuals' stories as well as my father's. So I set about inviting them to participate. But would I be able to track everyone down? And if I did, would they care? Would the idea be rejected? Well, to my absolute delight, I was able to find many of the people who were involved with *Guitar Player* magazine from 1967 to 1989, and not only did they care, but they were extremely enthusiastic about the project! Stories began rolling in, along with terrific, historic photos.

Now, in some cases, unfortunately, important folks were no longer with us: some of the musicians we all treasured, or the heads of guitar-related companies who'd placed their ads in *GP* back in the day. In other instances, some companies had since been sold and records from the early days had not been kept. In a few other cases, I simply could not make contact with some individuals, or when I did, they had various reasons for not participating . . . but overall, we were so very jazzed by the overwhelmingly positive response and the folks we were able to find; in fact, given more time, we likely could have filled several volumes with stories of these glory years. . . .

For readers of *GP*, both old and new, and for those of you who've contributed to this book, thank you for playing with us. . . . We've reconnected again, and it's been so damned much fun!!

Enjoy!

Dara Crockett

"Dad, have you thought any more about writing a book about your days at the helm of *Guitar Player* magazine?"

A portion of the proceeds from the sale of this book will go to the educational not-for-profit organization Guitars in the Classroom. GITC's mission is to make guitar and ukulele playing, singing, and songwriting a vibrant and integral part of learning each academic subject for students of all ages and from every walk of life. To learn about GITC's training programs and discover how you can get involved, please visit www.guitarsintheclassroom.org.

The Glory Years
by Jim Crockett

Bud knew the music business well, but not so much the magazine field. He needed someone to run *Guitar Player*.

"Glory years"? Yes indeed. A unique time in specialty magazines; a unique time for me. You see, for twenty years I was first the editor and then the publisher of *Guitar Player*.

I spent two years teaching radio and TV at the University of Idaho but was the first of a few hundred of the state's faculty members who resigned over a little matter called a "loyalty oath." But that's another book someday. Needless to say, I was then out of work, and with a wife and two daughters (one of whom has helped greatly with this book). We moved to Livermore, California, and I worked awhile at a North Beach art gallery in San Francisco while I did freelance writing—feature stories for the Sunday editions of the *San Francisco Chronicle* and *Examiner* along with the *Mercury News* in San Jose. Fine, but a bit difficult to support a family on.

I'd always believed if you did just one thing a day toward a goal, that was thirty things a month, and something had to break. My one thing that day in 1970 was to check the newspaper classifieds and there was a tiny, four-line ad: "Editor wanted for a music magazine," it announced. I'd no idea at all what kind of music magazine, but that didn't matter. It was a job opening, and I'd been involved with music in various ways nearly all of my adult life.

I went to a small, three-room office in Los Gatos to meet, and be interviewed by, Bud Eastman, who in 1967 had created *Guitar Player* magazine, and you'll read more about him and the very early days in his wife Maxine's and son-in-law Al Dinardi's recollections elsewhere here. Bud knew the music business well, but not so much the magazine field. He needed someone to run *Guitar Player* for them. With my years of music and writing, Bud felt I was worth a try, so we shook on it. I was the first full-time staffer.

I'd previously applied for a production position at a Sacramento educational TV station and was offered a job there. What a dilemma. After a year or more of scuffling for a gig, here I now had two possibilities. Bud was someone special, though, a real gentleman, and I agreed to follow his dream. My first paycheck bounced. What the hell had I done?

I figured if I gave up lunches, in a year I'd have an extra month to forge us ahead of other publications, though we were then alone in the music field— a magazine just for musicians, guitar players. This would be a kick. I studied guitar furiously: the players, the instruments, the equipment, repair, everything I could find. I even took lessons from Bud's daughter, Sheri. Instead of a publication for people who wanted to *learn* guitar, I changed the focus to a magazine for those who already played, but wanted to play *better*.

One day, early on, I did my first interviews—Andrés

Jim Crockett: GPI staff photo (Jon Sievert)

Segovia in the morning and Chicago's Terry Kath in the afternoon. And Segovia even made me tea. This was going to be great. Then I'd get on the phone and sell ads to manufacturers, then design and paste up the pages with a tiny hand waxer, convince printers to give us credit, talk a distributor into trying out this unheard-of type of magazine, make collection calls to previous advertisers and retail stores, dream up marketing and promotion schemes. The days went by quickly. At one point, I talked the Gibson Guitar Company into signing a contract for back cover ads in full color, which then allowed us to run color covers cheaply (our first, in February of '72, featured Chet Atkins). With that, and making up a few "assistant editor" names, we were looking better, and more successful, than we really were in those early stages. But only *I* knew. Everyone, it seemed, wanted to go with a winner, and we actually began making money. Paychecks would never bounce again.

Soon, though, it was clear that I needed to hire some staff. What I looked for, first and foremost, were people to whom the guitar really mattered. While I could teach people how to interview, how to write, how to sell ads on the phone, even how to do paste-up, I couldn't teach anyone how to love music and that instrument. A heart full of music was the number one ingredient necessary to join *Guitar Player*. It was Don Menn in 1973, Dominic Milano in '75, Chris Ledgerwood the following year, and Tom Wheeler the year after; Dennis Fullerton, Jas Obrecht, and Roger Siminoff came on board that same year and away we went.

My first feature story was an interview with the Ventures, bylined "Leonard Ferris" in the February '71 issue. The following month, Bud made me managing editor, and the following year, publisher/editor. I'd sort of felt that "Guitar Player" was a kind of awkward title and took up too much space on the cover, so I pitched Bud on changing it to "Guitarist." "You know what," he said, "we aren't guitarists, we're guitar players." And that said it all. A year later he moved the family to San Diego, but you can catch up on that story in Maxine's piece.

What were we doing in California? I was often asked. After all, the publishing capital was New York City. Singer/guitar player Paul Simon had a brother, Eddie, who ran a guitar school in Manhattan. He came to our Los Gatos offices on one of his rare visits to the left coast. Over lunch I was just starting to ask him how he could get anything done in New York with the noise, the frantic activity, and the seeming chaos. Just at that moment, Eddie said, "I can't imagine why you people stay in California; it's so laid-back, there's nothing pushing you, there's no *drive*." Then again, he was born and raised in New York, while I was from San Francisco. We stayed in Northern California.

I wanted the company to be "GPI," the new corporate name I came up with when we launched *Contemporary Keyboard* in 1975. "Guitar Players International," the initial corporate name, seemed a bit weird to be the publisher of a *keyboard* magazine, but it was time to expand our company's base.

For the two decades I ran the magazines, we focused on things differently from any business:

My first paycheck bounced. What the hell had I done?

- For one, we refused all non-music advertising. I wanted every page to be about music and guitar. We turned down car ads, travel locations, fashion. And we went from 60 advertisers in 1970 to 234 just ten years later.
- We had an advisory board that included Chet Atkins, Charlie Byrd, and Barney Kessel (great players, for sure) in 1967, to Will Ackerman, Laurindo Almeida, Chet, Jeff Baxter, Liona Boyd, James Burton, Charlie Byrd, Eric Clapton, Stanley Clarke, Larry Coryell, Herb Ellis, Buddy Emmons, John Fahey, Tal Farlow, Jose Feliciano, Jerry Garcia, Billy Gibbons, George Gruhn, Henry Kaiser, Carol Kaye, Barney, B.B. King, Albert Lee, Paco de Lucia, John McLaughlin, Joe Pass, Les Paul, Howard Roberts, Juan Serrano, Johnny Smith, George Van Eps, Doc Watson, Johnny Winter, and Rusty Young. All willing to pass on tips, respond to questionnaires. And even answer phone calls.
- We held in-house seminars, too, in order to tell the growing staff what was happening elsewhere in our expanding company. Some of the topics we covered were How We Put Magazines Together, Ad Concepts for the Upcoming Year, Accounting for Non-accountants, Music Theory, and much more.
- I initiated "ABCD Raises for staffers performing *A*bove and *B*eyond the *C*all of *D*uty.
- Like most companies, we had annual Christmas parties, but, as you might expect, ours were different. Fine restaurants, new dresses, and men in ties. Like that. But with a twist. We were all players, and many were singers, so we did our own entertainment. Jazz, blues, rock, bluegrass, folk, satire—you name it. It was then, too, that I gave out envelopes with, fortunately, profit-sharing checks. I'd opted to do that rather than establish a retirement fund, figuring people could invest wherever they wanted. Or blow it on a trip to Tahiti.
- We started an almost monthly, in-house newsletter, the *Mag Rag*, to keep us all appraised about the what and whom of the company.
- And every month, when the issues went out the door to the printer and mailing house we headed for the warehouse for our jams. By then the company was packed with talented musicians, and I wanted us to always remember what came first—music. So we ate snacks by the armload, played our hearts out for hour upon hour, and sometimes even had special guests join us—such guests as B.B. King (twice), Jerry Garcia, Country Joe McDonald, Santana keyboardist Tom Coster, David Bromberg, keyboardist Chick Corea, mandolinist David Grisman, and numerous others.
- And sports were not be sneezed at. We boasted a rather decent softball team, a pool group, and a bowling squad challenging local

We refused all non-music ads. I wanted every page to be about music and guitar.

Jim Crockett
at NAMM in
2013 (Roberta
Crockett)

advertisers, bands, and others in the business.

- When it came time for the two annual industry trade shows, the National Association of Music Merchants hosted twenty thousand to forty thousand industry leaders in, then, Chicago and Anaheim. I thought about what the most difficult thing to do at these gigantic gatherings was. Get breakfast! So each show, we hosted three or four hundred of our favorite advertisers, players, magazine types, and others, treating them to rather lavish breakfasts, delightful soothing music (harpist, guitar duets, a flute/guitar duo, others); we even had our logo on chocolate wafers—and guests, always guests, such as Chet Atkins, Al Di Meola, Les Paul, B.B. King, studio legend Tommy Tedesco, and Arlen Roth.

- As many other magazines did, we held a yearly Readers Poll, beginning in February of 1970. But ours was a bit out of the ordinary in that each year we commissioned an artist to create a dozen or so guitar-related awards that I'd present onstage. We had original sculptures and specially originated guitar artwork of various kinds, some of which, I'm told, is still on display in homes or management offices.

As personnel director Laurie Walters wrote in our two-part

Jerry Garcia visits the *GP* offices (left to right: Tom Wheeler, Dennis McNally, Jim Crockett, Jerry Garcia, Phil Hood) (Jon Sievert)

personnel manual (yes, at some point we needed to write it all down), "Perhaps one of the most unique things about GPI is an attitude of caring, a conscious effort to keep our working atmosphere mellow; to respect each other's area of expertise and to feel comfortable offering suggestions of any kind knowing they will be received with the same respect, and responded to with the same concern they are given. This conscious effort is to make GPI working conditions different from [those of] other, similar companies."

PR and promotion were very important to *GP*. We were on hundreds of newsstands, competing with every major magazine in the country, nearly invisible amidst all the biggies. That's why I had a designer create our little square icons of a guitar (and later a keyboard, a fretboard, and a drum) placed in the upper left corner of the cover. We might only get 1" of visibility with other mags overlapping most of our cover, but with that 1", if you were a guitar player, you'd see our icon and know this publication was for you.

But, with the freelance addition of PR experts Ernie Beyl on the West Coast and Ren Grevatt back east, along with our PR staffer Gretchen Horton, we went out there as much as we could in various ways. We had to, because *Guitar Player* wasn't a household name, like *Time* or even *Playboy*.

FROGGIE WENT A' COURTIN'

Dear *Mag Rag*,

Remember that picture you had of the frog and the girl in that last issue? I suppose you'll get some negative mail on it, because it's so risky and everything, but, I don't know, that picture really did something to me. I mean, I look at it pretty much every night or so, and I can't really describe it, but there is just something about that spiral curve of the body, those firm, upturned breasts, and those lips—a full, sensuous pout. And that creamy skin. It's sort of hard to write about. It just sort of did something to me. Don't like the girl, though. Too skinny.

A fan
—*Mag Rag* (in-house GPI newsletter), February 1980

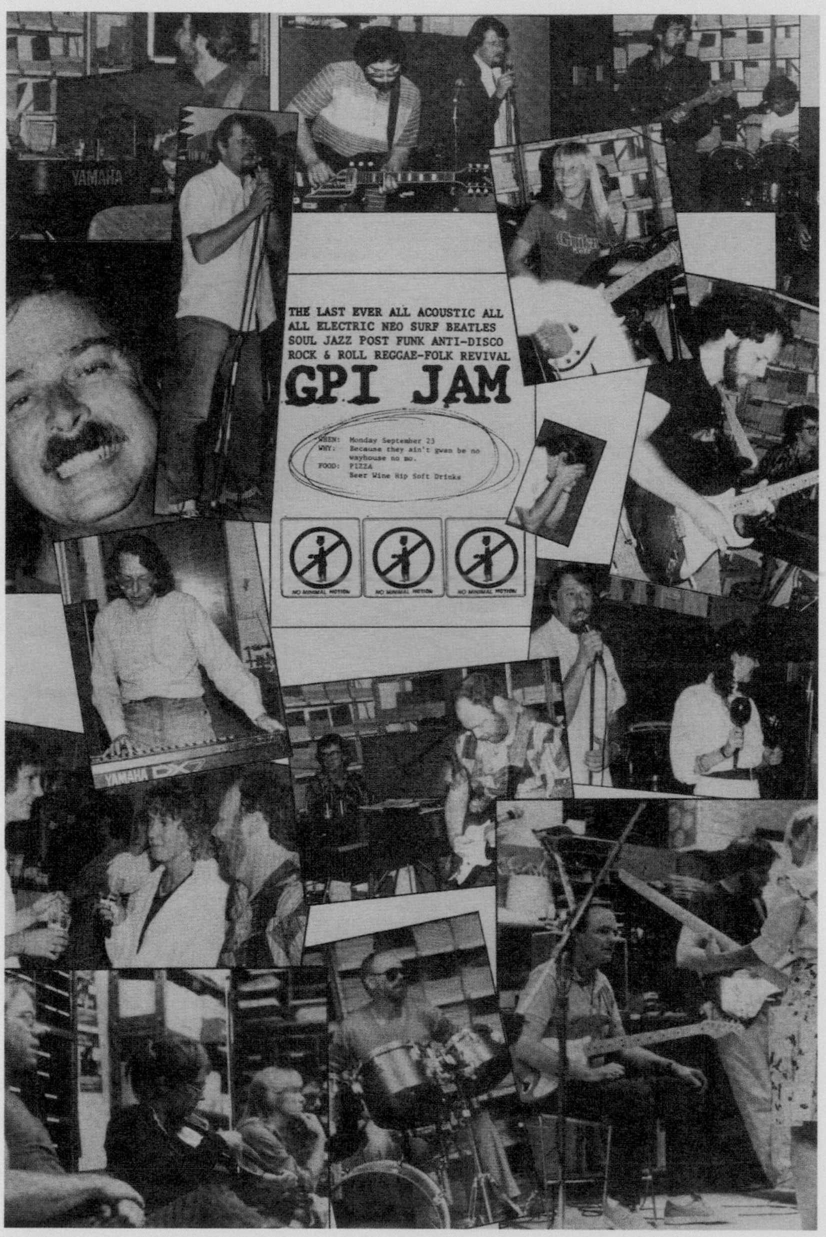

1985 *Mag Rag* back cover

We might only get 1" of visibility, but with that 1", if you were a guitar player, you'd see our icon and know this publication was for you.

In '74 we went monthly, and 1976 saw our first 100-page issue, and three years later we topped 200 (actually 220 pages, with George Benson on the cover). (In editor Tom Wheeler's '87 twenty-year retrospective, in issue No. 205, he tallied 1,500 artists and key industry personnel featured in *GP*, plus 2,500 how-to columns and 25,000 pages.) Our bound-in Soundpages (flexible discs of music related to an accompanying article), usually featuring unreleased original recordings, launched in 1984 with Steve Vai's "Attitude Song," followed by selections by the likes of Chet Atkins, Frank Zappa, Steve Morse, Eric Clapton with Robert Cray, Carlos Santana, Joe Satriani, Ry Cooder with Vai, and Frank Zappa with his son Dweezil.

Didn't we ever screw up? Mercifully, not often. We checked every word or comma. Over and over. And yet . . . "Hound Dog Taylor, British Folkie" the August '75 cover touted—a simple typo. A real blunder, though, that we still recall less than fondly. In 1977 I contacted MCA Records about doing a *Guitar Player* double album with Laurindo Almeida, Irving Ashby, Herb Ellis with Barney Kessel, Barney alone, Lee Ritenour, John Collins, and B.B. King. The double album was officially produced by jazz critic Leonard Feather and garnered us tremendous reviews and coverage.

To increase visibility and public acceptance of the magazine, Ernie, Ren, and Gretchen arranged numerous appearances, symposiums, lectures, and interviews for me, keeping me on my toes and on the planes. There was an appearance in front of 25 million viewers of NBC's *Today Show* with Jane Pauley, a shot on *CBS Nightwatch* and the network's *Entertainment Tonight*, plus interviews with the likes of the *Chicago Sun-Times*, the *Wall Street Journal*, *Newsweek*, the New York *Daily News*, the *Boston Globe*, the Gannett newspaper chain, the *Seattle Times*, *Folio* magazine, New Jersey's *Aquarian Weekly*, the *Philadelphia Daily News*, the *Chicago Tribune*, *Good Times*, *Cashbox*, *USA Today*; plus appearances on *The Merv Griffin Show*, *Nashville Now*, National Public Radio, CNN, Studs Terkel's radio show, and *The Larry King Show*. On one trip it was five cities in five states in five days. A guy could get pooped.

They sent me to hold seminars at NYU, Temple University, Rutgers, Berklee College of Music, the University of Maryland, the University of Denver, Stanford University, Columbia University, and other schools. *Guitar Player* was being recognized and acknowledged across the country.

I hosted and produced MTV's special for their *Rock Influences* series, "Guitar Greats" featuring Tony Iommi, Lita Ford, Dickey Betts, Johnny Winter, Dave Edmunds, Link Wray, David Gilmour, Brian Setzer, Steve Cropper, and Neal Schon. The "backup" band included Chuck Leavell of the Allman Brothers, Kenny Aronson of Sammy

Hagar's band, Santana's Michael Shrieve, plus Jonathan Cain and Paul Shaffer. The absolute highlight was the closing jam with everyone together for "Green Onions" and "Johnny B. Goode." A blast.

And this wasn't all. Through Ernie in '75 I did *Guitar Player Magazine Presents* radio shows for college stations across the country. The thirteen half-hour programs featured music selections and interviews with Chet Atkins, Les Paul, John Fahey, Juan Serrano, Barney Kessel, Happy Traum, Howard Roberts, Steve Howe, Doc Watson, and Wes Montgomery.

We received frequent media acceptance, too, through liner notes I wrote for Charlie Byrd, Joe Pass, Laurindo Almeida, Herb Ellis, Barney Kessel, and others.

GP editor Don Menn hosted a great event in Madison Square Garden's Felt Forum in 1984. The "Ultimate Clinic" brought Al Di Meola, Larry Coryell, Les Paul, Johnny Winter, and Steve Lynch before an audience estimated at more than three thousand players.

A great deal happened to our company over those "glory years." Our gross income expanded from $40,000 a year to nearly $15 million; our employee count grew from three to more than a hundred; and our 36-page issues six times a year became four monthlies, three monthly newsletters, and divisions for books, special editions, and records. Our *GP* circulation went on to include distribution throughout Europe and even a Japanese-language version out of Tokyo. We were actually in seventy countries and possessions by 1987.

Columnists? Outside writers/guitarists included Michael Lorimer, Larry Coryell, Frank Zappa, B.B. King, Lenny Breau, Johnny Smith, Rusty Young, Tommy Tedesco, Arlen Roth, Buddy Emmons, Craig Anderton, Stefan Grossman, Jerry Silverman, Rick Turner, Happy Traum, Arnie Berle, and others.

We were blazing trails, but we didn't think about it, or didn't even realize it. We simply wanted to make the best guitar magazine we possibly could.

"What are you going to write about after the first couple of issues?" we were asked by an early advertiser. We managed.

I learned a lot from these following reminiscences. Some stuff I either never knew at the time or had long since forgotten. Let's enjoy it together.

> We were blazing trails, but we didn't think about it, or didn't even realize it.

The Prehistory of *Guitar Player* Magazine

by the Eastman Family

Bud had a passion for everything guitar, and was determined to make his living doing what he loved.

No early history of Guitar Player *would be complete without a tribute to LaVaine Vincent Eastman Jr. (1936–1990), known to all as "Bud," who was the magazine's founder as well as its heart and soul.* Guitar Player *began as a labor of love, and all its employees were like family, including members of Bud's actual family, who were an important part of the* GP *story from the very beginning. Here, to honor Bud, we present memories of him and his work as shared by members of his family, interwoven with Bud's own words from past interviews, letters, and recollections. —JC*

Maxine Eastman Jackson, Bud's widow, remembers how he first conceived of Guitar Player:

L. V. "Bud" Eastman was first to envision a magazine exclusively for guitar players. He was a man of vision who, beyond good ideas, created plans and put them into action. Bud, as a young man, was a person who launched his ideas with an enthusiasm that drew other younger men alongside him. He trained them and set them out on an adventure doing something they never dreamed they could do.

At the foundation of *Guitar Player* magazine, Guitar Showcase, Musician's Supply, and Musician's Friend, Bud was the visionary who inspired these young men with confidence and the initial know-

Bud and Maxine at Guitar
Showcase in the 1960s

how to build these hallmark success stories of the music industry.
    He began playing guitar when he was fourteen, and by seventeen
he was playing on the radio and teaching guitar students. He had a

passion for everything guitar, and was determined to make his living doing what he loved. He started Eastman Studios in 1953, teaching guitar and training teachers in Utah. In 1964 Bud was encouraged by his Fender rep to move to San Jose, California.

That same year the "British Invasion" began as the Beatles' rockin' music poured live via TV into an estimated 73 million American homes. The revolution in rock music had begun.

We arrived in California and set up a teaching studio. A year later we opened Guitar Showcase. With ten years of experience in the guitar business, Bud was the right person to start a store for a new era in music. Rock players from the top local band, the Syndicate of Sound, instructed on electric guitar, bass guitar, and drums. The Showcase also sponsored a Battle of the Bands, awarding merchandise prizes to the winning groups.

First issue of *Guitar Player* magazine

Years ago, Bud Eastman reminisced about how he first got the magazine off the ground:

In 1966, Maxine and I owned and operated Guitar Showcase of San Jose. Teaching guitar and serving guitar-playing customers kept us abreast of the needs and frustrations of the guitar player.

In November of that year we decided there should be an organization players could join. Among other things, it would provide some sort of publication as a communications link. At first, a newsletter was envisioned. Then someone suggested a tabloid to include advertising. That idea evolved into a 32-page slick newsletter in which the news started on the cover.

Just prior to press time I decided that we could just as well put a separate cover on it, call it a magazine, and hit the newsstands. But at that time I lacked the experience to know that it is seemingly impossible to get such a highly specialized [magazine] on the newsstand with the

1985 *Mag Rag* cover

SNURFING?

A new fad has caught on like wildfire among the editorial staff. The fad is snurfing.

Snurfing could perhaps best be described by comparing it to . . . No, that isn't right. Well, snurfing is kind of . . . hmmm. What you do when you snurf is you . . . Oh, skip it. I could never explain it. But try it sometime. I guarantee you'll . . . Well, maybe you won't, either. You might not like it at all. Come to think of it, why are we all snurfing? Snurfing is disgusting, and isn't even fun! Everybody! Stop snurfing, right now!!!
—*Mag Rag*, Vol. 1, No. 3

first issue. Ignorance was strength, and with the enthusiasm of a new publisher with a new magazine, I somehow convinced Miller Freeman Publishing of San Francisco to at least test it with a few select dealers.

The first issue came out in April of 1967 and was not dated, since we couldn't be sure when number two would be printed. Number two, though, also 32 pages, had an August date and hit newsstands the first Tuesday in July. The third issue was dated October and came out in early September, establishing a frequency of six issues per year. Without missing a single issue, we held the bimonthly frequency until March 1970, when *GP* changed to an eight-issue [annual] frequency. In January of 1974, the magazine became a monthly.

Maxine recalls Guitar Player's *very first ad and first issue:*
To launch that first issue, Bud went to Gibson and convinced them to place an ad. After that, other companies wanted to purchase ads.

The magazine was priced at 35 cents, and the first issue featured Barney Kessel, Chet Atkins, Charlie Byrd, Jimmy Webster, and Jefferson Airplane. There was also instruction for beginning players through advanced.

The early days of Guitar Player *focused on going to concerts and interviewing the famous artists of the day for upcoming issues. Bud and Maxine's daughter, Sheri (Eastman) Dinardi, remembers one such excursion:*
The beginning days of *Guitar Player* included going to concerts and interviewing famous artists of the day. I was with Dad in early 1967 when he interviewed Jefferson Airplane for the first issue.

We went to their old Victorian-style house in the Haight-Ashbury district of San Francisco. Later, in June, we took a bus up to the Magic Mountain Music Festival held on Mount Tamalpais. This was the first rock festival ever during a key transition in rock music (Woodstock happened two years later, in 1969). Magic Mountain was the Doors' first large show and coincided with the rise of their first major hit,

> Just prior to press time I [Bud] decided we could put a separate cover on it, call it a magazine, and hit the newsstands.

Bud Eastman and Jim
Crockett jamming at a GPI
Christmas party in the early
'80s (Jon Sievert)

"Light My Fire." Dad photographed and interviewed band members while I took notes. We covered Jefferson Airplane, Grass Roots, the Seeds, the Byrds, and Country Joe and the Fish. Pictures of the event appeared in the second issue of *Guitar Player* in early July.

Maxine remembers one of the magazine's first subscription promotion efforts:
One key idea early on—in a world where no list of guitar players existed—was that we created an insert into guitar string sets advertising the magazine. The insert had "Guitar Player String Tips" [written] on the front. Inside, it described *Guitar Player* magazine as ". . . crammed with artist interviews" and other appealing features. It offered a one-year $3 subscription including a free gift of your choosing. This promo was a great way to get a subscription form into the hands of guitar players.

Money wasn't easy to come by, and Bud reflected on how tight the financial struggle was as he was determined to keep Guitar Player *afloat:*
How does a guitar-store owner get the first issue of a magazine on the newsstand? The same way he started a publishing company with one-tenth the required capitalization—I just didn't know any better. Indeed, the undercapitalization was so acute that the employees found themselves doing everything

from janitorial duties to licking address labels. My wife and kids helped out on the weekends and evenings.

Until you see 11,000 magazines stacked in a small room, you have no idea what you're up against. Somehow we got it out.

We obtained a second mortgage on our family home to raise funds for the first print run of the magazine. In spite of early setbacks, we hadn't lost hope. On the contrary, we were as enthusiastic as ever because we were seeing people turn on to *Guitar Player* in many important segments of the music business.

Maxine remembers how the company branched out:
While brainstorming a way to raise more money to pay for the magazine, we came up with the idea for Musician's Supply, an accessory mail order catalog. It kept *Guitar Player* alive and put food on the table.

One of Maxine and Bud's sons, Rob Eastman, recalls the continuing evolution of the family business and their flagship magazine:
Around then, my dad had another great idea. With the first and only subscriber list of guitar players, why not start a music mail order catalog? The company was called Musician's Supply and mailed its first catalog in 1968. This was another first for the music industry.

In 1970 he hired Jim Crockett as assistant editor. Jim was a professional drummer and writer with editing and graphic experience. The following year Dad withdrew from active management; however, he remained president and chairman of the board. He continued to consult, with responsibilities ranging from financial analysis to expansion and planning.

The magazine was priced at 35 cents.

Maxine reflects on those early days with Jim:
That same year [1970], Jim Crockett became publisher. The company continued to grow with Jim at the helm. Jim was a quiet, gentle man with a velvet hammer. He always seemed to have things organized and under control. I'll never forget his binders behind his desk. Anytime Bud had a question, Jim would go to the appropriate binder and the answer would be there. Jim's expertise in publishing helped transform the company into one with a unique collection of music magazines loved around the world.

Maxine continues with her memories of "fun friendships" with special guitar-playing friends:
Bud and I enjoyed meeting the artists and becoming personal friends with Chet Atkins, Les Paul, and Johnny Smith.

Over the years we enjoyed seeing Les at the NAMM shows. I remember watching him and Chet playing in the Gibson booth. Well,

Les, of course, really liked to steal the show every chance he got. Chet was playing away; then Les took his turn to solo. When it was time for Chet to solo again, Les reached over and pulled out Chet's cord and took off with another round of playing.

We were also close friends with Johnny Smith and his wife, Sandy. We spent time with them boating and fishing in Mexico. On one occasion we anchored our sailboats outside Rancho Buena Vista and rowed the dinghy in. A mariachi band was supposed to come and play, but didn't show. So Bud and John got their guitars out and were playing away when the mariachis finally showed up. Well, with all that guitar playing, they just turned right around and left. Bud and John kept playing well into the evening.

Al Dinardi, a brilliant guitar player, explains how he joined the family and what Bud meant to him:

In 1967 a fellow student handed me a business card that read, "If you play guitar, call this number for an important message from Charlie Byrd." Sure enough, the legendary classical/jazz guitarist's voice was heard, enthusiastically reporting about a new club just for guitar players. It was called Guitar Players International. One of the "benefits" of belonging to this club included a newsletter exclusively for guitarists. Little did I know at that time that this periodical would soon become what we all know and love as *Guitar Player* magazine.

Behind this visionary idea was a man who has a passion and love for everything guitar. His name was Bud Eastman. Not in my wildest imagination did I know that someday Bud would become my father-in-law. Nor did I know that the high school freshman girl who asked me to perform with her at a school music event was Bud's daughter.

Like all people who met Bud Eastman, I immediately felt as though I'd known him all my life. His quick, warm smile and enthusiasm for life was infectious. He always said people could do anything they wanted if they put their minds to it, worked hard, and didn't give up—advice given from his own personal life experience.

Some of my fondest memories of my father-in-law are of his passion for music—specifically, guitar music. Upon joining the family, I was immediately put to work—playing rhythm guitar behind him on pedal steel nearly every time we visited. We'd barely hit the Eastman home entryway and Bud would be ushering me downstairs to the music room to show me new songs he'd been working on—and was anxious to try out. I loved every minute of it, even when my hands hurt from playing for countless hours.

Bud was a real musician—complete with heart and passion. It is not by accident that history will remember him as the first publish-

Until you see 11,000 magazines stacked in a small room, you have no idea what you're up against.

er of a guitar magazine in the mid-1960s.

I remember Bud nearly every time I pick up a guitar. He inspires me still to this day.

Rob reflects on his father's leadership style:
I grew up working in a very entrepreneurial family environment. Dad would explain what we were doing, and then we all pitched in and did whatever it took to get it done.

He always communicated the endgame, so we all knew where we were going and when we would get there.

Dad was a great teacher and led by example. He had a knack for seeing the potential in people and bringing it out. His mentoring style was to give you the task with all the responsibilities that went with it, then to show complete confidence that you could do it. He was there if you needed him, but never micromanaged. He always gave you enough rope to succeed or fail.

Dad didn't read books on starting a business or mentoring employees. Instead, he had the confidence and drive to just do it. I believe this shaped his management style.

When *GP* started to grow into a real magazine, Dad looked for untapped potential, and hired Jim Crockett in 1970 as an assistant editor. Dad saw something special in Jim, and after mentoring him for less than two years, he turned the day-to-day operations over to Jim and retired from active management. Jim did a great job, allowing my parents to move to San Diego in 1972.

When I was thirteen Dad started taking me to NAMM shows. The first one I went to was in the basement of the Los Angeles Airport Marriott Hotel. It was a very small show and not well attended.

MEET TAYLOR YOUNG

Several years ago, the staff was attempting to persuade Crockett that another editor was needed most direly. How, after all, is one to produce a top-notch journalistic product with a bare-bones staff? Jim's answer was, "Wait."

That's how Taylor Young, the mysterious purple frog, became such an illusionary figure at the magazine. If they couldn't have a flesh-and-blood editor, then by God, they'd have a stuffed purple frog editor, and they even had an office for him.

—*Mag Rag*, Summer 1980

Guitar Player happened to launch at the perfect time. The music industry was quickly changing and was destined to grow, but a direct link from the manufacturer to the end consumer was lacking. *GP* was revolutionary in creating that link where guitarists could read about their favorite players, learn and grow in their own playing, and see all the new gear reviewed and advertised. For the first time, manufacturers had a forum, an advertising vehicle that was specific to their target customer. It was a win/win situation: Both *Guitar Player* and the manufacturers together grew and shaped the music industry. It was not until the '80s that other guitar magazines began popping up. In 1975 *Guitar Player* launched *Contemporary Keyboard* (later just *Keyboard*). Electronic keyboards and related equipment were also a fast-growing market, and manufacturers needed that same connection to the end user.

Sheri remembers Bud's passing in 1990:
Dad's memory lives on, and I will forever be grateful for the time we spent together and the lessons I learned.

On February 11, 1990, L. V. "Bud" Eastman breathed his last in this age and crossed over to his real home in eternity with Jesus Christ. I can't begin to express the loss and sadness we still feel as a family. He made a mark and left a legacy with everyone who knew and loved him.

Johnny Smith traveled from Colorado for Dad's memorial. He played a gorgeous guitar arrangement of "Send In the Clowns." Needless to say, there was not a dry eye in the place.

The family would like to conclude with two quotes they feel capture the kind of man Bud was. First, from Tom Wheeler's article "Remembering Bud Eastman," from the May 1990 edition of Guitar Player *magazine:*
Somehow we're still getting the magazine out more than two decades after that first issue, and Bud Eastman is very much a part of who we are and what we are doing. He founded not only a magazine and a company, but an industry. Today the racks are bulging with publications targeted at the popular guitar market; Bud Eastman was the first person to make it happen.

When I came to GPI in 1977, Bud had already turned over the day-to-day control of the company to Jim Crockett, although he kept his titles as president, board chairman, and consultant. Despite our seeing him only occasionally, Bud remained essential to the personality of our company. With a steel-guitar picker as our chairman of the board, the very special quality of GPI began at the top. Bud loved to play, and for our Christmas parties and warehouse jams he'd sometime bring along his steel. He held his own, no problem.

I remember Bud nearly every time I pick up a guitar. He inspires me still to this day.

Bud Eastman created a company that provided a uniquely rewarding experience for the many people who have worked here. He taught us by his example that it's possible to be a pleasant, caring person, and still succeed in business. And his presence reminded us that it was the love of music that brought us all together. With his ready smile and hearty handshake, he always seemed to lift the spirits of those around him. I don't think I had a single conversation with him in which we didn't share a pleasant chuckle. We were fortunate to know Bud Eastman, and we'll miss him.

And second, a thought from me, Jim Crockett, summing up the essence of what made Bud so unique:
Bud Eastman's entire professional life was dedicated to educating, encouraging, and entertaining musicians—amateur, semiprofessional, and professional—at every opportunity always treating them as colleagues who were as dedicated to their music as he was to his.

Today the racks are bulging with publications targeted at the popular guitar market; Bud Eastman was the first person to make it happen.

Staffers and Freelancers Reflect

I look back
with fondness
on the
fourteen years
I spent at the
magazine.

Each member of the Guitar Player *staff was unique in his or her own way, but the one thing that bound them all together was their love of music and their respect for the guitar and players.*

When artist interviews were called for, the writers thought, "What would you, as a reader and guitar player, want to know if you were sitting here?" Their job was to ask about guitar influences, not hotel mayhem, not hangers-on, not booze or drugs. Questions dealt with string gauges, instruments and accessories, fingerpicking vs. flatpicking, pickup placement, tremolo and vibrato techniques, guitar exercises. The stuff players *wanted to know.* —JC

Tom Wheeler

I came to the attention of *Guitar Player*'s staff after they were kind enough to run a positive review of my first book, *The Guitar Book* (1974, foreword by B.B. King). I joined the *GP* gang in the summer of '77, completed an update to *The Guitar Book*, and got to work on *American Guitars: An Illustrated History* (1982, foreword by Les Paul). By the time that book was published, I had succeeded Don Menn as chief editor, a position I held for ten years. I've been away from *Guitar Player* for longer now than I worked there, busy with my life as a family man, author, college professor, and occasional guitarist. But I look back with fondness on the fourteen years I spent at the magazine. Here are a few favorite memories.

Jim Crockett insisted that we run a Soundpage in every issue. These were flexible vinyl discs that you could tear out and play on your record player. (Records, kids, are these flat discs of vinyl.) In

Tom Wheeler (far right) with
B.B. King, David Bromberg, and
Dennis Fullerton at a GPI jam
(Jon Sievert)

all honesty, I was resistant because I could foresee all sorts of logistical problems, copyright issues, arranging for studios when we commissioned an artist to record something original, and so on, but Jim was right. The Soundpages were very cool. I wanted to kick off the series with something startling. I had just discovered Steve Vai and remember playing "The Attitude Song" for Jim. It was startling, all right.

Flash-forward just a bit. I got a call from Ry Cooder, who was putting together the music for the 1986 film *Crossroads*, based remotely on the legend of Robert Johnson. He was looking for a player who could record the music for the climactic duel with the devil's personal guitarist. I suggested Stevie Ray Vaughan, Johnny Winter, perhaps others. "No," Cooder said, "it has to be somebody who's really *in your face!*" Well, I had "The Attitude Song" on the turntable. I put the needle down and played it for Ry over the phone. After a pause, he said in that gravelly voice of his, "Uh, are you sure you played that at the right speed?" They not only signed up Steve to play on the soundtrack, but they took one look at the guy and cast him in the film as Jack Butler, Satan's own guitar player. Such interactions with artists I much admired are among my favorite memories.

Others include writing and performing songs at the annual Christmas party, like "GPI Deadline Blues," but more important were the daily nuts-and-bolts efforts to make the magazine as good as we could make it and to get it out the door on time. New owners and an offer of a job as a college professor are the reasons I left. We had become corporate. I departed in 1991, having accomplished pretty much everything I had dreamed of accomplishing as editor, and having had a good run and countless fond memories. Looking back, here is an extended excerpt (condensed and slightly altered) from my foreword to the magazine's fortieth-anniversary book:

> Like the Blues Brothers, we were on a mission from God. We saw ourselves as true keepers of the flame, heirs to the legacy, trustees of our readers' interests. We were also lucky as hell to have our jobs, and we all knew it. I described my role as editor of *Guitar Player* as the best job I'd ever heard of, and I meant it literally. Privileged to work every day with quirky, stimulating people, we listened to music we loved, discovered new artists, wallowed in swamps of new gear, watched from the wings as some of the most exhilarating bands on earth strutted their stuff onstage, interviewed people who inspired us, and shared the insights of our contributors and the tales of our interviewees with as many guitar players as we could reach. On top of all that, we actually got paid for it.
>
> My favorite time of the month was deadline week, when it all came together. In those days we used typewriters and then computers to write the stuff. Art directors pasted up the copy, ads, and graphics on "boards," as we called them, and then we shipped them off to the printer. I'd run down the hall with the crate of precious boards, sometimes to applause and even cheering. On many a deadline day my MG peeled out of the parking lot, top down and tires squealing, and I'd have one eye on my watch as I counted down the remaining minutes until FedEx's closing time.
>
> After the boards were shipped, it was time for the company jam. The editors, secretaries, warehouse folk, production people, and others from *Keyboard*, *Frets*, *Guitar Player*, and whatever other magazines we were publishing at the time gathered in the warehouse for food and music; sometimes with guests such as Chick Corea, David Grisman, or B.B. King sitting in. It was a great way to blow off steam, socialize with our pals, and celebrate completing another issue. And for those of us who didn't

Like the Blues Brothers, we were on a mission from God.

Tom Wheeler (Steve Spoulos)

gig as much as we used to, the warehouse jam was also a fine rationale for buying still more gear.

Memories such as these are among the *Guitar Player* legacies for those of us who were lucky enough to work there, but the greater heritage is found in print, photos and graphics, in thousands of stories, columns, departments, and ads covering almost a half century. These collected works are not merely the legacy of employees; they are a part of the literature of the broader guitar community—artists who inspired us, advertisers who supported us, and readers who told us what they wanted and needed and who let us know when we got it wrong.

For thousands of players around the world, *Guitar Player* was the Big Guitar Textbook, inspiring us with insights into the techniques and careers of worthy players famous and obscure, and walking us through chapter and verse of Guitar Basics 101. Long before I went to work there, I learned in those pages that if you carry your case with

ing masses. Our attitude toward readers was, we're all in this together, sharing the same journey.

Upon my arrival, Jim Crockett told me: "We don't consider ourselves experts except on one thing: We know who the experts are." Some of us did become experts in some areas. It was hard not to, given the almost unlimited opportunities we had to pick the brains of manufacturers, designers, repair people, educators, and artists of every style. At the same time, we had an aversion to self-aggrandizement, at least under our own bylines. Except in the columns, you won't find a lot of first-person journalism in *Guitar Player*'s early issues, a reaction to all the tacky music writing out there in which self-absorbed writers couldn't resist turning assignments into excuses to talk about themselves. It may seem ironic that a magazine so involved in rock music (among other styles) would be journalistically reserved, but I think our standards served readers well. I don't know if anyone actually told us that putting readers first was the most important thing, but no one had to. Our mission was understood.

Another benefit of seeing our job as a calling was our emphasis on ethics. On the staff at any time you could find people with years of teaching, recording, and gigging experience, but you'd be hard pressed to find anyone who'd had a course in media ethics. I don't ever recall saying, "What would Walter Cronkite do?" but I did think that way. We had almost as many conversations about fundamental fairness, obligations to our readers, and appropriate relationships with advertisers and interviewees as we did about strings, speakers, and pickups.

Scores of key employees contributed to *Guitar Player* over the years, far too many to list here. I mentioned Bud Eastman, who dreamed up *Guitar Player*, gave it life, and stayed out of the way as it evolved into a bigger and deeper publication than the one he had conceived. I also mentioned Jim Crockett, the publisher, who starting in 1971, turned *Guitar Player* into the magazine we now celebrate. He was a scuba diver and a jazz drummer who dug abstract paintings and fine wines. He was at the forefront of specialty music publishing, and his innovations and those of the people who reported to him can be seen in dozens of music magazines to this day. He was responsible for *GP*'s basic template and its philosophies of covering all styles, letting the experts do much of the talk-

Guitar Player was founded the year of the Summer of Love, of Sgt. Pepper's, Are You Experienced?, and other landmarks. Talk about good timing.

I don't know if anyone told us that putting readers first was the most important thing, but no one had to. Our mission was understood.

ing, keeping the spotlight on interviewees rather than on ourselves, being appreciative of our advertisers without crossing the line into inappropriate favoritism, and giving editors plenty of freedom and room to grow.

I'll mention one more. Don Menn is a Stanford graduate and the son of a distinguished Midwestern newspaperman. He grew up with a love of poetry and literature, and his sensibilities elevated the quality of writing in *Guitar Player* during the mid-1970s. I inherited the mantle of editor from him, and for my first several months I think my guiding principle was simply to live up to his standards and not diminish an already good magazine.

Since leaving *GP* I have continued to stay active in the world of guitar. I testified on behalf of Paul Reed Smith during the Gibson lawsuits, and contributed to the design of the PRS Limited Edition Signature guitar. Paul Smith is a dear friend, and I have had the pleasure of emceeing events at his annual Experience PRS events. I've also done a lot of work with my good friends at Fender—hosting concerts, making videos, etc. Since joining the faculty of the University of Oregon's School of Journalism and Communication, I've authored several hardcover books on Fender: *The Stratocaster Chronicles* (foreword by Eric Clapton), *The Soul of Tone* (foreword by Keith Richards), and *The Dream Factory* (foreword by Billy Gibbons); as we go to press, my latest book is in production: *The Fender Archives* (foreword by James Burton). Many of these opportunities arose in part because of the work I was privileged to do at the magazine. *Guitar Player* was a big part of our lives, and we cared deeply about what went into its pages.

Jas Obrecht

In April 1978 I sent my résumé to *Guitar Player* magazine. At the time, I was living on Detroit's west side and had been an editor at Gale Research Company for about a year. Every day, new magazines arrived at Gale, and during breaks I read every issue of *Rolling Stone*, *Billboard*, *Cashbox*, and my two favorites, *Guitar Player* and *Living Blues*. The front section of *Guitar Player* featured a column, Pro's Reply, bylined by one of the magazine's editors, Dan Forte. The column featured Dan's photo in the heading, and every month he interviewed a famous or historically significant player. From 2,300 miles away, I thought he had the best gig in the world.

I desperately wanted out of Detroit. Two deadly street gangs—the Black Killers and the Errol Flynns—were on the rise, and from my front porch, I could point up and down the street to where several murders had recently occurred. So I dutifully mailed my résumé off to all of the magazines I'd been reading, along with copies of Gale book chapters I'd written on Jim Morrison, e. e. cummings, and other writers. With its small editorial staff of just Don Menn and three assistant editors, *Guitar Player* seemed like the longest shot of all.

A few days later, much to my surprise, I received a telephone call at work from *GP*'s office coordinator, Clara Erickson, asking if I'd be available to speak with Don Menn at five thirty that afternoon. Dan Forte, she told me, had just parted ways with the magazine. "The drive home from downtown Detroit is really stressful," I responded, "and I like to unwind by watching *My Three Sons* when I get home. So could he call a half hour later?" When Clara told Don what I'd said, he reportedly quipped, "Oh my God. He has a sense of humor—let's hire him!" They arranged for me to fly out a few days later.

A week earlier, I'd foolishly followed my father's advice and worn a three-piece suit to an interview at *Creem* magazine, where the lady editors squinted at me like I was some kind of narc. For the *Guitar Player* interview, I went casual. Good thing, because Don Menn showed up barefoot and tousled, in cutoff jeans and a King Tut T-shirt. I liked him instantly. Hanging behind his head in his Cupertino office was a numbered Les Paul guitar that had been smashed onstage by Pete Townshend. Within a couple of hours, I'd also met Jim Crockett, Tom Wheeler, and Tom "Ferd" Mulhern, and I'd been hired as *Guitar Player*'s new assistant editor. I was sent home with some copy to edit and instructions to pack up and move to California ASAP.

And so, on Ascension Thursday, I flew to sunny San Jose, California, to begin my new life. My timing was unassailable. Guitar-intensive music was a huge attraction during the summer of 1978, and there were no other guitar magazines being published in the United States. As soon as I arrived at the office, Don asked me to write an album review in the next two hours, to fill a space in the new issue that was about to ship. I chose a Mance Lipscomb album, put on some headphones, and got to work.

From the very beginning, the work we were doing at *Guitar Player* seemed important—not just for the company, but for fans of guitar music

Jas Obrecht in 1978 (Clara Erickson)

I was sent home with some copy to edit and instructions to pack up and move to California ASAP.

all over the world. My assignments during my first four months at *Guitar Player* reveal much about the ecumenical nature of the magazine's coverage. By the end of the year, I had edited other writers' cover stories on Ritchie Blackmore and Roy Clark, as well as freelance articles on the band Kansas; jazz guitarists Remo Palmier, Ed Bickert, and Al Caiola; and luthiers Jimmy D'Aquisto and Matt Umanov. I had collected and edited columns by Tommy Tedesco, Jeff Baxter, Craig Anderton, Barney Kessel, Michael Lorimer, and Jimmy Stewart, and prepared the annual Readers Poll ballot. Under my own byline, I had written feature articles on bluesman Fenton Robinson, feminist indie Meg Christian, young Eddie Van Halen, and Steve Morse's new band, the Dixie Dregs. My Pro's Reply columns had featured rockabilly pioneer Paul Burlison, Woodstock star Country Joe McDonald, John Oates of Hall & Oates, country singer Emmylou Harris, and singer/songwriter Shawn Phillips.

Of these 1978 assignments, the Eddie Van Halen interview—his first published in a national magazine—would prove the most newsworthy. And it came about accidentally. That June, Don sent me to Bill Graham's Day on the Green concert to interview Pat Travers. It was my first in-person interview for the magazine, and I dutifully showed up, my little tape recorder and carefully prepared questions in hand. After Travers's set, I knocked on his trailer door. Inside, he was surrounded by a pair of scantily clad women. When his manager announced, "Hey, Pat, the guy from *Guitar Player* magazine is here to interview you," Travers briefly looked up; said, "Not today, man"; and dismissed me with a wave.

I did not want to come back to my colleagues in Cupertino empty-handed. To steady my anger, I started shooting hoops at a small basketball court Bill Graham had set up backstage for performers, photographers, and journalists. Soon, a lean, wiry guy about my age came over and asked, "Hey, man, can I shoot with you?" I said sure, and we played spirited one-on-one. He was fast and had a decent hook shot. Afterward, we sat at the side of the court to cool off. "What band are you in?" he asked.

"I'm not in a band," I responded.

"Well, what are you doing here?"

"I came here to interview Pat Travers, but he blew me off."

"Pat Travers blew you off? I can't fuckin' believe it. Why don't you interview me? Nobody's ever interviewed me."

"Who are you?" I asked.

"Edward Van Halen."

Praise God Almighty! A few weeks earlier, when the first Van Halen album came in, Don Menn had called Tom Wheeler and me into his office. Tom Darter, editor of *Keyboard*, was also standing there. Don lowered the phonograph needle onto the track called "Eruption" and asked, "What is that—a guitar or keyboard?" None of us were dead certain. It was Eddie doing guitar finger-taps, but at that moment the technique was so revolutionary that even music journalists were mystified. And now the man himself was asking me to interview him. I switched on the tape recorder right there at the side of the basketball court. The story ran in the November 1978 issue and today is pirated all over the Internet. Eddie liked it so much he offered me his first cover story interview, another assignment I happily accepted.

After that, the interviews and articles came fast and furious: cover stories on Bad Company, Jeff Beck, Jeff Baxter, Billy Gibbons, Steve Morse, Duane Allman, Charlie Christian, Andy Summers, Randy Rhoads, Brian May, Muddy Waters, and the list goes on and on. At the same time, my monthly Pro's Reply column brought the opportunity to interview virtually anyone I wanted—from my childhood hero Ricky Nelson to psychedelic guitar pioneer James Gurley to Charo, George Gobel, and the guys in Devo. What a blast.

From the beginning, I made it my mission to introduce people not only to up-and-coming players such as Van Halen, Satch, Vai, and Yngwie Malmsteen, but also to the living pioneers from the 78 era. Interviewing Nick Lucas, the first "guitar star" in American history, was a big thrill, as was finding electric guitar pioneers Eddie Durham and Floyd Smith. At *Guitar Player*, we were all committed to covering players of all styles and from all walks of life—as long as the music was there. My lifelong love of blues led to long talks with John Lee Hooker, B.B. King, Buddy Guy, Otis Rush, Johnny Shines, Johnny Winter, Sam Chatmon, Albert Collins, and so many others.

In those days, *Guitar Player* was highly respected by musicians and industry figures alike. Told of my upcoming cover story on Charlie Christian, Benny Goodman and Columbia producer John Hammond were happy to contribute their memories of the man they knew. When I did our Duane Allman cover story, Gregg Allman, Dickey Betts, and Duane's studio pals from Muscle Shoals all volunteered for interviews, as did Billy Gibbons and Duane's best friend, the bluesman John Hammond (son of the Columbia producer). These cover stories are just two examples among many.

While *Rolling Stone, Creem, Circus,* and other rock-oriented magazines tended to veer into the gossipy parts of celebrities' lives, at *Guitar Player* we were able to focus almost exclusively on the

LES PAUL HIMSELF

A new series of house ads will contain quotes from famous artists, attesting to the value of the magazine. As Crockett said in his publisher's note, "Don't take it from me, though, I'm prejudiced. Take it from Les Paul."

What did Les Paul, electric guitar pioneer, have to say? "I read *Guitar Player* faithfully. Keeps me in touch. It's the bible." —*Mag Rag*, Fall 1981

music—on how famous songs were written, how unforgettable solos were recorded, how the player's gear influenced tone and note choice, how inspiration can be enhanced, and so on. Before every interview, I'd consciously put myself in the place of the interviewee's most dedicated fans, and I tried to ask the questions they'd ask. I'd listen to every song on every record, find all the press clips I could, and try to explore new ground. With musicians such as Andy Summers, Keith Richards, Brian May, and especially the old-timers, this proved very effective. It also helped that we were allowed a lot of editorial space in the magazine, so the interviews and features could go much further in-depth than the vast majority of today's print music journalism.

For me, the very best of the twenty years I spent on staff at *Guitar Player* were in the late 1970s and early 1980s, while we were still in the Cupertino office on Lazaneo Drive. From our front door, we could look out on rows of apricot trees and a farmhouse with a Shetland pony tied to a nearby tree (these same fields are now the site of Apple Computer's world headquarters). During our years on Lazaneo, GPI was still owned by Bud and Maxine Eastman—fine people, but we seldom saw them. Our publisher, Jim Crockett, directed the company's day-to-day operations, and at *Guitar Player* we had a small, intensely creative crew. These were happy, productive times—the magazine's "glory days," from my perspective.

Don Menn planned the issues, giving each of us our monthly assignments on handwritten little squares of paper, which I still have and cherish. Tom, Ferd, and I wrote and/or processed the copy on typewriters, while Bill Yaryan and later Carla Carlberg and Dominic Milano designed and laid out the issues. John Lescroart, known as "Capo" around the office, was ad director when I arrived, and man, what a fine guy and wicked poker player. Dennis Fullerton came in when Capo left to pursue his dream of becoming a published novelist. An excellent guitarist who'd played in 1960s rock bands, Dennis got along well with everyone, a class act through and through. Our office managers, Clara Erickson and, later, Judie Eremo kept us all in line. Jon Sievert, our staff photographer and later an on-staff editor, opened a lot of doors for me into big-time rock 'n' roll. Grand and good-hearted, Jon became like a brother to me. In fact, GPI often seemed like a big family.

Jim Crockett was wonderful to work with—I have nothing but love and praise for "JC," as we called him in those days. He treated everyone with dignity and respect, and he knew how to get out of the way and allow creative people to flourish. His extraordinary generosity was evidenced by our salaries and annual Christmas bonuses. When the Toyko-based Rittor company began reprinting our

I made it my mission to introduce people to the living pioneers of the 78 era.

articles in Japanese, Jim split every incoming reprint fee 50-50 with the original writer. His From the Editor column ran in the front of every issue, and I edited the column with pleasure for many years.

Sometimes after we sent an issue to press, we'd have a jam session in the warehouse. B.B. King, Chick Corea, Jerry Garcia, Barney Kessel, Tommy Tedesco, and Pete Seeger were among those who jammed alongside GPI employees. Tom Mulhern, whose razor-sharp wit and unwavering dedication were essential to *GP*'s morale and success, usually played bass at these jams while Jim manned the drums. When it came to playing guitar, Tom Wheeler could easily out-jam all of us—that held until Joe Gore came on staff.

I rapidly discovered that being an editor of a popular music magazine would bring endless opportunities for the excesses associated with big-time rock 'n' roll, from unspeakably beautiful women bearing controlled substances to offers of illicit junkets and all sorts of swag. Luckily, for us editors the copy on the page came first, and our love for writing about guitar music kept our core staff sane and on-track while some of our office mates and industry associates fell prey to the excesses. Tom Wheeler, bless his heart, handed me my first opportunity to freelance for *Rolling Stone*, while Jim encouraged me to branch into producing one-shot magazines and books. Tom and Jim encouraged us to interview any artist or write about any scene we felt worthy of coverage.

For decades, people have been asking me who my best and worst interviewees were. The worst is easy: George Thorogood, whose ego and attitude in the early 1980s seemed to extend far beyond his abilities. Ugh. Choosing the best is trickier. Two musicians were remarkable for their insight and ability to speak in perfect Queen's English: Andy Summers and Keith Richards, who need no editing. Eric Johnson stands out for his warmth and friendship, and what an exquisite player! James Honeyman-Scott from the early Pretenders had the sweetest personality. Ry Cooder was always great to talk to because of his deep knowledge and passion for American roots music. I only spent one day with Rory Gallagher, a great favorite of mine, but I just loved talking with him. My favorite interviewee, though, is probably John Lee Hooker, who epitomized my concept of what a good man is all about. (While I did three *GP* cover stories with John, our best interviews were done near the end of his life for *Living Blues* magazine.)

The other question people ask is what I liked best about my twenty years on staff at *Guitar Player*—the close encounters with famous musicians, the rock 'n' roll lifestyle, the recognition, the swag, the freedom to choose what to write about each month, the ability to shape people's thoughts about music. Actually, none of the above.

> My favorite interviewee is probably John Lee Hooker, who epitomized my concept of what a good man is all about.

Jas Obrecht (Saroyan Humphrey)

For me, as surprising as it may sound, it was sitting down one-on-one with Tom Wheeler to refine our copy. My friend Tom is, without doubt, the best editor I've encountered. He's exceptionally lucid, a brilliant writer, really knows language and grammar, and adores good music. Some days, especially early on, we'd have animated discussions on the placement of a single word—or a comma, a semicolon, or an em-dash. Tom and I united in wanting the writing to sparkle with streamlined editing and lots of active voice. Today, those meetings with Tom over manual typewriters and well-used jars of Wite-Out deeply inform my approach to teaching college-level comp and creative writing.

Tom Wheeler is also a *profoundly* ethical man. Under his stewardship, *Guitar Player* was safeguarded from the demands of angry advertisers and other outside interests. Sadly, this was not always the case after his departure. As editor in chief, Tom always encouraged us to pursue our interests, scout new talent, and write from the heart. During his tenure, other new editors came onboard: Jim Schwartz, with whom I'd attended grad school at Ohio University; the expert jazz and classical guitarist Jim Ferguson; method book author David Alzofon; Jon Sievert; the returning Dan Forte; and Matt Resnicoff, whose insights occasionally bordered on pure genius. While not as well-known as the editors whose photos ran in every issue, three classy women rounded out our little family later in the 1980s: art director Peggy Shea, effervescent office coordinator Janine "J9" Cooper, and office manager Lonni Gause, later promoted to managing editor.

Another high-water mark in *Guitar Player* history was set in the early to mid-1990s, when Joe Gore, James Rotondi, Andy Ellis, and Art Thompson were on staff. Joe is actually a much more accomplished guitarist than many of the people who've appeared on our cover. Clever, full of attitude, and musically informed in a way our writing had never been before, Joe's words energized the magazine when it really needed it. Roto is as cheery and charming a guy as I've encountered. He's always fun to hang with and looks very much like an Italian version of Johnny Depp. He's a soulful and witty writer, too. Andy and Art broadened the magazine's coverage of music lessons and gear, and I've always respected their talent and insight. Saroyan Humphrey was our visionary art director during some of this second golden era.

In 1997, I announced my decision to leave *Guitar Player*. It had never been my intention to be there twenty years, but the work was so interesting that the time just flew by. By then, I'd interviewed John Lee Hooker at least six times, Eddie Van Halen six or seven times, Keith Richards three times, and so on. It was time to give someone else a voice. Plus, I had two books nearly completed, a newborn daughter to raise, and a strong desire for change.

As I flip through my handwritten address book from the *Guitar Player* days, bittersweet memories float up from the names on the pages, and there are stories to go with every one of them: Chet Atkins, Jeff Beck, Jason Becker, Lurrie Bell, Liona Boyd, Gatemouth Brown, Paul Burlison, James Burton, J.J. Cale, Craig Chaquico, Albert Collins, Ry Cooder, Willie Dixon, Eddie Durham, Elliot Easton, The Edge, Rik Emmett, Tal Farlow, Rory Gallagher, Jerry Garcia, Billy Gibbons, Benny Goodman, Arvella Gray, Stefan Grossman, Buddy Guy, John Hammond, Ben Harper, Michael Hedges, Al Hendrickson, Mitch Holder, James Honeyman-Scott, John Lee Hooker, Eric Johnson, Doc

As Shakespeare once wrote, "We few, we happy few, we band of brothers."

Kauffman, Jorma Kaukonen, Carol Kaye, Phil Keaggy, Barney Kessel, B.B. King, Donald Kinsey, Robby Krieger, Alex Lifeson, Alan Lomax, Nick Lucas, Steve Lukather, George Lynch, Yngwie Malmsteen, Curtis Mayfield, Brownie McGhee, Joe Pass, Les Paul, Poison Ivy, Vernon Reid, John Renbourn, Keith Richards, Howard Roberts, Jimmy Rogers, Otis Rush, Carlos Santana, Joe Satriani, George M. Smith, Pops Staples, Tommy Tedesco, Steve Vai, Eddie Van Halen, Stevie Ray Vaughan, Joe Walsh, Muddy Waters, Leslie West, Johnny Winter, Neil Young, Frank Zappa . . .

For thirty-five years and counting, Tom Wheeler, Tom Mulhern, Jon Sievert, and I have remained the closest of friends. We're often in communication, and whenever we get together in person, it's like no time has elapsed. And all of us are delighted every time we hear from Jim Crockett or Don Menn. I feel the same way about Joe Gore and Roto. As Shakespeare wrote, "We few, we happy few, we band of brothers."

Tom Mulhern

[*Ed. Note: The following is excerpted from "Strumming, Picking and Shredding: An Oral History of* Guitar Player*" by Steven Ward, originally published November 5–9, 2007, at Rockcritics.com.*]

Although I started at *GP* in June 1977, I moved from the Chicago area to California in January '77 to do freelance editing for their book division—to sustain myself while starting a band with my old friend Dominic Milano, the assistant editor at *GP*'s sister publication, *Keyboard*. The freelancing fell through, and over the next months I had a couple of crappy jobs elsewhere. In June, Don Menn called and asked if I'd want to come to work at *GP*. This was on a Friday; I started on the following Monday.

I began as an assistant editor, which was probably better than I deserved, considering I was fresh out of school with a background in electronic music composition, rather than in journalism. Youth and enthusiasm, not to mention the needs to feed myself and pay the rent, motivated me to work very hard. I realized how green I was when, confronted with a gibberish-like piece of text from one of our columnists, I edited it and got it back from Don with more red ink than black on it. I then got really intimately acquainted with my copy of *The Elements of Style*—I didn't want to lose this gig.

We were in a cozy place—Don, Dan Forte (the other assistant editor), and Steve Caraway (the ad director), sharing one big room in a space that *GP* rented upstairs from a carpeting store. Glamorous it was not. Less than two months later, Tom Wheeler came in, which, sadly for him, placed him in a storage closet—literally. The good

We were in a cozy place, sharing one big room rented upstairs from a carpeting store.

Tom Mulhern (left) with Jas Obrecht
(standing) and Jim Ferguson in 1982

news was that we were moving to a brand-new building in about a month (it would hold *GP*, *Keyboard*, and all the GPI people until the early 1980s).

I liked our columnists and was largely in awe of them. Who wouldn't be? Tommy Tedesco was about the most widely recorded studio guitarist ever; Howard Roberts was a jazz legend, as was Barney Kessel; and Larry Coryell was a pioneer of leading-edge jazz-rock. The list of titans willing to write a column for us was long. Among my favorites was Craig Anderton, who was unique in that he was not only a guitarist but a designer of cool effects that guitarists could build. He's still unmatched in the guitar world, and is still influential in the world of recording and many aspects of the guitar, plus he's a big presence on the Internet.

I was nurtured by our staff and inspired by our columnists and regular contributors—and I'm indebted to them for their patience and insight, believe me. I eventually worked [my way] up from assistant editor to senior assistant editor to managing editor. Titles were largely symbolic, since the staff really operated symbiotically. Naturally, someone had to be the head honcho, and Don was able to juggle a lot of needs from the editors, printer, publisher (Jim Crockett), and more.

Our staff was mostly non-journalists, at least when it came to formal training. Dan Forte was a bona fide journalist and had the task of copyediting my material at first. When Tom Wheeler came, we did a sort of "round robin" style of copyediting each other's work, which I thought was a brilliant way to hone our stories. Once the story was "done," meaning that Dan, Tom, and I had all put our paws on it, whoever wrote it or was the assigned editor would tweak it and give it to Don for a final copyedit.

A year later, when Dan left and Jas Obrecht came in, we kept this round-robin editing approach, which you almost never see anymore, anywhere. Each of us had a different perspective, a different background, and this helped strengthen the stories. Did we have some arguments? You bet. We also nitpicked over format, including such arcana as apostrophes with plural nouns, the age-old *who* vs. *whom*, etc. We took it very seriously.

I'd have a hard time picking a favorite among those I worked with. We had very little staff turnover in the thirteen and a half years I was there. I still think of all these people as friends, mentors, and some of the best folks I've had the luck to have known.

My favorite screwup with a happy ending was when I interviewed Les Paul over the phone for about an hour, with a borrowed tape recorder capturing the conversation. I was still new and green, and really felt I'd had a chance to talk to the guru, the Wizard of Oz. After

Our staff was mostly non-journalists, at least when it came to formal training.

hanging up, I discovered the tape was blank. I didn't know what to do, and after unknotting my stomach, I called Les back. "No problem," he said. "Tape machines do that all the time. Let's just do the interview all over again." What a guy.

Guitar Player was alone in its field until the early 1980s, so we didn't have to respond to competition. This made *GP* a unique place, and the style was also unique. A lot of friends and friends of friends worked in the company (GPI), and while virtually everyone had a love of music, more people came in with a lot of ambition and not necessarily all the talent. However, most people grew into their jobs and the jobs grew organically. Sounds like a bunch of hippies or utopians, but it's true. And it worked.

At *Guitar Player*, we felt our primary mission was to inform guitarists about the world's great guitarists, whether they were well-known or unknown, alive or dead. We wanted to dig out and expose interesting phenomena and techniques and weren't constrained by such concerns as whether ideas or personalities came from rock, jazz, classical, or any other style. It was about guitar. And above all, we wanted truth. We did our own fact checking and were rarely comfortable taking anything or anyone's word at face value.

We plotted our own course and weren't trying to ride anyone else's wave—we certainly weren't shills for the record companies or advertisers. We were always open to suggestion, but never did tit-for-tat journalism the way most magazines do ("We'll run ads if you cover our company/artist," or, "We'll give you exclusive access to so-and-so if you put him/her on your cover"). Each month we'd try to come up with our own hit list of who we wanted to write about, and Don would sift through freelance stories. The point was to come up with issues that gave guitarists a balanced diet, instead of something lopsidedly tilted to one style or another. Sometimes we were faced with an embarrassment of riches, forcing us to decide between putting, say, Andrés Segovia on the cover or instead have Steve Howe. Segovia was the world's greatest classical guitarist and Steve Howe was Yes's guitarist and a perennial winner—by far—in the annual Readers Poll.

We covered famous guitarists like Billy Gibbons of ZZ Top, Eric Clapton, and Frank Zappa, but we also graced the cover with people who weren't household names, like Jim Messina, Albert King, Rory Gallagher, and Larry Carlton. Non-12-tone music, roundtable discussions of the impact of Japan's guitar industry, and overviews of wireless transmitters and the emerging guitar synthesizer were routinely mixed in with stories on long-dead classical guitarists, living bluegrassers, and guitarists' guitarists like Tuck Andress and Ted Greene.

The mission of *GP* changed over time, mostly in subtle ways.

We were mostly viewed by the people we interviewed as either peers or allies, but never as adversaries.

Tom Mulhern (Susie Mulhern)

When *Guitar World* came along as our first competitor, we pretty much ignored them. I think the widespread belief was that they'd disappear pretty quickly—history seemed to be on our side, as most magazines fail in their first year or two. Eventually, *Guitar for the Practicing Musician* came along to add to the competitive pool. Both magazines went after our advertisers, urging them to jump ship on us and to go with them. More unexpected fallout: We also found ourselves in the awkward situation of having to explain to record companies or managers that, no, we weren't the ones who had just called and interviewed their artist.

When GPI was sold in 1987, the agreed-upon terms were to pretty much keep everything and everyone intact. Unfortunately, the small company that bought us was leveraged to the hilt, and when the stock market plunged 22 percent in October, they found themselves in deep trouble and had to unload GPI. Not long after, they sold the company to Miller Freeman, an old company that had only produced trade journals and didn't know consumer magazines from shinola. Miller Freeman wasn't bound by any terms such as keeping the staff intact or maintaining the status quo, and they made it eminently clear from day one that we were their "property." That was a turning point when the focus of the magazine was transitioned into a "compete or die" mode.

GP has always been underrated, except by the hundreds of thousands of players who have read it each month for four decades. It would be difficult to compare *GP* to other magazines. It grew organically from a newsletter for a guitar store into a bimonthly and eventually the most respected monthly in the music industry. We had an extremely small, tightly knit staff who weren't driven by fame and fortune. And we were mostly viewed by the people we interviewed as either peers or allies, but never as adversaries who pried into their personal lives. We weren't looking for exposés. We wanted to connect what they knew with what we wanted to know about what made them tick as musicians. Dan Forte, Jas Obrecht, Jon Sievert, and Jim Schwartz had the schooling and the journalistic nuts and bolts well in hand. Guys like Tom Wheeler, Don Menn, and I weren't journalists by training, but Wheeler wrote probably the most important book about guitars ever, *The Guitar Book*, and had incredible dedication and chops; Don had a lot of musical training, a love of writing, and great empathy for the staff and readers; and I had a mix of musical training, a strong "like" of writing, and a lot of adrenaline. Probably one of the most important things I learned at *GP* was: "We're not experts. Our job is to find the experts and get the information from them." It's important for journalists to keep that in mind if they truly value journalism.

Guitar Player paved the way for other magazines such as *Musician* and *Guitar World*. The only guitar magazines before it were short-lived, and existed in the 1930s and late 1950s. *GP* came along as the electric guitar was on an unparalleled upswing that didn't level off for a long, long time. It was only a matter of time before someone else would compete. It's like in any other industry: There isn't just one kind of car, one kind of toothpaste. And that's good in some ways, bad in others. It's good in that it makes the magazines all strive to serve the reader, a bonus if you read guitar magazines. It's bad in that too much focus has to be placed on competing and not enough on charting your own direction. You often see the same people on the covers of two guitar magazines simultaneously, and you rarely see obscure, but highly talented, guitarists on the cover.

And while you see *GP* and *Guitar World* today, many other guitar magazines have come and gone. And spun out of *Guitar Player* is a true jewel, *Bass Player* (originally a part of GPI), which has taken what was considered a minuscule slice of *GP*'s audience and built it into its own sustained community.

I left *Guitar Player* at the end of 1990 when I realized that our editors had to toe a corporate line or be cast out. The place had changed, the focus had changed, and the culture had been badly eroded. I'd had a run of thirteen and a half years at *GP*, my only real job of my adult life, and I thought, "What are you going to do when you grow up?" Leaving *GP* required one of the hardest decisions of my life, even though I was completely stressed out and depressed by the prospect of cutting loose. One evening I called Tom Wheeler and said, "It's time for me to go."

Looking back at the old days of *GP*, we had almost unlimited access to guitarists, without interference from record companies or managers. We didn't have to worry too much whether we made a bad "who's on this month's cover" decision. But times change. The

TAYLOR YOUNG COMMENTS

Aspirin? You journalists are all alike, aren't you? You all use drugs. If there's one thing I can't stand it's a drug-crazed journalist. The stories I've heard are true, I can just tell by looking at your bloodshot eyes, your sunken cheeks, your sullen, loutish sneer—and that haircut! My God. I don't know what the world's coming to, when impressionable young girls are exposed to the kind of pelvic filth you journalists purvey. You travel around month after month, living in rat-infested motel rooms with nothing but a typewriter and your large, economy-size bottle of NoDoz, just waiting for the chance to assault a poor, defenseless musician with your filthy, probing questions! Go away! Get out of here! I'm an artist. I don't have to put up with this.

—*Mag Rag*, Summer 1980

world is a more corporate environment, the guitar and its players are very mainstream, and the audience has many more ways to get, share, and disseminate information. For the first thirteen years of its existence, *GP* had no competition, MTV and VH1 and other music-centric networks didn't exist, instructional videotapes and DVDs hadn't come along yet, and the rise of the World Wide Web was still more than a dozen years in the future. The world was different, the guitar was different, and the magazine was different. I feel fortunate to have been part of the magazine at what I consider its zenith.

Jon Sievert

Born and schooled in northwestern Ohio, I got my first job as a working photographer in the summer of 1965 at the *Toledo Blade* following my graduation from Bowling Green State University with a BS in journalism. I took the job as a summer intern because it was the time of the huge buildup in Vietnam, and I knew I was going to be drafted. When the notice arrived in October, not seeing any alternative except jail, I reported for basic training.

Following two years in the army as an information specialist for the post newspaper in North Carolina and Alabama, I took a job in advertising in Worcester, Massachusetts, about an hour from Amherst, where two of my oldest friends were in grad school. Nineteen sixty-seven was a glorious time for music, with great albums coming out every week and excitement all around. Every Friday night I drove to Amherst and returned on Sunday. I went to a lot of concerts and discovered pot and LSD, which did not encourage my continued participation in the corporate state. Buried in the snow and cold of Massachusetts winter, I was getting letters and photos from my younger artist brother living in Santa Cruz, California, talking about smoking a joint and going to the beach. In April 1969, at age twenty-six, I hung up my suit and tie for good and headed for California with no job prospects or any real desire to find one. Within a week of my arrival, we drove to San Francisco to see the Grateful Dead and the Jefferson Airplane perform a free five-hour concert in Golden Gate Park. I knew then, for sure, that I had made the right decision. I delighted in sending photos of topless dancing hippie chicks back to my corporate pals in Massachusetts, who, until then, hadn't understood why I did what I did.

Though it was cheap and fun living in a three-bedroom house with five people who smuggled weed from Mexico, I was older and too conditioned to be a hard-core hippie.

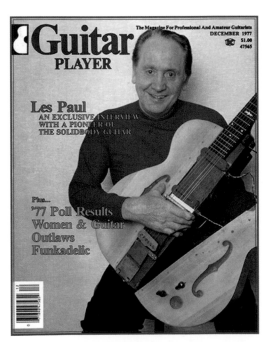

December '77 (Cover photo by Jon Sievert)

I never liked soggy brown rice and veggies much and really wanted my own place. I lasted three months before my savings gave out and I moved to San Francisco to find a job at Brooks Cameras, the biggest and longest-established camera store in town.

At first I sold cameras before fortuitously being moved to the darkroom sales department, where I met the real photographers who printed their own photos. It was very inspiring. I met many working pros who eagerly showed me their work and made me realize there was a higher standard to reach for than I knew. There were also talented students from the San Francisco Art Institute, including Annie Leibovitz. I remember how excited she was the day she showed me her first *Rolling Stone* press pass. I heard Jim Marshall before I met him when he smashed a store pay phone and ripped it off the wall with "colorful" language because it wasn't working right.

I started taking my camera to concerts, which you could still do then. At the time there weren't even passes required to get backstage at Bill Graham concerts. If you looked professional and confident, you could just walk in past the door monitor.

My first paying music gig came in 1970 when a writer friend, Alec Dubro, asked me to accompany him on an interview of the Youngbloods for *Rolling Stone*. The magazine liked the photos enough to publish three images, and the band hired me to shoot the cover for *Good and Dusty*, the last Youngbloods album. A couple of months later we did another story together on John Lee Hooker, who had just moved from Detroit to Oakland. Thus my first published music photographs were in *Rolling Stone*. It was six years before I had another in that magazine.

I discovered *Guitar Player* in a small music store in March 1972 and was intrigued by the eclectic concept. The issue featured Chet Atkins, James Burton, Jerry Byrd, Roy Buchanan, Leo Kottke, Oscar Ghiglia, Carol Kaye, and Jesse Fuller. Four days later Alec took me along for an interview with a new band called Copperhead for a Berkeley entertainment weekly. The lead guitarist for Copperhead was John Cipollina, the former lead guitarist for Quicksilver Messenger Service and arguably the most distinctive-sounding guitarist to come out of the San Francisco '60s "psychedelic" scene. John and I hit it off and, before contacting anyone at the magazine to see if they were interested, I asked John if I could interview him for *Guitar Player*. I don't know what made me so audacious, since my entire guitar knowledge was limited to about ten chords and a little theory. Fortunately, that was all that was necessary in those days, and publisher/editor Jim Crockett liked the story enough that he asked me to shoot a cover photo. The piece appeared in the January/February 1973 issue. John was thrilled and told me it meant more to

At age twenty-six I hung up my suit and tie for good and headed for California.

Jon Sievert
(Betse Davies)

him to be on the cover of *Guitar Player* than on *Rolling Stone*.

Even then the magazine had established a unique niche with a select appeal to musicians. The entire editorial staff for the 50-page publication consisted of Crockett, assistant editor Michael Brooks, and editorial assistant Jim Aikin, who later became a distinguished, longtime editor for *Keyboard* magazine. Crockett apparently liked my work enough that he offered me a job as an assistant editor when Aikin left the magazine in the summer of 1973. I declined because I wasn't sure I was up to the job and wasn't ready to move from San Francisco. I always say it's the best thing I ever did for *Guitar Player*, because Don Menn was hired instead. His presence and talent took the magazine to the next level.

After that, Jim began to call on me to photograph musicians when they came to the Bay Area, and I started writing a few more features. There was nothing official, but, in time, I became the de facto staff photographer. It became official when *Contemporary Keyboard* was founded based on the same editorial approach that had made

GP so successful. *Keyboard* editor Tom Darter asked me to fill the same role I had at *GP,* and my name went on the masthead of both magazines in January 1976.

At the time, *Guitar Player* was growing rapidly. In 1976, it went from 75 pages to 106 pages, 60 percent of them advertising, and more editorial staff appeared, with Dan Forte and Patricia Brody joining Steve Caraway and Don Menn, who became managing editor. Steve was an important transitional figure in that period. In his three years with the magazine, from 1974 to 1977, he served at different times as ad director, art director, assistant editor, and photographer, and wrote several cover stories.

I also wrote cover stories on Dickey Betts and Joe Pass in 1976. In my opinion, 1977, 1978, and 1979 marked the full maturation of *GP,* with Don becoming editor and the arrival of Tom Wheeler, Tom Mulhern, Jim Schwartz, and Jas Obrecht. By July 1979, it had reached 200 pages. Those were my most active years as a writer *and* photographer for the magazine. In those years I had sixteen cover photos and wrote cover stories on Les Paul, Jerry Garcia, Roy Clark, Bill Wyman, Lee Ritenour, and George Benson. Between *Guitar Player* and *Keyboard,* I was shooting as many as seventy-five concerts/musicians a year. And with all the advertising, we were given all the room we wanted to write. *Guitar Player* had no competition for stories or ad dollars until 1980, when *Guitar World* was founded with almost total editorial coverage devoted to rock.

The eclecticism was the best part. I got to hear so much great music and get exposed to the world's greatest musicians in all idioms. All of my photographer colleagues were shooting pretty much one kind of music—rock, jazz, or blues. I got to do all that plus folk, classical, flamenco, ethnic, country, and experimental music. In one twenty-four-day stretch in 1978 I photographed Joni Mitchell, Van Halen, Tony Rice, Eric Clapton, Oscar Peterson, Jerry Garcia, Willie Nelson, Tal Farlow,

October '78 (Cover photo by Jon Sievert)

B.B. King, Doc Watson, Carlos Montoya, Rory Gallagher, and Bonnie Raitt. The respect the magazine got from the musicians made it easy to work with a minimum of hassle from management. In January 1979, *Frets* magazine, which covered acoustic-stringed instruments, was launched, and my musical world expanded again.

In the early '80s, Jim Ferguson became the music editor and our preeminent authority on jazz and classical music, and Dan Forte returned to create the persona of Teisco Del Rey. We all knew we had the best jobs in the world, and we had the highest respect for each other's talents. I was especially fortunate to work alongside such great writers in the field and accompany them on interviews. Those guys are still some of my best friends, even today though we are spread all over the country and beyond. It's important to note that it was not just the editorial staff that made the magazine great, however. It was the whole staff working together that made the atmosphere so exceptional.

In 1986, *GP* was ready to hire another editor and I asked for the job. After so many years as a staff freelancer, I was ready for a new challenge and a steady paycheck so my wife and I could buy a house. For five years, I made the drive from San Francisco to Cupertino and thoroughly enjoyed writing features, editing copy and columns, proofing, and writing two of the most popular columns in the magazine, Questions and It's New. I also created two new columns, Skeletons (which featured quotes and photos from the same month X years ago) and From the Advisory Board. Naturally, I also still photographed concerts from time to time.

By the end of the decade big change was in the air. The magazines were sold to a large corporate entity that felt that the best way to meet the challenge of competitors such as *Guitar World* and *Guitar for the Practicing Musician* was to become them. When the corporate hatchet man came around to interview the staff, I failed the audition and went off to write and publish my book, *Concert Photography: How to Shoot and Sell Music-Business Photographs*.

At seventy-one, I am regularly reminded in some way how much *Guitar Player* magazine shaped and influenced my life and how lucky I was to be a part of it. All of us have the memories and some back issues to remind us of those days, but I also have the photos of some of the greatest musicians who ever lived thanks to Jim Crockett, who agreed from the start that I would retain the copyright to everything. My carefully dated contact sheets are my diary, and contain shots of musicians, family members, girlfriends, equipment, and GPI staff members. I was in the right place at the right time with the right skills, and I will always be grateful for it. That confluence doesn't happen for everyone.

I was ready for a new challenge and a steady paycheck.

Roger Siminoff

There are those things in our lives that have such an impact they become frontal in everything we do—it might be a time, a place, a friend, a job, a memory, a trip, or even a loss.

Being at *Guitar Player* was all of these in varying proportions and at various intensities over time, and I'm pleased to have been asked to participate and share my views of *Guitar Player* magazine, the why and how.

Roger Siminoff at a GPI jam (Jon Sievert)

Guitar Player wasn't just another monthly publication; it was a vision illuminated by an amazing publisher and shared intensely by a "family" of talented people whose joint efforts raised the bar for what publishing really means. And it set the magazine, its sister publications (*Frets* and *Keyboard*), and GPI Publications (the overarching publishing company) apart from all other similar publishing entities in so many ways.

Most publishing companies (and I've worked for several) hold advertising and subscription revenue—and the resulting profit—as their primary target and goal. Getting there at all cost is foremost in their minds. Growth and profit, after all, are what one expects and strives for in any business. GPI, under the watchful guidance of Jim Crockett, was on a different bent. As a drummer who struggled through his musical endeavors, Jim ("JC" to us) wanted to reach out to musicians everywhere and provide them with golden editorial content that would enrich their lives and musical careers to help them in a way he wasn't helped.

JC recognized that there were tons of talented folks who could share their knowledge and experiences, and he wanted to package this and provide it on a silver platter to musicians eager for real content. This became the mantra, and the objective was for us to deliver editorial excellence. It was assumed—and it came to light—that if we delivered well on that mission, we would be successful, and the subscribers and advertisers would follow.

Monthly columnists—all of whom were leading professionals with individual expertise in their particular fields—provided a wealth of content in varied areas such as technique, musicology, vintage instruments, how to play certain pieces, instrument repair, and much more. These prominent contributors added strength and variety to the magazine's main editorial thrust in each issue and greatly bolstered *GP*'s rather impressive credentials. Staff editors worked closely with their assigned columnists, and they jointly developed a work flow and process by which content was shared, processed, proofed, and—in the case of tablature and notation—tested and played note for note.

JC directed the editorial staff to "challenge everything!" and to ensure that all content was read, reread, spell-checked, and read again. (In the pre-computer days with no automatic spell checkers, this meant reading everything letter by letter, period by period.) All references and dates had to be verified, instrument model numbers checked, the names of places and venues substantiated, musical scores played, artists' names spelled precisely, and more. No stones unturned. Or else!

The "or else"? Immediately after each issue of *Guitar Player* was published, JC went through it cover to cover, page by page, mil-

> *Guitar Player* wasn't just another monthly publication; it was a vision.

limeter by millimeter, with his fine-point red pen in the smallest handwriting anyone is capable of, and he marked up the issue commenting on questionable facts, things being out of place, asking why certain photos were used, inquiring on the positioning of ads, calling out a line that was not pasted up straight, and so on. The dreaded "marked-up copy"—with JC's comments written in the most considerate way (except for an occasional "arrrgh!")—was circulated to the staff and received as a gift from On High. It was the way we learned, it was the way JC taught us, it was proof that Daddy cared and was watching, and it was a testament to the very elegant nature of the vision we all shared in delivering excellence. Hard to imagine, but we all looked forward to receiving the dreaded marked-up copy.

On one hand, the editorial excellence was a true bonus; on the other, it caused some anxiety. A good portion of *GP*'s monthly content came from outside writers, most of whom were proficient in their craft. These articles, when diligently reviewed and polished by *GP*'s editorial staff under the excellent leadership of editor in chief Tom Wheeler, delivered the promised editorial excellence laced with a tone and voice that was unique to *Guitar Player* magazine. The content was so tight that the magazine rightly deserved to be named the "bible" of music magazines, as it was by many. While this virtue might seem an expected value that most readers would anticipate from any magazine, most publications are less diligent in the processing of their content; many publishers are content to print articles exactly as they receive them. So, the upside was that the content was tight; the downside was that it took time for outside authors and staff editors to gain each other's trust and respect. Editors who were new to the magazine were set back a bit when they discovered that their content was questioned or tampered with, but the end result quickly turned the new authors when they learned how much better their published articles had become. This also meant that many important but poorly written articles were rejected. The magazine's mission and values were unshakable.

GP editors also made sure that content followed the "format book." In order to ensure consistency, we agreed on certain conventions and terminology common to the music industry, and some of them unique to *GP*. We ensured that such words as *soundhole* were not published as *sound hole* and so on. (Each magazine—*Guitar Player*, *Frets*, and *Keyboard*—had its own format book with words and descriptions that were specific to its market, instruments, and readers.)

The idea of "providing the reader with editorial excellence" extended to mean anything that existed between the front and back cover. Editorial excellence didn't mean "forget the advertiser." There were strict guidelines on how and where ads could be positioned

We were directed to "challenge everything!" and ensure that all content was read, reread, spell-checked, and read again. No stones unturned. Or else!

Roger Siminoff
(Rachel Neumann)

throughout *GP*. Ads for competing products couldn't face each other, coupons couldn't back other coupons (so that readers could use one without violating the other), coupons could only back ads (so readers could use them without destroying valuable *GP* text or photos), and so on. Ads were considered a critical part of the magazine's editorial content, and the rules dictated how the ads would interact with text. The problems associated with properly positioning ads and editorial content presented the art director with a real jigsaw nightmare, but the end result was well worth the effort.

Instruments and accessories that were received for product review or for evaluation purposes in articles and columns had to be returned to the manufacturer or dealer when the review was completed. This was a house rule. JC didn't want advertisers to create a situation where the very folks sending products for evaluation would ever get the impression that they could soften the blow of the editorial gavel by providing the staff with "goodies." Of course, it was assumed that things like strings and picks could fall below the radar.

Aside from those ad positions listed on our "rate card" (the document that provides advertisers with rates and ad production information), an advertiser couldn't buy his way into an article (ask to have his ad appear next to or within an article about one of his endorsers, for example). If a Fender Stratocaster appeared on the front cover of *GP*, it was strictly the editor's choice and not the result of some special favor between the advertiser and someone on staff.

I joined GPI in 1979, coming from a Madison Avenue publishing company that had acquired a magazine I owned, titled *Pickin'*, and I was part of the deal. *Pickin'* was an acoustic music magazine that I founded in 1974 and sold to the New York publisher in 1977. JC and I had known each other professionally, and while *Pickin'* was not really competing with *Guitar Player* for advertising revenue, we were nonetheless in similar markets, with some overlap of advertiser and subscriber interest. Jim knew that I'd previously owned a publishing and commercial printing company and envisioned that my skill set might be an asset to GPI. At the June NAMM show in 1978, JC and I spoke about the possibilities of my joining GPI, and it wasn't but an hour into the conversation that I became enamored with Jim, his focus, his ideals, and his vision. The die was cast (and I had to say yes).

I had dual citizenship at GPI: I was to serve as editor for *Frets* magazine, and to take on the responsibility for the production (publishers call it "manufacturing") of GPI's three magazines and the book division. As time went on, we became highly advanced in our production processes, and performed all graphic design, mechanical assembly and typesetting, in-house, where cover graphics were created as well. I instituted advanced processes for image replication, and we had a top-notch darkroom, a large flatbed camera, and advanced photostat and image assembly capabilities (graphic arts processes were analog in the late 1970s, and we moved to digital "desktop publishing" in the mid-1980s, trading our typesetting, camera, and darkroom equipment for computers, printers, and scanners).

The printing companies who produced our magazines were selected for their ability to work with our production techniques, provide bulk-ship services for our music dealer sales, and handle fulfillment services for the portion of our print run that went on the newsstand. Cheryl Matthews (Cheryl Fullerton now) and I made it a point *never* to visit our printers for a "press check." It was a common practice at that time for publishers to send their production people to check the publication while it was being printed, but coming out of the printing business, I knew the downside of press checks and realized that the ideal situation was to visit the printers when our magazines were not on press, do our preparation well, and select a printing company that knew what it was doing at the outset.

Within two years of joining GPI, I championed a program to bring our subscription fulfillment services in-house, something most publishers didn't do. We wanted full control of our subscriber data and for our staff to have immediate access to all information at their fingertips; we wanted subscribers to be able to call us directly rather than talk to a non-GPI person at a fulfillment service with questions about their accounts or expiration dates. If a reader called GPI

> The magazine's mission and values were unshakable.

because he or she didn't get their copy, someone on staff would see that they got one, pronto. The computerization of GPI was no easy matter, but after a period of about two years our advertising, subscription, dealer sales, and accounting services were all connected through a common computer system. What I found most enlightening as the process was under way was that though JC really didn't like computers, it was clear to him that the computerization of GPI was absolutely essential to its growth. JC was the first to have a terminal at his desk, and he was on it almost every day.

As an outcome of working on so many projects together, Jim and I got to be very good friends—with a bond and trust that was rather powerful. We scuba dived together, I supported his race car driving interests as a member of his pit crew, and we had lots of time away from the office to talk about the growth of GPI. He knew me well, understood my creative needs, and knew how to allow me ("make me" might be a better term) to be my best. In some ways, I look at my tenure at GPI as being my most creative time. I loved that JC gave me free rein, but I also knew that he was behind, controlling the horse.

A particular incident comes to mind that I'd like to share. We had just moved into a new building that we designed and built. One of the entrance areas featured a large stair tower between the first and second floors. Shortly after we moved into the building, the huge blank wall above the stair tower "spoke to me" and motivated me to create a six-by-six-foot three-dimensional GPI logo, which I proceeded to craft in my home shop over a period of about three months. Without asking JC's permission, I went in one Sunday to put the logo on the wall and then paint it the same color as the wall so that it was basically a subtle but especially elegant relief element that caught your attention when you walked by the second-floor balcony. I don't think I'll ever forget that Monday morning when the door to my office gently opened six or eight inches with Jim just standing there, not speaking a word, but sharing every thought through eye contact, and then he just as gently closed the door. I don't remember that we ever had a discussion about the wall after that; we didn't have to.

The staff was a wonderful mix of highly talented music-oriented individuals who were, variously, studio musicians, regular performing artists, doctorates of music, luthiers, highly recognized authors, those with recording studios, flute makers, consultants to the music industry, and composers—all dear, sweet people. Music was the core tenet and was the bonding element among the staff. Our regular monthly jams not only brought us closer but also allowed us to share normally hidden sides of our personalities that would

If a Fender Stratocaster appeared on the front cover of *GP*, it was strictly the editor's choice and not the result of some special favor.

not typically reveal themselves in the course of run-of-the-mill employment. And staff were hired on the basis of having a strong music background in addition to being skilled in the underpinnings of their job title. To this end, when *Guitar Player*'s ad director Dennis Fullerton spoke to an advertiser, he did so with the combined responsibility of an experienced ad director and the background of a seasoned studio musician.

Our monthly jams were rather special and included an eclectic mix of electric guitar and bass folks (*Guitar Player* staff), acoustic string folks (*Frets* staff), and keyboards (*Keyboard* staff). We took turns jamming separately and together, but we were always connected. JC was our full-time drummer, and as I always liked to remind him, "It's great to have all these musicians and a drummer!" Artists traveling through the area knew of our jams, and we were often joined by the likes of Jerry Garcia, David Grisman, B.B. King, David Bromberg, and Country Joe McDonald, just to name a few.

Staff meetings and editors' meetings were regularly scheduled events orchestrated by JC in the most sensitive, fun, serious, rich, informative, and meaningful way. Through our staff meetings we were all connected in regard to the daily goings-on as well as being engaged in long-term projects. As a result of the interface, our growth happened by design, coupled with a mutual trust and driven by a sincere dedication to our mutual goals and mission.

Editors' meetings were separate from the regular staff meetings, and these were usually held off-site. Those in attendance at these meetings included JC, Tom Wheeler for *Guitar Player*, me for *Frets* (I also represented production), Tom Darter for *Keyboard*, and Don Menn, who was assistant publisher. It was in these meetings what we shared immediate and long-term content goals, spoke about mutually beneficial content and artist contacts, and discussed issues relative to newsstand sales and distribution, staffing matters, and other such things that pertained to the management and growth of our titles.

Jim's approach to business and employee latitude was unusual, but it fostered trust, loyalty, and stability. Rather than trying to suppress what is typically considered "conflict of interest"—where an employee worked on projects for other music companies—JC fostered it; in fact, I think he thrived on it. Many staffers had outside gigs either writing or consulting. For example, I consulted to Gibson for many years, and also worked with NAMM on computerizing their organization. Most business executives would see these efforts as a pure conflict of interest, but JC saw it as an asset and strength for GPI rather than a threat. He took great pride in knowing—and publicly sharing—that his staff was deeply seated in the music com-

> In some ways, I look at my tenure at GPI as being my most creative time.

MAKES PERFECT SENSE

From Roger Siminoff: If lawyers are disbarred and clergymen defrocked, does it follow that electricians can be delighted, musicians denoted, cowboys deranged, models deposed, tree surgeons debarked, and dry cleaners depressed?
—*Mag Rag*, Summer 1981

JC was our full-time drummer, and as I always liked to remind him, "It's great to have all these musicians and a drummer!"

munity. He also realized that our connection to the various facets of the industry was a highly valuable asset for GPI. It was a rather stellar approach and an example of respect and trust that I don't believe any fellow employee ever wrongly took advantage of.

You couldn't be a "slacker" at GPI; if you weren't running with the pack, you'd be run over or run out—not in a malicious way, but just because attrition only happened at GPI in the normal course to those who couldn't keep up or didn't fit in. The employee roster was rather stable, which led to great consistency and time-honored relationships.

The hidden machinery keeping GPI and *GP* going was an incredible accounting team and an equally incredible mailroom/warehouse team. While they were not part of the editorial production force, these folks kept the gears greased, made things happen seamlessly, and allowed us to do what we did best, and I'd be remiss if I didn't include them as part of the whole story.

We had a great presence at the NAMM conventions. *NAMM* stands for the National Association of Music Merchants, an organization that has been supporting dealers and manufacturers in the music industry for over a hundred years. NAMM held two shows a year— a winter show (usually in California), and a summer show that toggled between Chicago, Atlanta, and New Orleans. Our booth —a long white pristine space with the three publication titles brightly emblazoned on the back wall—both stood out and fit in. Three illuminated towers featured giant backlit blowups of the current issues and also held piles of free copies for visitors. We hosted an "advertiser breakfast"—usually on Saturday mornings (NAMM was a four-day event) where our advertisers could escape waiting in the long hotel restaurant lines, come to our suite for a quiet but excellent breakfast, meet with fellow industry folks without being hounded by one of our ad directors, and get to their booths on time. There was often some form of live music—a guitarist, a string quartet, a harpist—to sooth their early morning ears and prepare them for the intense day's work ahead. It was "style" in the most ultimate sense, and *GP*'s advertisers knew it. For many, it was one of the highlights of their weekend.

My tenure with GPI continued through 1989; the company was sold to another publisher and then rather quickly sold again to yet another publisher. JC and many of the staff went on to other things, and the core fiber of *GP* changed slowly over time as the emphasis, guidance, and leadership changed. We of GPI see each other from time to time—often at a NAMM show—and the bond has never changed. It was a wonderful time with wonderful people. Speaking for myself, being part of the GPI family was the best of times, and

I'm sure many of my former colleagues would agree. We shared in the joys of weddings and births, and embraced each other in times of loss. While my memory grows veiled as I grow older, the indelible relationships and visions of my days at GPI will never fade.

Where pertinent, I've mentioned names of some staffers, and I don't mean to omit anyone; everyone aboard GPI was a valuable member of the family. I'm hopeful that other folks who are nameless in my contribution will be mentioned elsewhere in this book.

They say that software programmers often embed special code for folks in the know to find. On that cue, and just to rub a feather under the chins of my *GP* comrades, I offer "deadline day" and "continuous format."

Chris Ledgerwood

In 1976, I was asked to come to work at *Guitar Player* and her sister magazine, *Keyboard*, by my good friend Don Menn. Don and I had become friends as undergraduates at Stanford in the late '60s. I majored in art and design. In my junior year, impatient to get some experience in the "real world" of applied arts and design, I decided to take a leave of absence from the student world and jumped into such jobs as architectural and industrial scale-model making, and piano tuning and rebuilding. During this period, Don and I had remained close friends. In 1976, I was looking for my next job when Don mentioned to me there was a need for a full-time music copyist at this small magazine publishing company he worked for in Saratoga called GPI. Would I be interested? Don was a very talented writer, and was funny, entertaining, and warmhearted to boot. I figured anything he was involved in would likely include a lot of fun and excitement. So on a hunch I said sure, why not, I'll give it a try. My hunch turned out to be more than right. Just about everything at GPI was to be fun and exciting. Little did I know then that I would still be working for this same, small but growing company some fourteen years later!

In 1976 there was no such thing as a personal or desktop computer or a software program designed specifically for the magazine publishing industry. Technically, the publishing world was a very different place. When I first walked into my new office as music copyist for *Guitar Player* and *Keyboard*, I was confronted with this rather odd-looking wide-carriage manual typewriter called a "Musicwriter," a specially designed typewriter with all its keys associated with music symbols rather than with the characters of the alphabet. From quarter notes to whole notes, to stems and flags, and numerous symbols . . . you name the musical character . . . it was on that Musicwriter. I

Little did I know then that I would still be working for this somewhat small but growing company some fourteen years later.

Chris Ledgerwood (Jon Sievert)

had a lot to learn and learn fast I did: how to space out measures and symbols correctly on preprinted staff paper, how to add the appropriate press-on materials to the typed symbols and characters, and how to finish off musical details with a Rapidograph pen and use thin black tape of varying thickness cut to length using an X-Acto knife. It was a challenge to translate a penciled music transcription handed to me by an editor or one of the numerous columnists for *Guitar Player* and *Keyboard*, to somehow morph that penciled scrawl into a professional-looking piece of music, ready to place for publication in either of GPI's two magazines. Though the work was tedious, I enjoyed the challenges music copying presented, especially when viewing the finished product on the published page.

In the early 1980s, Don and I were offered the chance to produce a freelance project brought to us through the friendship of GPI's publisher, Jim Crockett, with Monterey Jazz Festival organizer Jimmy Lyons. The project was to design, produce, and publish the magazine programs for the annual Monterey Jazz Festival, which took place every fall and lasted three days. Don would act as editor in chief, and I would do the design and physical production, even though I had no previous experience designing anything of the sort! This was how I got my feet wet as a magazine designer. Trial by fire! I essentially taught myself what was, at least for me, a new process of design. Don, of course, was an experienced editor with many years of writing and interviewing under his belt. Jim Crockett was kind enough to allow us to use GPI's facilities to put this project together. Above and beyond our work for GPI, Don and I did the festival project for two years running. It was extra work, which we had to find time to do on our own time. And it was a heck of a lot of fun, mainly because at the end of the publication process we would rent a house in Carmel and hang out with our friends and families at that great festival for three days of wonderful music and camaraderie.

Well, Jim must have seen something he liked in those jazz festival programs, because he asked me to become art director for *Keyboard* magazine shortly thereafter. Of course, I jumped at the chance. I was already a part of the GPI family as music copyist, but this was going to be even more creative. It sure would beat banging away on that Musicwriter!

What did a magazine art director at GPI do in the early 1980s before the personal computer and desktop publishing? Well, aside from having the responsibility of designing the look of the editorial content of the magazine, the art director basically was the final person in the line of production who was responsible for physically putting all of the physical aspects of the magazine together . . . and I do mean physical! It was the art director who had the responsibility of figuring out how to puzzle-piece all visual aspects of the magazine in a logical and eye-pleasing manner. At GPI, the art director would first create a "dummy" of the next magazine issue. A dummy is a miniature mock-up of the entire magazine's layout that would all fit onto one or two 8.5" x 11" pages. The finished dummy would be approved by the editor, the ad director, and finally the publisher before production began. Then the actual physical piecing-together process would start . . . without any computers, mind you!

At that time, all of the physical aspects of the final magazine product would be placed by the art director onto what were called "boards" (thick pieces of fine white artist cardboard with a preprinted non-reproducible blueprint of the underlying column structure of each magazine page; virtually all magazine boards were two pages wide), which were then shipped off to the printer. If a magazine was going to be 160 pages that month, there would be 80 of these two-page boards to produce. Placed on these boards were cutout portions of typeset galleys of text, the accompanying photos and artwork, music examples, and advertisements of all sizes. All of this was "waxed" into place.

Manually typed editorial text would be sent to the typesetter. Photos and artwork would be sent to the darkroom, where halftoned photographs would be developed and printed, in advance of the offset printing process. Physical ads would be gathered from the various advertisers. Waxing machines would add a thin coat of wax to the back of the typeset galleys; photo halftones were also

At the last moment, all boards would be shipped to the printer halfway across the country. We all prayed the plane would never go down!

Chris Ledgerwood and family
(Heather Klausner)

waxed, sized, and cut to fit. Artwork, sheet music, and ads were all waxed as well. Then all would be rolled with hand rollers down onto the boards, placed in final position ready to be proofread by the editorial staff. Fine, hand-penned ink borders would be drawn on the cut edges of each individual photo halftone, and Rapidograph-penned ink lines would be hand-drawn between the margins of text and ads. Last-minute text corrections of typos would be ordered from the typesetter, those corrections waxed through the waxing machine and cut and rolled into place on top of the appropriate red-lined typos already existing in place on the boards. Finally, each board would be proofed multiple times, then subjected to one final proofreading by the editor . . . then, usually at the very last possible moment, all boards would be gathered and packed together in one box and shipped off to the printer somewhere halfway across the country. We all prayed the plane would never go down in midflight as those boards were the one and only result of an entire month's worth of collective blood, sweat, and tears!

The last day or two of the monthly publishing cycle were always the most stressful for everyone on staff, but from my direct experience I believe the art directors carried the heaviest weight of that stress, as they were always the last people in the line of production to finish off those damn boards! There were many late nights and sometimes final twenty-four-hour workdays to get the finished boards out the door on the appointed day of our monthly deadline. So still, to this day, I can't say loudly and proudly enough: My hat's off to all of the wonderful and creative art directors and assistants with whom I worked at GPI and *Guitar Player*: Carla Carlberg, Peggy Shea, Lachlan Throndson, Courtney Granner, Saroyan Humphrey, Rich Leeds, Paul Haggard, Rick Eberly . . . month after month you all did such a wonderful creative job, always handling the stress and constant pressure with such grace!

After working as *Keyboard*'s art director for a few years, I had a hankering to get back into musical-instrument making. So I asked Jim if he would allow me to continue being *Keyboard*'s art director part-time while I also pursued my other interest part-time. He graciously said yes. So for a straight two weeks every month I worked and focused as art director, and then for the next two weeks straight I would work as a musical-instrument maker's apprentice in Berkeley, learning the craft.

Toward the end of that apprenticeship, I met a wonderful woman, Liz, who ended up becoming my wife and who also became (and still is) the music copyist for *Guitar Player* magazine. With my instrument-making apprenticeship at an end, Jim asked if I would return full-time as GPI's managing art director. GPI had grown to include four full-time monthly music magazines and a book division. I accepted his offer and happily came back to a full-time position working along with the greatest bunch of people I have ever had the chance of knowing under one roof.

For me, in a nutshell, it was the people who worked there that made GPI so special. Everyone had a unique set of talents. Many were multitalented: excellent as writers and as musicians, some were also visual artists and instrument makers. One thing we all had in common was our love of music and musicians—all kinds of music and all kinds of musicians. And of course there was the mixing of the people who worked there with the people whom we wrote about. There was the usual monthly jam session held in the shipping room or the under office garage for the musicians who worked there, and often people from outside casually would drop by to join in those sessions . . . such people as B.B. King, Jerry Garcia, Pete Seeger, and many others. What a treat to see your musician friends playing with the likes of those guys! One day I was working in my office putting together a part of *Keyboard* magazine for later that month when Chick Corea casually walked in and asked if he could take a peek at what I was working on. That's the kind of place it was. It was a heady time. I have to give great credit to Jim Crockett, publisher and part-owner, for bringing together such a special group of people who worked there and for creating an atmosphere I can only describe as a very relaxed mix of casualness, headiness, and creative energy. This atmosphere permeated all of what was *Guitar Player* and GPI for the fourteen years I worked there. I have never experienced

One thing we all had in common was our love of music and musicians.

One day Chick Corea casually walked in and asked if he could take a peek at what I was working on. That's the kind of place it was.

anything else that came close to that working experience, not before or since.

Personal memories—there are just way too many! But here are just a few very personal ones: just hanging out with Don; Tom Darter's bachelor party in San Francisco; dinner and parties at Jim's in Los Gatos; watching Bob Doerschuk play the piano at a fancy restaurant in Palo Alto while he, at the same time, casually read and flipped the pages of a novel; many dinners with Phil and Connie; and with Tom and Ann; listening to Darter's great band in their Berkeley hangout. *Concerts remembered*—two in particular: Paul Simon's early and intimate *Graceland* concert in Berkeley and Stevie Wonder's December 8, 1980, concert at the Oakland-Alameda County Coliseum, where he announced the death of John Lennon to the audience.

Suffice it to say that GPI—that small, intimate company made up of so many wonderfully talented, quirky individuals—was ultimately sold to a corporate group of bean counters. Those bean counters, by their very nature, had little to no understanding of the multiple talents of the carefully chosen people who were GPI up to that time, or of the uniquely created family-like work structure of individuals who made up *Guitar Player* and her sister publications. Many of these individuals were let go on the very first day the bean counters walked in the door as the new owners, including myself. Many others were to leave of their own accord over the next few years, unable to adjust to a much larger corporate culture so different from what had previously existed.

I can only speak to one aspect of *Guitar Player* after 1989: that of its design and art direction. As my wife, Liz, continued to work for the publications that remained, I received a copy of the magazine every month. It was obvious to me that *Guitar Player*'s art direction continued to peak far after 1989, first with the continuation of Peggy Shea's and Paul Haggard's strong efforts and then, in the mid-1990s and beyond, with the art direction of Richard Leeds. I had hired Rich when he was fresh out of college during the last half of the 1980s as assistant art director for *Keyboard*. In the beginning, Rich worked under my direction, but it didn't take me long to realize he needed no directing. Over many years, Rich raised the design of the *Guitar Player* to breathtaking heights, winning so many magazine design awards along the way. One of the many multiply talented individuals who worked for *Guitar Player*, as its art director extraordinaire and as a performing guitar player . . . Rich finally went his own way too. Rich, you made us all very proud!

In 1990, Liz and I moved to Orcas Island in the beautiful San Juan island archipelago off the northwest coast of Washington State. We've been here ever since. We have two wonderful children: our

brilliant daughter, Ana, as I write this, now in college, and our multitalented son, Reid, now in high school. After 1989, I continued
working as a freelance graphic designer and art director for various
companies: among others, a catalog company, Musician's Friend,
in Oregon; a locally produced magazine in the islands; and even a
fledging television network with a creative office located on Orcas
Island. Over the last six years I have chosen to work solely as the
county's cartographer for the 130-plus-island archipelago that sur-
rounds us here, and I plan to do so until I retire. Liz continues to
work part-time as a freelance music copyist for *Guitar Player*, which
is under its latest corporate metamorphosis, working with a very
much reduced staff of guess what . . . multitalented writers, editors,
artists, and musicians.

In closing, I would just like to thank everyone whom I had the
chance to work with at GPI for those wonderful years from 1976 to
1989. You were all the most amazing group of people that I've ever
had the privilege of working with and knowing. There are too many
of you to list here, but you all know who you are . . . My hat's off to
all of you, wherever you may be!

John Lescroart

I was in a major transition in my life when I first joined *GP*. For
the previous three years, I had been the leader of a working band,
Johnny Capo and his Real Good Band. On my thirtieth birthday, I
decided to give up the idea of a music career—the band was working steadily, but there was no record deal on the horizon, so I decided to call it quits. While writing a novel (*Sunburn*, which went on to
win the Joseph Henry Jackson Award for best novel by a California
author under thirty-five), I needed to make a living. As an English
major from Berkeley, I thought I should check out the local magazine market. My first stop was *Peninsula Magazine*, which went well
for a couple of editions but turned sour on my second or third pay-
day, when the publisher had no money to pay me. Next stop, *Guitar
Player*.

I got the original *GP* gig as an editor for Guitar Player Books. Jerry
Martin, then the leader of that division, gave me a manuscript to
take home and edit—Rusty Young's *Pedal Steel Handbook*. Rusty's a
hell of a musician but wasn't so clear on the basics of writing. So
I worked on the pages for a couple of days and then brought them
back to Jerry, who hired me to work with Rusty, Craig Anderton
(*Home Recording for Musicians*), and maybe on another book or two. It
was a great month or two before *GP* moved to its later locale—I got
to know Jerry and Jim Crockett and Don Menn and Steve Caraway

I felt like this
was going
to be a great
place to work.

John Lescroart (Jon Sievert)

. . . and felt like this was going to be a great place to work.

But . . . meanwhile, things in the rest of the company were in flux. Suddenly, Steve Caraway, the ad director, got fired over creative differences with Jim. At the same time, it was clear that Guitar Player Books didn't have enough manuscripts to keep me busy. I didn't want to have to go back on the job market, so I made the rather bold move of applying for Steve's job. I went in and made my case to Jim, who was understandably reluctant to hire someone with no experience in advertising, but I made the case that I hadn't had any experience as an editor, either. If it didn't work out, there would be no hard feelings. If he gave me a month, I'd either sink or swim.

Luckily, I came up with a filing and tracking system for the monthly advertising, and just as the "glory days" were beginning, I found myself as part of the team. I found that I very much enjoyed the technical aspects of getting ads ready for the magazine, talking to the owners of these legendary companies—Fender, Dean Markley, etc. Plus, the company was growing and it was just plain fun working in tight quarters with Don Menn and Jas Obrecht, Dan Forte and Bill Yaryan. Everybody was young and idealistic and we had mostly a terrific time . . . plus, we put out terrific product.

A particular and regular highlight was the jam sessions that we had, I think it was every month. The amazing thing I came to realize is that almost everybody was a terrific musician—Jim an excellent drummer, *GP* editor Tom Wheeler a whiz on guitar, Jim Aikin brilliant on six-string bass (which I'd never seen before)—these guys were as good as my old "real good band." It was a great time. The other great thing about these days was that if there wasn't production work to do, creativity was allowed to thrive. In my little windowless office, I wrote lots of fictional sketches plus many songs—"Guilty of Rock & Roll," "Mediterranean Sea"—that have appeared on my CDs. Also, I took up jogging during lunchtime for the first time, heading out nearly every day with Yaryan and learning the important lesson that if you couldn't talk while you ran, you were going too fast.

My feeling about those days is that they were truly magical. Working with folks who shared many of the same interests, who all loved music, who didn't wear suits and ties to work, who were young, was a great experience. The only fly in my own ointment is that I wasn't really looking for a career as an advertising director. I wanted to be a novelist. and over time, every day spent not writing novels became more and more untenable for me, until eventually I gave my notice. Sometimes, especially when you're young, you don't know when you're in the middle of something unique and valuable. I can't say how many times I wished I hadn't left *GP* when I did. As it turned out, it took me nearly fifteen more years to begin to make a living as a novelist, and some of those years were dark indeed, with "day jobs" that in no way compared to the vibrant, interesting, youthful environment at *Guitar Player*.

John Lescroart (William Mosgrove)

The good news at the end of this story is that my dream of writing novels did eventually come to fruition. In 1994, I published my seventh novel, *The 13th Juror*, which featured my series character Dismas Hardy and went on to become a *New York Times* Best Seller, and then an international bestseller, translated into twenty languages. Since then, I've come out with about a book a year, and all of them have been *New York Times* Best Sellers, sixteen and counting.

Phil Hood

I definitely want to share my remembrances of GPI. What a momentous time in life it was for me.

I came to the company in 1984 after the party had already been going for fifteen years. How I came to be there is still something of a mystery to me and shows the beauty of how business sometimes got done in those heady days.

My hiring was a benefit of lucky circumstances. Someone—perhaps it was Don Menn, though I no longer remember how I met him—invited me to hang out at a GPI party in the garage behind the building

Phil Hood (center) with Mark Hanson and Elisa Welch (Diane Gershuny)

What a momentous time in life it was for me.

on Stevens Creek. It was probably something like a fifteenth-anniversary party. What a great bash. East Bay Ray of the Dead Kennedys was one of the guests at the jam. But I was particularly taken by a couple of young guitarists, one of whom was Mirv—Marc Haggard, who was the younger brother of the company's then graphics assistant, Paul Haggard. He and I hung out later, and I recommended a bunch of older jazz and fusion guitarists for him to listen to.

At that party I talked to Don about opportunities at GPI. I was working then as an editor for an automotive magazine and was ready to make a move. Less than a week or two later, I was brought in for an interview with Jim Crockett. We talked for perhaps a half hour about editorial philosophy and what Jim saw as a delicate personnel situation at *Frets*, the company's acoustic instrument magazine. Roger Siminoff had recently dropped all his duties there, and Jim wanted to shake up the staff. I had no idea what I was getting into, but it sounded good to me.

The next day Jim called and said I had the job. I was expecting to go through at least a couple of rounds of interviews, but Jim and Don had seen something in me that maybe I didn't even see. Lucky me.

Phil Hood (Connie Hood)

In that initial interview Jim had warned me that editors who worshipped stars too much were ineffective. He told me not to be a "starfucker." You needed to keep your distance. Fortunately, I didn't have any big lessons to learn in this regard. When you interview someone famous you aren't their friend. Your job is to be friends of your readers and to be objective, albeit supportive, with artists. And they are rarely looking to be friends with you. Sometimes you feel a real sympatico vibe with an artist you meet, but it's the exception, not the rule, in my experience. In fact, the bigger they are, the more likely they are to have managers, publicists, and others involved who want to use you to meet their goals. Getting the best story, by journalistic lights, is not their goal.

Jim said something else that stuck with me every day since. "The instruments," he said, "are more important than we are or the music is. The music will change over time, but the instruments will probably still be here." It was just another way of saying, Pay attention to reader needs, not your own prejudices. Since then I've worked with many editors—and hired some—who thought their job was to cover every one of their personal favorite drummers or guitarists or keyboardists. They were 180 degrees wrong. The job is to figure out what your readers want and what they need to know, whether it's a style or artist you care about or not. One of the secrets of traditional journalism is that you sometimes get to set the agenda, but you can rarely make the public dance to your tune. Magazines don't make stars; the public does. We just reported on them and on how they did what they did.

I was a Grateful Dead fan when I went to work at *Frets*. Not a Deadhead but a fan. I didn't own a tie-dyed shirt or drive five hundred miles to see them in various cities during tours. But I'd seen them a few times over two decades. I had all the records. I'd ingested the substances. I'd played their songs. So I was pretty excited the day Jerry Garcia was visiting the office. I had some dealings with Dennis McNally, their publicist and historian. Dennis could be very demanding when dealing with magazines, but was a pro. But also in those days the Dead were still the Dead. They were operating by their own rules, carving a post-hippie path through world civilization. A fog of smoke and magic hung over everything they did; hazy clouds of countercultural chaos ruled. To attend a Dead show, or be in the presence of people in and around the band, was to enter a reality-distortion field every bit as strong as the one Steve Jobs wound around Apple in that era.

Dennis and Jerry visited the office on the event of the company's twentieth anniversary. When they came in that morning, someone ushered them into my office—I'm not sure why they came to my place first. I had a great corner office in the northeast corner of the building. I got off my call to a freelancer and said hi. Jerry responded with that big grin: "Hey man, good to be here." Then he and Dennis sat down on the small couch in the office and proceeded to light a joint. "Want a hit, man?" Well, not really. Five or ten years before, such behavior might have been okay at GPI, but not in 1987–1988. From nine to five it was mostly business, and here people were in my office toking up at ten in the morning. I'm sure I was thinking that it would be bad form to get high, and I had to work in the afternoon anyway. What if Jerry had a secret line to superstrong weed? He no doubt did. I'd be too wasted to get the issue out. So I refrained. As it turned out, it didn't matter. Jerry just wanted to talk guitar a little and go around and see Jim and others in the building.

The man's aura, if you want to call it that, was huge. I think we all carry our life and our own little geography with us as we move through space and time. To be in Jerry's presence you were definitely experiencing his version of reality. And in that reality, whatever is happening, you just go with it—whether that means getting high in my office in the morning or taking a thirty-minute guitar solo.

When you interview someone famous you aren't their friend. Your job is to be a friend of your readers.

Bonnie Schoenemann and a guest at a GPI party (Jon Sievert)

Bonnie Schoenemann

Just before coming to GPI I had been unhappily working in an all-woman superintendent department for the Cupertino school board as one of the secretaries, when I applied for an ad in the newspaper for GPI seeking a secretary for the president. That was September 1979. I got an interview with the head honcho (JC) and arrived in my best interview suit, nylons, and high heels and was led out to the small outdoor sunroom where the boss was sunning. I kept my cool and answered all his questions professionally, then beat it home. He called me back within a few days to meet again, and I was very happy to see him in his actual office.

GPI was more like a family fun outing as most of us had relatives of some sort either working in some capacity and/or coming to the monthly jams and listening to wonderful music for a few hours, which were better and far more fun than most concerts. I, however, could never bring myself to smoke the weed that was passed around. I certainly didn't object to it, but I just couldn't put my lily lips on something touched by everybody else's, even though I loved you all!

The rest, of course, is history—the best, most wonderful, fun, interesting, intelligent people I have ever had the honor to work with. And the only day I ever cried at work (in Dave Williamson's office) was when we had just found out we'd been sold. I still think of everyone often and love to catch up on comings and goings.

> … the best, most wonderful, fun, interesting, intelligent people I have ever had the honor to work with.

Bonnie Schoenemann (Bill Schoenemann)

Dennis Fullerton

Dennis Fullerton: GPI staff photo (Jon Sievert)

For nearly fifteen years prior to my joining *Guitar Player* magazine in October of 1978, I had worked in a number of music-related operations, primarily in California. Those included retail and wholesale music businesses; music product manufacturers, for whom I did R&D; and recording studios. I also participated in professional live performances. In 1976, I experienced and survived a disabling stroke, which halted my career as a professional guitarist.

While recovering from my stroke, I had written and produced a manuscript that focused on guitar theory and instruction. I had also been a *Guitar Player* subscriber since *GP*'s third or fourth issue, and in early 1978 I noticed Bill Yaryan's name listed in *GP*'s masthead. I contacted Bill with the intent to have my manuscript considered for publication by the Guitar Player Books & Records division. I was invited to visit *Guitar Player* magazine and discuss the prospect of my book being published. Shortly thereafter, however, I learned that *Guitar Player* intended to dissolve their books and records division. Nevertheless, with that change, a new opportunity was presented to me to be directly involved with *Guitar Player* and its display advertising sales efforts.

I was hired by Jim Crockett in October of 1978 to be *Guitar Player*'s display advertising salesperson. My tenure at *GP*/GPI ended in July 1988.

Jim Crockett often enjoyed sharing his publisher's wishes and advocations via succinct, handwritten notes placed on the chairs of his respective recipients. Jim often distributed those notes at night and after normal working hours. It was Jim's "See me / JC" notes that always seemed to offer recipients a special feeling of cause for concern and wonderment. And of course, one did know a prompt follow-up was always Jim's expectation.

Jim did, however, share a few thoughtful and appreciative notes of comment from time to time. One in particular that he shared with me is as follows:

> 10/2/86 . . . Dennis—8 years ago this month you conned me into giving you a chance with *Guitar Player*. Thank heaven. Happy anniversary; I hope you're still having a good time. —Jim

I also recall Jim making a comment one time where he described me as being "one who has a mind like a steel trap," and, thanks to my keen eye for spotting ants in the carpet (aka an eye for detail), Jim thought I might also make "an excellent proofreader of cartography." Yes, Jim's sense of humor does bring forth enjoyment, appreciation, and a few chuckles or moments of downright laughter.

When I look back at where *Guitar Player* was physically located at that time (Central Coast/ Santa Clara Valley) and what we did each day of each week of each issue cycle, I can happily say my work at *Guitar Player* was the absolute best "job" I ever had. The bonuses, in part, were the monthly jam sessions we did in the warehouse at the conclusion of each month's issue cycle. Our "downtime" was truly filled with music and fun!!!

Guitar Player was a great place to be at work. And for those years I was there, the magazine maintained a very creative spirit in work and in play. Of course, my role with the advertising sales was made very clear to me when I first started. There existed a line of separation between advertising and editorial. *GP*'s editorial content was never to be

My work at *Guitar Player* was the absolute best "job" I ever had.

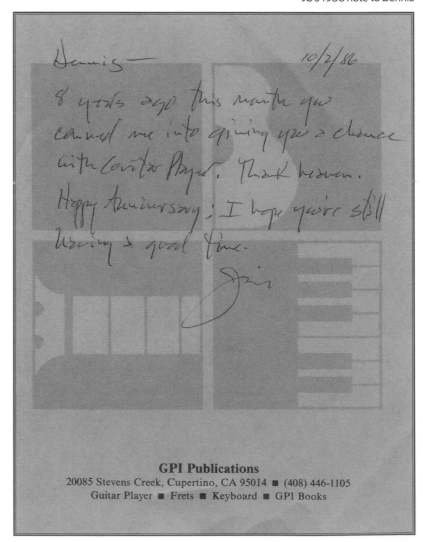

JC's 1986 note to Dennis

GPI Publications
20085 Stevens Creek, Cupertino, CA 95014 ■ (408) 446-1105
Guitar Player ■ Frets ■ Keyboard ■ GPI Books

Dennis Fullerton
(Cheryl Fullerton)

compromised, nor disrespected, nor jeopardized in any way, shape, or form. *Guitar Player*'s editorial staff was considered to be the most respected team of editors in the music industry. We at *Guitar Player* magazine represented and delivered honest information and value, both inside and outside of our workplace. *Guitar Player* subscribers demanded and expected nothing less than the best from *GP*. And our advertising clients during that period truly appreciated and respected *Guitar Player*'s credibility, its reach, and much, much more.

Jim Hatlo

As a *Frets* magazine guy first and foremost (I think I had the distinction of being the only *Frets* staffer who was on the mag's masthead in vol. 1, no. 1, and was still on there for the final issue), my view into *Guitar Player*'s sphere of operations was limited. I did a little moonlighting for *Keyboard* (I shot one or two concept cover photos, as I recall), but none for *GP*. At least, not directly. I authored a section on Guild Guitars for Tom Wheeler's *Guitar Book*, but that

Marshall came into the office to meet with Tom Wheeler and me. After exchanging pleasantries, we discussed the issue and how Marshall's shots would be perfect for it. The conversation then turned to money. I excused myself and went back to my office, which was next to Tom's.

Our offices were connected by a door, so I could hear most of what was being said, even when the volume was at normal conversation levels. But it didn't take long for things to heat up. Marshall was infamous for having a temper—and there were plenty of folktales about how far his temper could go off track. When things finally settled down, I knocked and peeked my head through the doorway.

"Is the coast clear?"

Marshall chuckled and said something like, "Come on in, it's safe." He reached inside his sport coat and tossed me a dark-colored object, saying, "If things had gotten out of control, you'd have known it."

Looking down to see what I'd caught, I was surprised to see a clip loaded with what looked like 9-mm ammo. After a moment, I handed it to Tom so he could see it for himself, but instead of looking, Tom just took the clip and passed it straight to Marshall. It disappeared into that sport coat with a *snick*—the sound a clip makes when getting inserted into the butt of a pistol. Oy.

We worked with Marshall on and off for years after that. He was a character, but under all his bluster he was a sweetheart of a guy. In the years following GPI's sale to Miller Freeman, my boss, Pat Cameron, and I bought something like twenty large-format Marshall prints for the office. The subjects of those photos ranged from the Stones to B.B. King and Mike Bloomfield, Cream, Jimi Hendrix, Duane Allman, Woody Guthrie, Ray Charles, Johnny Cash, Grace Slick, and Janis Joplin.

The heyday of *GP*/GPI was a magical time. Everything was new—people hadn't done some of the things we were doing. At least not when it came to special-interest consumer music magazines.

We were early adopters of digital publishing. When I joined the company, we were using type set on IBM Selectric typewriters by an outside service run by a couple named Al and Louis and supplemented by the folks at Doubert Printers, a small operation that was directly below *CK*'s corner of the Reed's Carpets building in Saratoga. Within a year, JC had purchased a fancy Compugraphic typesetting machine. Staff editors still worked on typewriters, hand-correcting manuscripts with pens, correction tape, and Wite-Out, but we had our own in-house typesetter named Frank Fletcher. What I remember most about that fancy machine was that it used punch cards as its memory system: the typesetting room was often covered in little pieces of paper, which had been punched out of a card.

JC never said, "This is how much you can spend." Instead, he trusted us to put out "the best music magazines in the world."

Dominic and Susan Milano

Over time, we added two more Compugraphic machines and brought on more in-house typesetters. We also adopted Kaypro computers—early CPM-based microcomputers that the editors used to input and "code" stories—which had special codes for changing fonts, for example, from roman to bold or italic. Before those Kaypros, the editorial staffs of *GP*, *Keyboard*, and *Frets* all shared those three typesetting machines. Typically we each had a few hours every couple of days to input the stories and columns we were responsible for writing and editing.

Kaypros saved data from a program called Perfect Writer onto big 5.25" floppy discs, which we handed off to Leslie Bartz's typesetting department. And then someone brought in an early Macintosh—I think this occurred around mid-1989, about six months before we were sold to MFI—and the way we handled production started really getting digital, although I don't think we made the full transition until after we'd been sold to Miller Freeman.

We did issues with Soundpages in them—Eva-Tone flexi-disc recordings you could play on a turntable. Each month we presented something new for the readers—I remember Tom Wheeler playing me the portion that had been edited out of "Crossroads"—Eric Clapton's signature solo from *Wheels of Fire*. Tom Dowd, Clapton's engineer and producer, sent it to TW for inclusion on a Soundpage to go with a cover story on Clapton. There were other, similarly stunning recordings bound into issues of *GP* and *Keyboard*.

Rather than rely on one of the big distributors to get the magazine into specialty outlets, JC created our own network of music stores—one of my roles in the early days of *CK* was to cold-call music stores to get them to carry the magazine. Eventually, we had an entire telemarketing department devoted to handling that task.

After records went the way of dodo birds, we started a thing called Notes On Call—an interactive phone service that let you listen to, and play along with, recordings of the lessons in the pages of *GP*.

We didn't rely on editorial budgets, at least not in any traditional sense. Former *GP* editor Don Menn as associate publisher, along with the head of our accounting department, Tom Murphy, used to give the chief editors monthly breakdowns of what we'd spent, newsstand and subscription sales figures, and other stats that are typically associated with editorial budgets, but JC never said, "This is how much you can spend during a given month on editorial." Instead, he trusted us to put out, as he'd put it, "the best music magazines in the world."

That gave the editors a lot of room to flex our muscle. For example, while I was the editor in chief of *Keyboard*, we did a special issue on digital sampling that involved spec testing that had never been done before. It took six months to get the tests perfected, completed, and printed up. During that time, I paid a freelancer to work out of our offices and practically live and breathe sampling. I can't tell you how much it cost, but the issue sold out and went into a second printing. I don't know of another publishing house that would've allowed that kind of follow-your-gut-and-hope-for-great-results approach without insisting on focus groups and other marketing data to make them comfortable spending money on something like that.

JC instilled in us a focus on what was important to the readers, and that served us very well. And it was amazing that we could pay attention to obscure musical styles and not get locked into a commercial formula that forced us to put rock stars on every issue's cover. If anything, we seemed to go out of our way to do the opposite—people landed on the cover because their stature as guitar players warranted it. Not because they sold a lot of records.

In the years that followed the heyday, business and economic conditions changed. Some of the companies that owned *GP*, after JC and Bud Eastman sold their interest in it, didn't know how to deal with flat or declining circulation numbers or advertisers that didn't like it that we didn't negotiate rates.

If there's one thing that those companies that followed JC and Bud did that I think we should've done long before, it's that JC didn't let us travel. As a result, advertisers got the impression that we lived in some kind of ivory tower—I suspect our competition helped foster that perception. But letting both editorial and advertising staffs travel and meet with companies on their home turf instead of waiting for a NAMM show to have any meaningful face-to-face contact made a huge difference in the post–JC and Bud years.

GPI in its heyday was a closely knit family. A pool of incredibly talented people working their butts off to create world-class music magazines based not in L.A. or New York or Nashville or London (the usual places people thought of as being music meccas) but in the heart of the Silicon Valley. I'm not sure if other staffers felt this way, but I never thought of myself as a "music journalist." Thanks to JC's philosophy of putting readers first, I was a musician writing for my peers. *GP* editors had access to musicians and could ask the questions readers wanted answers to, such as, How did so and so get that incredible tone? What strings do they use? Like I said, it was a magical time.

We could pay attention to obscure musical styles and not get locked into a commercial formula . . . to put rock stars on every issue's cover.

Bill Yaryan

When I left my job in January of 1975 as West Coast A&R and publicity director in Hollywood for Atlantic Records, I thought I was leaving the music business forever. My girlfriend and I packed our things in a U-Haul truck and migrated from Venice Beach to Northern California to live a carefree lifestyle. We moved into a house under the redwoods in the Santa Cruz Mountains that we shared with a couple of UC Santa Cruz students. My plan was to write poetry while collecting unemployment. But a year and a half later I was knocking on Jim Crockett's door at his sumptuous suite of offices over a carpet store in Saratoga to ask him for a job.

Bill Yaryan in 1978 (Jon Sievert)

My girlfriend—not that one but the next one—was pregnant. Unemployment had run out, and I was working part-time for a weekly Santa Cruz newspaper setting type and laying out pages for the printer. The free paper had an insert covering local culture, and occasionally I contributed reviews and stories, just as I had for the *Los Angeles Free Press* during my five years in the music business. After a year on unemployment and poor-paying part-time work, the need for a larger income had become insistent.

It was quickly apparent I was not a good fit for GPI, the magazine publishing company Crockett had developed almost from scratch, starting with *Guitar Player* and growing into *Contemporary Keyboard* (later *Frets* and others). They were magazines for musicians written by musicians. I thought of myself more as a writer than a musician, and my guitar skills were extremely limited.

Jim and I had talked occasionally on the phone when I was a

Hollywood PR man and tried to talk him into writing about my recording artists. But we'd never met. At my appointment I saw he was a trim fellow with a goatee who moved and talked slowly, but with deliberation. GPI did not need another writer. What it needed was someone to take over preparing the issues for the printer who could paste up galleys of type, ads, and photographs according to Jim's design. It was only part-time work to start with, at a less than modest salary, but I was given the glorious title on the magazine mastheads of art director.

Those early days in Saratoga with the *GP* and *CK* staff were nearly forty years ago, so I no longer remember much of the details. It was informal and fun. Of course we didn't wear ties, it being California casual every day. There was lots of play and socializing during the sunny days, which meant that getting the magazines out on time frequently required evening hours. Since I had a wife and baby at home and had to commute long distances over the hill from Santa Cruz to the office, I protested at staff meetings about the unpaid overtime. This was not a popular view, with Jim or the employees, most of whom were single, lived not far away, and enjoyed the excitement of the deadline crunch. I was seen as the guy who kept banker's hours.

The move to Cupertino was highly anticipated. We posed for photos on the land where construction was to take place. The completed offices with a large warehouse were impressive, the inside windowless offices less so. Jim ruled his domain from a tastefully decorated corner suite. My art studio was very well appointed, although I continued to cut galleys with an X-Acto knife, once accidentally slicing my hand and bleeding all over the layout pages.

Our neighbor, as many here will mention, was a start-up computer company called Apple. Gradually they would grow to take over all the nearby buildings and eventually practically the whole town, their skyscrapers plastered with the Apple logo. I remember when they went public and I contemplated buying stock—a road not taken. What I remember is the donut store at the end of the block and the Japanese restaurant in front of our building. Some of us would go running around the campus or swim at De Anza College not far away. There was room in the warehouse for back issues, supplies, and the regular jam sessions with notable musicians joining in and Jim banging the drums. I even played the sax and clarinet a couple of times. Workers from Apple would come over to listen, and some of them even joined in.

The number of employees increased with the move, but we still felt like a family. There were picnics together in local parks, parties at people's homes, the annual Christmas shindig, and even the wed-

Bill Yaryan (Nan Yaryan)

My plan was to write poetry while collecting unemployment.

My art studio was very well appointed, though I continued to cut galleys with an X-Acto knife.

dings of a couple of staffers. My wife and baby would join in, but the distance always set us a bit apart from the social scene. Some of the employees shared recreational drugs, at work and also after hours, and I must confess to being one of them. But of course that was long ago. And I will mention no names other than my own.

My wife and I also became friends with Jim's wife at the time, Rebecca. When they divorced, she would come to visit us in Santa Cruz. Looking through our photograph albums one day she picked up photo one and said, "Who is this handsome man?" A couple of days later I introduced her over the phone to my friend Jerry Hopkins, who lived in Hawaii. And a week after that she went to visit him. Their marriage lasted ten years. Now Jerry lives in Bangkok and is married to a Thai woman with a farm up-country. He's my oldest and closest friend these days.

As art director, I was occasionally given freedom to design layouts, but they were never as good as Jim's. The editors would provide photos to illustrate their stories. I remember I used one of the Grateful Dead that came, I was told, from their manager's office. When the issue was published, I got an angry call from photographer Jim Marshall, who had been a friend when I worked for record companies and hired him for jobs. Marshall used to come to my office to examine my music book collection to see who was using his photos without permission. Then he would call his lawyer to sue. He was notoriously volatile, and was upset over the Dead photo that he claimed was his. He said he would kill me because I stole his art. For a while I was genuinely concerned because I knew he owned a gun and was famous for threatening those who did him wrong. We had done drugs together at Willie Nelson's Fourth of July picnic in Texas, and it was rumored that cocaine was his downfall. As I remember it, we eventually paid him something for the photo. It was cheaper than a funeral for me.

Gradually I became more involved in magazine publishing and the business side of the enterprise rather than the editorial or art content. After leaving the music business in Los Angeles, I'd stopped keeping up with new innovations (were there any?) and could contribute little to office conversations about so-and-so's playing ability (for we were a magazine for musicians, and not for simply fans).

With Jim and others on the business side of the staff, I attended magazine conferences and read the publishing trade press. The idea of modeling circulation and production excited me, and I convinced Jim to sign up for Kobak Business Machines (KBM), an East Coast company that provided this service via phone line and printer. I moved up to the position of circulation director and was involved in choosing a new printer in Long Prairie, Minnesota. This required trips to a tiny town in upstate Minnesota where everyone worked for the same company; in snowy winter it was lots of fun. Taking estimates on circulation and ad sales from the ad directors, subscription rolls and newsstands, I would input figures into the program to predict our P&L for each issue. I found it fascinating, and occasionally accurate.

After four years with GPI, events conspired to my leaving. Our landlady in Santa Cruz broke up with her husband and needed to live in our house. My wife's sister in Connecticut had gotten romantically involved with a drug dealer and we wanted to separate them. But most importantly, I now had visions of using my GPI experience to climb the ladder of success in New York publishing. So I resigned in the summer of 1980. At my going-away party, Jim gave me a beautiful handmade leather shoulder bag. (I'm sad to report that while drunk one night in Manhattan I left it behind in a taxi.)

My family and I moved east, where I worked in circulation at Billboard Publishing and as general manager of *Theatre Crafts* magazine. At *TC*, I got RadioShack computers for staff writers and learned how to convert their files to type for the printer. Magazines were beginning to figure out the possibilities of computers, and I was a bit of an innovator on a minor scale. Jim and his wife Bobby came back to visit. Two years of commuting by train to the city finally got to me. And after our son was born at Yale Hospital, we packed up a U-Haul and moved back to California. Instead of returning to GPI (another road not taken), I got a job in the Alumni Association office at UC Santa Cruz. A year later I returned to complete my bachelor's degree, and continued to study for eighteen years until I received a PhD in history. Now I teach English to Buddhist monks in Thailand and keep in touch with my old friends from GPI on Facebook, where it seems they all have pages. What a long strange trip it's been!

Cheryl (Matthews) Fullerton

Getting to GPI was not any well-planned or thought-out process on my part, not like it was for those folks who had known about *Guitar Player* from an early age and revered the magazine from its inception, who loved their music and went to school to learn how to write about their favorite music, musicians, and gear. My path was circuitous and serendipitous.

I learned there was an opening in dealer sales from a musician friend of mine, Randy Bush, whom I'd been introduced to by Juice Newton, who was not directly involved in GPI but knew Jim Ferguson, who was working in dealer sales at the time. It was 1979,

> The number of employees increased, but we still felt like a family.

Cheryl Matthews in 1988
(Arden Syman)

and I was looking for a job so I could go back to school and finish my art degree. I had just completed a stint in Seattle working in a boutique music store, University Music Center, in the heart of the university district. We carried high-end classical instruments and a few moderately priced guitars. The owner had inherited some really fine antique Gibsons (The Gibson) and New York Martins from his dad. They were all pre–World War II, fine vintage instruments. There was also a collection of French violins. The store was very cool, and I loved selling guitars, but things started to unravel. (I learned years later that the owner never wanted the music store; he wanted to be a helicopter pilot!) I lasted about a year and a half before the rain, and lack of business, drove me back to sunny California.

A few days later, I was in the reception area of GPI Publications waiting for an interview with Tom Brislane, head of dealer sales. The receptionist told me Tom would be along soon, so I waited. In the meantime, I chatted with the friendly receptionist, who filled me in on what GPI was all about. This was sounding interesting—musicians, writers, designers, huh? What's not to like? Three hours later, Tom breezed through the door. Smacking himself on the forehead, he apologized dramatically and profusely, so genuinely devastated was he for having forgotten about the interview. I think the reason he hired me was because he felt so guilty about forgetting our appointment. So this was my introduction to GPI and the many talented characters I would come to know and love so well. They called Tom "the Breeze," as some of you might have guessed. He had a light, airy, ethereal quality about him. He was like a zephyr, disappearing and reappearing without, it seemed, any effort. He had big clown hair. Tom had a mischievous sense of humor and delighted in teasing me about Dennis Fullerton, *GP*'s ad director, who I had a little crush on. Tom would make up stories about Dennis's escapades with women at the NAMM shows, telling me that dozens of women lined up at Dennis' hotel door. When I refused to believe his concocted stories, he would drag Jas Obrecht in for support, and Jas would gleefully chime in that it was indeed true! All the women loved Dennis!

Cheryl (Matthews) Fullerton
(Dennis Fullerton)

I did pretty well with dealer sales, but when I learned there might be an opening as a production assistant to the art directors, I wondered if my art background might help me get my foot in the door. Dennis encouraged me to talk to Roger Siminoff, who was in charge of that position. Roger was the last person I wanted to talk to at GPI. Every time I saw him he was racing off in some direction with a huge scowl on his face. He barely glanced at me if we passed in the hallway. I think I was really afraid to approach him. I finally got the gumption to ask him about the position, and he agreed to have a look at my portfolio. I was offered the job. In the beginning it consisted of shooting halftones (converted photos to be ready for printing) for all three magazines. It had become problematic for all three art directors to shoot their own and schedule the time in the darkroom to get it done. We needed to have more process in place. Working with Roger and our printer, I learned how to get the best shots for print. At least, I tried. Sometimes the photos we had to work with weren't the best quality and we had to improvise. Yes, kids, this was before the digital revolution. Each and every photo was placed into a vertical camera and a screen placed over it to create the dots needed to burn the plates that were hung on a press, and from which the photos were printed. I know it's hard to believe, but believe it. Sometimes the work was backbreaking, and nonstop the closer we got to deadline. The stress was intense at times. Sometimes an impatient art director came pounding on the door insisting he have the shot "now!" All three magazine deadlines had to be at the same time to meet the distribution deadline, so it made it triple hard on the production people.

Roger was, in my opinion, a Renaissance man. There was nothing he couldn't do. He could build instruments; play guitar, banjo, mandolin, and bass; and write books and articles about it all. He was the best mentor anyone could ever have had. He convinced me and Jim Crockett and all the editors that we could save money and have more control over our covers if we "stripped them in-house," and he would teach me to do it! Roger had a strong print production background, and no one doubted him. So I began the grueling, difficult process of "stripping." You know all those little hairlines around the pictures? They were created by manual means. This meant hours in the darkroom creating just the right amount of "shrinks" and "spreads" on the film to make those little hairlines that are, most likely, taken for granted by the casual observer. There were no temperature controls on the chemicals, and we counted out loud to get the desired effect. I admit the learning curve was huge! One deadline night, or should I say morning, at around 4 A.M., I discovered I had been burning plates without film in the plate maker! I literally fell on the floor and cried because I had to go back to almost square one. This is probably too nerdy-geeky for most readers to appreciate, but take my word for it, it was a bummer.

Then there was the famous Stanley Jordan fiasco. We had sent our colored cover shots out to separation houses, where they would literally separate the colored photos into four separate films (magenta, cyan, yellow, and black) screened at the correct angles to produce the same colors as were in the photo. Flesh tones were the hardest to get right. Not all folks have the same perception of color, so Stanley came out too dark for Stanley, and he was extremely upset by the mistake. Stanley, if you read this, I apologize! Sometimes we flew by the seat of our pants!

Another cover headache ensued when Tom Wheeler showed Gary Richrath of REO Speedwagon his cover photo proof. Gary happened to be visiting our offices at the time. He went into a tizzy and made us choose a completely different photo of himself. This meant that I basically had to redo the cover. Argh! A lesson learned—you never show a cover to a star before it's published. Tom was so proud of that cover and the action shot. He thought we had captured the moment perfectly! Oh, well, all you can do is your best.

The coup de grâce of all covers, though, was the Charlie Christian one. We only had a black-and-white photo of him [likely taken in the '30s], so it was decided we should add that old-fashioned sepia-tone effect to give it depth and richness. This was a labor of love on my part. I worked for hours upon hours to get the desired effect. I used the four different colors in varying degrees to get the rich reddish brown we were looking for. In those days we proofed by using "color keys." I exposed the four separate films I created to the four color-key acetates and then washed them with process chemicals. I

At around 4 A.M. I discovered I'd been burning plates without film in the plate maker.

think there was something in those process chemicals' fumes, because something terrible happened. You couldn't see it on the proof, though. It wasn't until the cover was printed and delivered that you could see the hideous moiré pattern on the cover photo! I thought my life was over! But, strangely, only art director Peggy Shea noticed. Everyone else thought it was a cool graphic effect! The angles for two of the colors weren't far enough off, therefore creating a ripple effect. Just to prove I'm a production geek, again.

Roger started making noises like we could do our own separations in-house! Groan, "Please, not separations!" He agreed to put it on the back burner for a while. I eventually got some help with the addition of Paul Haggard, aka "Bosco," to my department. We started to split the work. I taught him how to do covers, which he seemed to enjoy a lot, and I took over the advertising materials, scheduling and inspecting the ads to make sure they conformed to our printer's specs. Most of our advertisers were always on time and gave us the correct materials, but there was one incident with a late ad that will go down in my memory as among the most epic excuses in advertising history. I can't remember the company, but they used an advertising agency in New York. The ad exec was a particular favorite of mine, Robbie Kline. He was usually late, but of course, I had to let him in the issue. One month we were literally down to the wire. I called Robbie to try and speed things along and found him in quite a tizzy. He yelled through the phone at me in his thick Brooklyn accent, "Cheryl, there's a catastrophe in the garment district! Nothing can get in or out! I can't get you the materials!" Well, knowing nothing of New York and its traffic peculiarities, I couldn't fathom what Robbie was talking about, so I said I'd get back to him. I immediately went down the hall to Roger's office, knowing he was an expert on all things New York, and said I thought Robbie had just come up with the most creative excuse not to get the ad materials to us by the deadline that I'd ever heard. Roger told me that the excuse was quite plausible. It was then that I learned that there was a tunnel into the New York garment district that, if blocked in any way, nothing could move into or out of. I called Robbie back and we came up with a work-around solution.

One Christmas, Dennis somehow persuaded me to do a song for the Christmas party. It was really an off-and-on thing leading up to the party. I practiced and practiced, and then I would say, "No, I can't do it." He kept saying it would be all right. Easy for him, because he had been performing so long, it was like ducks in water. He gathered the most illustrious trio that ever an incompetent greenie like me could, in their most vivid imagination, ever conceive of: Tom Darter on bass, plus Tom Wheeler and Dennis Fullerton on gui-

> You never show a cover to a star before it's published.

> **POLITICAL WISDOM**
> If you voted for Bush in '88, speak softly and carry the BIGGEST stick you can find.
> —*Mag Rag*, February 1989

tars. Wow! I did it, but it wasn't easy. Bless those guys for making it okay for me. That was the beauty of GPI. We all ultimately supported each other. And that was what I was destined to be, never a star, but a star supporter.

Certainly one of the highlights of my tenure at GPI was to be able to speak with B.B. King on the phone. It was the day of one of the most anticipated events in GPI history. Gretchen Horton, GPI's publicity director, had arranged for B.B., Herbie Hancock, Country Joe McDonald, David Grisman, and David Bromberg all to be there for our monthly jam in the warehouse. News stations had been informed, and television crews were in place to film, but B.B. was nowhere in sight! After much pacing and hand wringing, the phone eventually rang and it was B.B. "B.B.," I said, "where are you?" He said, "I'm lost!" Gretchen and Jim immediately went to fetch him and lead him back to the warehouse. My impression of B.B. was that he is the most gracious and humble musician I've ever met.

Paul Haggard moved on to be the art director for *Bass Player*, and I found a replacement for him in Joe Verri. Of course, no one could replace Paul! But Joe had been working for a printer in Pittsburgh before moving to the West Coast to play reggae. I interviewed him and went to see him play. I knew he would be a good fit for the company and could add a lot to the production team. He would be the one Miller Freeman kept when they bought us out in 1989.

It was a good time to leave, I suppose, but very hard to say goodbye to all my buddies. I went on to work for a printer, took some high-tech production-related jobs, and eventually got my teaching credential in art and foods. Teaching was a lot of fun, but my days with *Guitar Player* were some of the best days of my life. It is a tribute to Jim Crockett for gathering such a creative, motley crew together and producing some of the most-loved music magazines in the business. Oh yes: I married the "guitar god," Dennis Fullerton, and we are still together. I'm now supporting my son in his aspirations to become a great musician.

Sherry (Cronic) Thomas-Zon

I was a college student by day, silicon-disc inspector by night. My roommate at the time, Mike Formosa, had landed his dream job: part-time gig at *Guitar Player* magazine in late 1980 selling wholesale copies of the magazines to music dealers. He encouraged me to apply for a similar position as a way out of the night-shift rut I'd been in. It was the early days of tech in Sunnyvale and Mountain View, California, and I had worked more than enough swing and graveyard shifts. Thinking back, Silicon Valley was just coming alive

My days with *Guitar Player* were some of the best days of my life.

with opportunities. I had worked for a number of tech pioneers prior to *GP*, including Fairchild and Atari, while attending college during the day. It became clear I needed something that allowed me to both study and sleep within a twenty-four-hour period, so I accepted a position with GPM. This was my first part-time, commission-based telesales job, which allowed for time to study and have fun, simultaneously. I hadn't expected it to turn out to be such a fun job that exposed me to some of the brightest, most dedicated and creative people around. I ended up staying almost ten years.

I hadn't planned it this way, but I stayed awhile, primarily because it was fun and allowed me time to figure out my college path. I bounced around the company for about five years, averaging one new job each year. I'd been work-

Sherry Cronic: GPI staff photo (Jon Sievert)

ing on the business side, developing circulation, harassing music-store owners in telesales, and even programming, under the tutelage of Roger Siminoff, for our mini mainframe computer system (just dated myself). So when Jim Crockett asked me one day what I wanted to do at the magazine, or with my life, I paused and then quickly recovered. I took the opportunity to speak up for a job on *Guitar Player*'s advertising team and ultimately moved over to the ad director position after some time training with the pro, Dennis Fullerton. Needless to say, I had rather large and experienced shoes to fill at *Guitar Player*.

I think this impresses me because I ended up working in tech. But I remember one monthly jam in particular, the one that B.B. King attended. It was, of course, a thrill to meet B.B., and it's funny now to think we had B.B. play in our humble magazine shipping area, of all places. What were we thinking? I'm sure everyone who jammed with the blues master has a great memory of that afternoon. In addition to the buzz of having B.B. on-site for our monthly staff jam, there was this oddly quiet, uninvited group of early Apple employees who wandered over to our building to enjoy our barbecue as well as B.B. As it turns out, Apple and *GP* shared a distinct Lazaneo Drive address. The

GP was my first part-time, commission-based job. I ended up staying almost ten years.

difference was that we had fun out loud. Apple staff rarely mixed with the neighboring companies. I didn't even know who they were until I saw a small group of ten or so of them breaking the veil of Apple secrecy by joining our B.B. King party. I never saw those folks again.

These were the occasional music giveaways held in Tom Wheeler's office. It was part auction, part Christmas. Tom sat behind his desk while the staff waited patiently for Tom to raise a worthwhile throw-away recording among the albums sent to *Guitar Player* that period for review. In terms of who got what, it was generally accepted that editors ranked higher than the business hacks for take-home albums. Some were naturally set aside for the editors associated with a particular style of guitar, which made sense: Tom Mulhern, progressive; Jim Ferguson, classical or jazz; Jas Obrecht, blues; Tom Wheeler, whatever he wanted; the leftovers, the rest of the team.

Certainly the most memorable and lasting impression for me is of my meeting my future husband, bass maker Joe Zon. Actually, it's important to note that young Cordell Crockett technically introduced us at the 1986 Anaheim NAMM show after the advertiser breakfast. Editor Tom Mulhern personally escorted me to Joe's trade show booth more than once during that January show, which enabled yet another meeting with the man I would marry seven years later in Kenwood, California. We celebrated our twentieth anniversary in 2013.

The entire experience of working at *GP* was amazing. I have so many great memories, especially of my time as part of the *Guitar Player* team. It was such fun working around that talented group, hunkering down at deadlines and celebrating after every issue shipped to the printer. The editors were amazingly fun, interested, devoted, and wonderful. They also became some of my best buddies, big brothers, and lifelong friends. As far as the direction of the mag, I can't think of a thing I would have done differently, other than perhaps not selling the asset to Miller Freeman Publishing . . . but I'll skip that.

I was too young during my time at *GP* to comment on anyone's editorial direction or objectives. The magazines all served their respective audiences so well, and each succeeded as one of the most dynamic and committed content sources for young, devoted, and aspirational musicians. That dedication and commitment to the product is a testament to Jim and to the stated values he promoted.

I mentioned I work in technology now. I left *GP* sometime after its acquisition by United News publisher Miller Freeman. I returned to finish graduate work in digital media and film. After spending a few years working in docu-

Sherry (Cronic) Thomas-Zon
(Keaton Zon)

mentary film, repertory theatre, and what they used to call "new media" design, I returned to publishing with a small group focused on the video and animation. In 1993, Joe and I were married and moved to San Francisco, where we live today with our wonderful twin boys. I've continued to work in the digital media and now technology fields. I moved into leadership roles within technology start-ups during the 2000s. In 2009, I became CEO of a Mountain View–based Internet search start-up, which was acquired in 2011. Recently, I ended up back at school doing some academic work at Stanford University, and I'm still very active within the technology field. Today, I'm primarily focused on "big data" for retail and search technologies. I split my time between San Francisco and the Los Angeles area for work, and spend much more time now writing, researching, speaking at tech conferences, and, of course, thinking fondly of my early years at *GP*.

P.S. One of my twin boys plays guitar and worships Dave Grohl and the Foo Fighters. The other has played piano for three years and worships Bach.

Janine Cooper Ayres

At twenty-three years old, I thought I'd died and gone to heaven when I was chosen to be the office coordinator of *Guitar Player*!

Janine Cooper with Tom Wheeler in 1986 (Jas Obrecht)

My previous post had been receptionist of GPI Publications. At the time, I'd already been playing bass guitar and singing in several bands (for almost six years).

Part of my job was to transcribe interviews with such amazing guitarists as Eric Clapton, The Edge, Eric Johnson and Yngwie Malmsteen. I also assisted Peggy Shea (the art director) during boards each month doing the paste-up of the magazine. It was a fascinating process!

The creative energy in the office was incredible! It was an honor to work for the editor, Tom Wheeler, and writers Dan Forte, Tom Mulhern, Jim Ferguson, and Jas Obrecht. I have no doubt it was the hippest place to work in the Bay Area!

Janine Cooper Ayres (Alex Ayres)

I was also responsible for opening mail and receiving such things as photos for the interviews. One photographer in particular was not easy to work with. His name was Jim Marshall. He was well known for his photos of the Beatles, Hendrix, and Janis Joplin, to name a few. One day he became irate with me on the phone. I can't remember the details, but I know it didn't go well. About a week later, I received a large manila envelope in the mail (the only time I received something addressed to me). It was a print of Lennon and McCartney signed by Jim Marshall! I still have it today and understand it is quite valuable.

After working at *GP* for nearly a year, I was told by Dan Forte that he heard that the band Let's Active was looking for a new bassist. He suggested that I audition. A few weeks later I was heading for North Carolina! It went well, but the band's leader, Mitch Easter, told me he didn't want to take me away from my job for two short tours.

A few months later I did leave my post at *GP*. I moved to Los Angeles with my fiancé at the time. The bass player that Mitch Easter had chosen was not working out. When he found out that I was no longer at the magazine and was available to tour, he flew me back out to North Carolina. I did two tours with Let's Active, on the second of which we opened for R.E.M. It was a highlight of my musical career and would not have happened if not for *GP* and Dan Forte.

Jim Aikin

My friends and I had been hanging around Jim Crockett's bookstore, Books Universal, in Livermore in the mid-1960s. In 1970, Jim played drums a few times with a band that I had started with Tom Darter (who later became the editor of *Keyboard*). But the bookstore went the way of all bookstores, and by the time I came back from the East Coast in the summer of 1971, Jim was working in Los Gatos at a tiny publishing endeavor called GPI Publications. I worked there as an editorial assistant at *Guitar Player* that summer. I remember very little about what went on, but I do remember that my first job was transcribing a long and rather depressing tape-recorded interview with a big-band guitarist named Billy Bauer, who felt that he had lost out because he never learned to read music. (In later years, I got to know that tape recorder quite well. I used it at *Keyboard* to transcribe jazz piano solos for Leonard Feather's columns.)

The following summer, 1972, I was hired as an assistant editor. By that point Bud Eastman was no longer part of the day-to-day opera-

Jim Aikin

tions. I worked at *GP* for six or eight months, but at that time I had an opportunity to play full-time in a band (not the same band, although it was also formed by people from Livermore), so I left *GP*. I believe my replacement was Don Menn. To be honest, I had gotten tired of writing about string gauges, amps, and the types of picks players used. Those topics didn't interest me at all.

The office in Los Gatos had about five rooms, four downstairs and one upstairs. My office was the upstairs room. It was also the warehouse; all of the back issues were stored there.

In those days, we had nothing resembling typesetting equipment, and certainly no office computers. The typesetting was done by a separate company in downtown San Jose (or possibly Santa Clara). Someone would drive downtown with the edited copy and drive back a couple of days later to pick up the galley sheets. If there were typos, we would type them out (on paper, using a typewriter—remember typewriters?), noting carefully that this was a two-line correction, so the second line needed to be justified. A batch of corrections went downtown along with the next batch of copy. The columns of type in the galleys would be neatly cut from the large sheets with an X-Acto knife, run through a waxer, and laid down on one of the boards. The boards were the size of two-page spreads, and all of the layout was done on them.

Photos were handled much the same way, I believe. A shop somewhere would turn the photos into black-and-white halftones, and the halftones would be run through the waxer and pasted onto the boards. Headlines were created one letter at a time by transferring rub-on letters from large sheets of decorative type.

Jim was always very concerned about containing costs for the fledgling enterprise. There was no color in the editorial pages—it was all black-and-white. When I started at *GP*, the covers featured black-and-white photos, with a band of solid color (different from month to month) filling up the cover. Eventually Jim decided to try a four-color cover. Strictly black-and-white editorial in the inner pages continued, however, until 1978, when Tom Darter convinced Jim that *Keyboard* really did need color photos for our cover story on Keith Emerson. After that, color started creeping into the editorial pages.

Jim and Bud Eastman tried out several business ideas during those years. Bud was keen on the idea of a national guitar players' club. By the mid-1970s, however, the company had focused on what worked best: magazines. There was also a GPI books division in those days.

As early as 1972, Jim had mentioned to me that he might want to start a keyboard magazine along the lines of *Guitar Player*. When that happened, in the summer of 1975, Tom Darter was hired as editor, and Tom convinced Jim that, even though I had been flaky and run off from my gig as assistant editor at *GP*, they should hire me at *Contemporary Keyboard*.

I started work at *CK* (the name was changed a few years later to just *Keyboard*) in December of 1975. At that time the offices were above Reed's

November '76 cover painting by Jim's artist father, Ben Aikin

Carpets on Los Gatos/Saratoga Road. By that time there were fifteen or twenty employees in all. The *GP* editors shared a room, as did the *Keyboard* staff, but Jim Crockett had a private office. When *Keyboard* started, the galleys were still being printed by a separate company, but it was downstairs in the same building. Shortly thereafter, Jim purchased typesetting equipment, which was operated by Frank Fletcher, but waxing galleys and typing out corrections would still be the norm for years to come.

In late 1976 or early 1977, ground was broken on a new office building on Lazaneo Drive in Cupertino. A few months later, we moved into those offices, which were much nicer than the setup above Reed's Carpets! I believe the other half of the building was rented out to a small start-up called Apple Computer. Shortly thereafter, the staffs of *Guitar Player* and

Jim Aikin (Barbara Stanton)

Keyboard, along with other musicians in the other departments and folks who dropped by, starting having a monthly jam session in the warehouse. For most of the year, the weather was warm enough that the warehouse's metal door could be rolled up, so that people could sit out in the parking lot and listen to the music, drink beer, or whatever. The jams were a high point of those days.

One of Jim's ideas was to use the jams for a bit of publicity, to show readers that the people creating *GP* were actual musicians. That was the main pivot of the company's sales pitch, in any case—that these were magazines *by* musicians, *for* musicians. It was never the case that rock stars dropped by to jam on a regular basis, but once in a while somebody famous or semi-famous did show up. Sometimes this was an arranged PR "event." When B.B. King played at a jam, I'm sure it was arranged. On the other hand, a Santa Cruz piano player named George Winston did drop by once and bang out some chords at a jam, using *Keyboard*'s electric piano. This was a year or so *before* George's first album became a huge hit and catapulted Windham Hill Records into the stratosphere. After we moved to the Stevens Creek Boulevard office, I know Jerry Garcia played at a jam. Again, I'm sure that was an arranged event.

Some of the music at the jams was both spirited and quite respectable. On the other hand, some of it was just a lot of fooling around. Jim was careful to invite everyone at the company to participate. Whether they were a good player or had very limited skills didn't matter. He shared drumming duties with Ed Sengstack, who was the ad director of *Keyboard*.

One of the things I've always admired about Jim Crockett was that he had a clear view of the separation between advertising and editorial. His policies toward advertising changed a bit over the years, but he was always very clear that our editorial content was not to be dictated by advertisers. After Jim left and the Miller Freeman gang took over, that gradually changed. I was on the editorial side, so I really don't know the details of what business decisions were made—and there would be no point in dredging up anecdotes about Miller Freeman at this late date! The point is, Jim had started on the editorial side of *GP*, and before that he had run a bookstore, so he understood how important it was that the printed word be independent of outside influences. (If memory serves, he stocked Mao Zedong's *Little Red Book* at Books Universal, which I'm sure infuriated some of the conservatives in the community.)

Joe Gore (Jon Sievert)

Joe Gore

Sadly, my time at *Guitar Player* overlapped only briefly with Jim Crockett's—the mag changed hands mere months after I was hired at *GP*. But I say "sadly" because Jim had created such a lovely community as well as a successful company. He was always very kind to me. I only got to work under Jim for a few months—but then I spent several decades hearing everyone say, "Man, it was so much cooler when Jim Crockett ran the place." A quarter century later I'm still touched by

Joe Gore with Tom Wheeler, Tom Mulhern, and Jas Obrecht at NAMM 2013 (Claudia Lopez Rhea)

how, even though I didn't report to him, he went out of his way to give me supportive feedback on my work and tell me that he was glad I was working for the mag. It meant so much to me as a young guy starting out in the field.

Peggy Shea

I was working in Palo Alto for the Equipment Guide-Book Company as a production artist and finishing my last year at San Jose State in graphic design/art direction. One of my vendors, Darrell Monda, who worked for Federal Envelope, told me about a job opening up at GPI, in marketing. Karen Bland was moving on, and they were look-ing for a production artist. I interviewed in August of 1979 and got the job. Roger Siminoff grilled me in the conference room for what felt like hours.

I was the production artist in the marketing area with Lucienne O'Connor-Marrow and Joan Kreamer. After about two years or so,

Peggy Shea with
Michael Hedges
(Jay Blakesburg)

Dominic Milano, who was the art director at *GP*, was very ill in the hospital and Crockett came to me and asked if I could help produce *GP*. I was art director there until August of 1990.

I remember the jams in the warehouse on Lazaneo and then in the back underneath the building on Stevens Creek. I still have dreams about both buildings.

I remember Crockett always saying: "We're not here to win design awards." Heck, could have fooled me. I would have loved a few design awards. But it was always about the quality of the content of the magazine, which was not a fanzine.

I was attached at the hip to Tom Mulhern ("Ferd Dog"). If it hadn't been for him being the managing editor, the magazine wouldn't have happened. I loved all the stuff he acquired from *Frets* assistant editor Lachlan Throndson in his office, such as the window switch plaque with flowers on it, the velvet painting, and the beaded doorway to the record room. Oh, can't forgot the other gems: one-legged Minnie Mouse (or was it Mickey?) that was in the outer office on

may be a bit biased when I say that the years 1974 to 1980 was their true high-water mark.

Oh, and coincidentally, those were the six years when my by-line appeared.

Rick Eberly

I'd been working as an electronics technician building Prophet synthesizers for Sequential Circuits in San Jose, California. I was also playing bass on the weekends in a three-piece power trio, a couple of hours north, in Sacramento.

While at Sequential Circuits I was cartooning for the internal employee pub, the *Toilet Paper*, for Greg Armbruster and others. Greg later joined *Guitar Player*'s sister publication, *Keyboard* magazine, in an editorial position. One day I got a request for a spot illustration. I worked on it for two weeks and got $35. Wow! My first published drawing!

That continued for a couple more years until one day I was dropping off a piece, and the company's art director, Chris

Rick Eberly

Ledgerwood, took me aside to offer me a full-time position as a graphic artist and illustrator, launching my art career in magazines, allowing me to escape from electronics.

I remember a photo shoot for a *GP* cover with Van Halen and Sammy Hagar a bit north in Marin County. It was at an old school that was then the production studio for the Gumby animated TV show. There were different sets in different classrooms. Sammy was daring Eddie to jump in the air and do the splits, but he didn't want to rip his pants open.

And there was that day Jerry Garcia came to GPI and jammed down in our warehouse area. Before the jam I was sitting on the platform stage with my bass in my lap when the door opened and Jerry walked out of the offices. He stood for a moment looking around, then walked

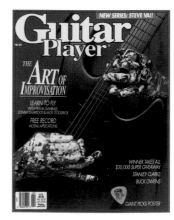

February '89 Rick Eberly cover

Rick Eberly (Self-Portrait)

over and sat next to me. I told him what an honor it was to meet him, and that my friends and I listened to the Dead and Country Joe and Jimi Hendrix and Cream and Led Zeppelin etc., nonstop. I played him that melodic bass line by Phil Lesh from "Walk Me Out in the Morning Dew," and explained how it had influenced me.

Jerry chuckled and said, "I love doing these things." I think he meant showing up at *GP* and being around the people and jamming.

Personally, I consider my time at *Guitar Player* one of the high points of my career, although I arrived a little later in the "glory years" timeline. I felt that the authors, and I, as an illustrator, were very respected and appreciated for what we created.

As I write this now, I'm a contractor for Cisco Systems, creating high-level PowerPoint presentations for executives.

Illustrations by Rick Eberly

Neil Zlozower

I was a young little punk kid living at home with my parents, and I was just sort of shootin' photos for a hobby to, you know, hang pictures of my favorite rock stars on my bedroom walls. I went to concerts like Deep Purple, Led Zeppelin, Rolling Stones, the Who, or whatever it was. . . . Back then, they were a little bit more liberal about bringing cameras in; you could just walk right in and bring a camera, and that's what I did, more or less.

I was never on staff for *Guitar Player*. They had a staff photographer, Jon Sievert, at the time, but I was just a contributor. We probably pestered the hell out of Jim Crockett and every so often called him up, as there was no e-mail back then. I'd just tell him, "Hey, we're gonna shoot Led Zeppelin tonight," "Hey, we're gonna shoot Eric Clapton tonight," "Hey, we're gonna shoot Rory Gallagher tonight, you need any photos?" and we'd make the prints and send 'em some!

I don't know the date, but I think the first picture I ever sold him, which would have been one of the very first pictures I ever had published in my whole, entire career, was Ritchie Blackmore from Deep Purple, and I remember Wes Montgomery was on the cover. They used two of my shots, actually, and Ritchie Blackmore was probably my all-time favorite guitarist, so I was ecstatic about having a couple of my photos of one of my idols in the magazine. That was a lot of brain cells ago for me. . . .

I don't remember my first cover for *Guitar Player*. I've had a lot of covers in *Guitar Player* over my forty-five-year career. But *Guitar Player* was probably the first magazine I really remember of any national quality that I had photos in, and obviously there wasn't *Guitar World* and there wasn't *Premier Guitar* and the foreign market hadn't been born yet, so *GP* was the guitar magazine of choice back then. I go to my baby brother Zakk Wylde's house, and he's got old vintage *Guitar Player* magazines all over the place lying around. *Guitar Player* magazine was *the* magazine, if you were a guitarist, to be in, ya know?

Hopefully JC remembered to give me photo credits; he was pretty good about that stuff, and he ran a professional ship, and it was a professional-looking magazine, ya know?

A bit of trivia: I remember doing the first Eddie Van Halen story that Jas Obrecht did, and I remember we started off at my studio.

Neil Zlozower (Self-portrait)

January '77 (Cover photo by Neil Zlozower)

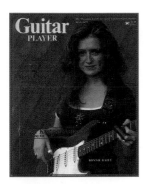

May '77 (Cover photo by Neil Zlozower)

April '78 (Cover photo by Neil Zlozower)

September '78 (Cover photo by Neil Zlozower)

April '80 (Cover photo by Neil Zlozower)

Neil Zlozower (Jamie Barker)

. . . Eddie was my friend, so he wanted to take the event to my place, where I lived, for certain reasons which I won't go into in detail, but . . . so me, Jas, and Eddie ended up driving to my apartment, and we hung there for quite a long time. Back then, the whole music industry was more fun, and now it's turned into more of a cold, sort of pathetic business. . . . It's not like it was in the '70s, that's for sure. It was fun back then; everybody had fun. Now it's just a moneymaking tool and there's not a lot of loyalty. It's a business now, a scientific business. Back then, if I wanted to get in touch with a musician, I'd just call 'em on the phone, basically. It was a lot easier to get in touch with someone. Now you have publicists and managers and all of that to go through.

artists and their music. I can't remember how many shows we did, but they were highly successful. We not only had a prominent radio show, but we received favorable publicity about the show itself. For a long time I had copies of those reel-to-reel taped shows. I wish I still had them, but they long ago disappeared.

Another project we developed was the annual *Guitar Player* Magazine Awards. Jim developed categories for the awards—Best Blues Guitarist, Best Rock Guitarist, Best Hawaiian Slack Key Guitarist, or whatever. Besides naming artists "the best . . ." we decided to present them with some unusual kind of memento. We didn't just want to give them a framed certificate or a brass plaque. I recall two such "gifts" we gave our winners: The first was a custom-designed and created bracelet fashioned of rosewood and sterling silver. I found a street jewelry artist in San Francisco and commissioned him to create the brace-

Ernie Beyl (Fred Lyon)

lets based on a rough design by Jim and me. The bracelet was designed like the neck of a guitar with a rosewood board and silver frets. I gave mine to my daughter and she still wears it.

Another year's memento for winners in various categories was a beautiful framed abstract color print of a guitar. It utilized something like ten colors, which meant it had to go through a hand-fed press ten or so times. Each print was numbered and signed by the artist. They were terrific. Again, we printed a few extras and I eventually gave mine to my son Jeff—a guitar player—who has it hanging in his home.

As I said, I believe Jim and I made a good team. He was willing to try anything, and I was coming up with some unusual PR ideas.

Lonni Elrod (Jon Sievert)

I think the program we developed together was highly imaginative and perhaps ahead of its time. We were roundly praised for the things we did.

I can't recall how Jim and I ended this relationship, but I continued on in "the PR biz" for many years and represented all kinds of clients in travel and tourism, music, etc. When I finally retired from PR and closed my business, I reverted to my first love—journalism. Briefly, I do a lot of freelance writing—mostly about food, restaurants, San Francisco history, and fly fishing. I also have a steady gig as a columnist for a San Francisco neighborhood newspaper, for which I write a column called Sketches from a North Beach Journal.

Lonni Elrod Gause

I had recently graduated from West Valley College, in Saratoga, in Northern California. I was definitely the baby of the staff, only twenty-one years old when I started, and everyone else was about ten years older than me.

My sister, Luanne Giacalone, who worked in circulation and advertising, told me about the opening for an office coordinator at *GP* and encouraged me to apply.

I started out as office coordinator with the November 1986 issue. From '86 to '89 I was

Tom Wheeler's assistant, transcribed interviews, solidified copyright permissions, helped proofread, coordinated deadlines and payments with the monthly columnists, and supported the editorial staff.

I loved the family vibe of the office.

I remember going backstage at a David Lee Roth concert to talk to Steve Vai and bassist Billy Sheehan, and he introduced Tom Wheeler and me to Joe Satriani and told us we should do a story on this guy and that Joe had taught Steve everything he knew. Meanwhile David Lee Roth was in a separate room surrounded by about twenty women with big hair and little clothing!

I was invited for a backstage tour at the Grand Ole Opry while attending the summer NAMM show in Nashville and loved the awesome vibe that permeated the entire theater.

I also remember how hard/fun it was to obtain an exclusive Soundpage for the magazine. I loved the excitement that surrounded packing up the "boards" and racing them off to FedEx to meet the print deadline. When we later moved to digital production, the party/celebration vibe was lost.

Lonni Elrod Gause (Mike Bromberg)

As I mentioned earlier, *GP* was a family when I came on board. It wasn't about budgets and the bottom line; it was about putting out a quality magazine every month. We featured "real" guitar players and were proud of every issue we produced. We took pride in discovering the real talent, not the newest hit maker.

I am a librarian now, working in education. I am passionate about children's literature and getting children excited about reading.

Jim Santana
by Andre Santana

"It's not what you know, but who you know" and "Timing is every-thing" are two sayings that led to Jim Santana's relationship with Jim Crockett and *Guitar Player* magazine. My father, Jim Santana, was a freelance photographer for *GP* in the early 1970s. He and Jim Crockett (JC) met in college. JC later married Jean Reyburn, who knew my father as a teenager growing up in Stockton, California. The memories that are strongest are of visiting the Crockett house-hold in Livermore, California, on the way back from weekend trips to the foothills. At that time, Crockett owned a small bookstore, and my parents would stop by to visit and catch up on how things were going. It was after one of these visits that I remember the discussion on the final leg of the trip home that JC was working to get into the magazine business. I was only about eight or nine years old at that time, so it is only a vague recollection.

Growing up the son of a photographer could be described as "in-teresting." I was amazed at the level of effort to take a picture of a pot or a candle for an advertisement. There were lights, backdrops,

In the 1970s, a photographer relied on his knowledge and skill and then shot fifteen rolls.

Jim Santana in 1976 (Self-portrait)

Jerry Garcia (Jim Santana)

flash umbrellas, batteries, and cords all over the place. Our living room was often turned into a photo studio. It was not unreasonable to take forty or fifty shots to get the right picture for a stationary object. What it took to capture images at a performance in a dark venue, with lighting out of your control and a subject who was moving onstage, was a skill that I only now truly appreciate.

The pictures that stand out strongest in my mind were on the cover of the February 1971 *GP* featuring Chuck Berry. It was the first time that I saw my father's work on the cover of a magazine. He had another cover photo of Jerry Garcia in the April 1971 edition of *GP*. My dad would work all day as a ships clerk for the longshoremen's union and then come home, eat dinner, gather his cameras and photography equipment, and head out for whatever concert he might have been assigned to. The next morning I would awake and see his camera bag, and it was not unusual to see ten to fifteen rolls of film (thirty-six exposures) shot and ready to be processed. In those days I never really knew what he did while he was gone at those concerts, but I have a much better idea now. Much like a sniper, my dad would survey the area and look for hazards and for the best angles, lighting, and locations that would enable him to get the best shots of the subject. This was not like shooting the static objects in our front room, but shooting a moving individual with lighting and actions that were random. There was no way to know if you had it right, and you had one chance to get the picture. Today's digital equipment allows for test shots with instant viewing and adjustment of the camera. In the 1970s, a photographer relied on his knowledge and skill and then shot fifteen rolls to capture the image good enough to be published.

As the child of a photographer, I learned that photographs were the product of work and strategy to capture the subject and tell a story. Images of legends such as B.B. King, Carlos Santana (no relation to me), and Chuck Berry, and of up-and-coming performers such as Jerry Garcia, Jorge Santana (brother of Carlos), John McLaughlin, Commander Cody, and Jeff Beck were just a few of the subjects from my dad's "other job." I would often spend time with my father in the darkroom and watch the magic of photography as negatives were developed and reviewed to see which ones appeared to have the best lighting. My dad would wear a jeweler's loupe and go over the three or four hundred shots to try to identify the best pictures to enlarge. He then would enlarge and dodge or burn where needed to come up with ten to twenty of the best pictures to submit to *GP*. Of those submitted, maybe one or two would be selected for publication.

There were other perks to being the son of a *GP* photographer. There were times we would visit Jim Crockett at the *GP* offices. To keep us occupied while he and my father talked business, Crockett

I would often spend time with my father in the darkroom and watch the magic of photography.

would send my brother and me into a room with what seemed to be countless records sent to *GP* for review. If they had been reviewed, Crockett would allow us to take one or two that interested us. On one visit in the early '70s Crockett picked out an album knowing that my brother and I were into R&B. He stated that it was the first album of a new group and they were supposed to be pretty good. I still have that record (with quite a few scratches) today and that new group did pretty well for themselves; it was the Commodores.

Guitar Player magazine was many things to a lot of entertainers, musicians, writers, and fans. For me it was a place where my father's "other job" was highlighted and gave him his fifteen minutes of fame.

Tim Lundell

Over the course of my forty years of legal practice, my ten years as legal counsel for *Guitar Player* and GPI Publications certainly stand alone as a one-of-a-kind experience.

In 1982, when I had become acquainted with publisher Jim Crockett, it came to light that, after fifteen years in the business, it might be time to have a regular attorney to advise the staff and handle any legal disputes that might arise in the often litigious world of publishing. It was an easy engagement to enjoy, though the culture clash between my then-customary business suits and the denim-and-sandals look of company management took some getting used to.

Our conference room meetings to review fundamentals of copyright practice were often followed by a jam session in the back parking lot, though I am sad to say that, unlike just about everyone

Tim Lundell (Matthew Crosby)

LOST IN TRANSLATION

Fachblatt is a music magazine in West Germany, and a pretty good one at that. They distribute our magazines there. For a brilliant, stellar example of how sometimes things get lost in translation: Tom Wheeler's *GP* interview with Michael Bloomfield was reprinted in *Fachblatt's* March 1980 issue.

Wheeler quoted Bloomfield saying he wanted to be "B.B. to the tits," referring to our beloved B.B. King. The Germans, being of European orientation, figured that "B.B." meant Brigitte Bardot, so it came out sort of like Bloomfield wanted to have tits like Brigitte Bardot.
—*Mag Rag*, Summer 1981

LEARN A NEW SKILL:
Playing The Guitar Is Easy!

A few months ago I bought a guitar instruction book and tried to teach myself to play the instrument. The book said I would be popular at parties, but I have no way of knowing; nobody has invited me to a party. While I have been waiting and practicing, I've also been making a few revisions in the instruction book to bring it closer to reality. I'll begin with the instrument:

Description:

The guitar looks like a large ukulele and has six steel strings. The four lowest ones are wound with wire and unravel with wear. The highest string often breaks when the guitar is first tuned. It doesn't matter. There are still five left and, after all, you only have five fingers anyway. The guitar obviously was invented by someone with six fingers. Anyone who attempts to play the guitar with only five fingers starts off with a severe handicap. When playing a chord (a group of notes that sound terrible together) one finger frequently must press down two or more strings. This is called a "barre." Playing a barre makes a deep groove in your finger. Pretty soon you can't stand the pain and you give up and go down to the neighborhood barre and have a beere.

Selection:

When buying a guitar, examine it carefully. Make sure it has a strong neck, as this part could split if the guitar is hit against something solid. Like a tree. Check the frets, the little metal strips on the neck. Frets are important. When you push a string down on a fret, the guitar often makes a buzzing sound. Choose a guitar that has a pleasant buzz, because you will be hearing a lot of that.

Tuning Up:

Always tune the guitar before playing. Do this very slowly, ear close to the strings. Pick the strings while turning the little tuning keys this way and that. Assume a thoughtful expression. Don't over-tighten the strings as one may snap and tear your ear off. Some successful amateur guitarists spend an entire evening just tuning up. People go away saying, "What a wonderful sense of pitch!" or "He certainly has a fine ear!" If he has never broken a string, they say, "He has fine ears!"

Playing:

Three chords are all you need to play most songs on the guitar. They are called "E" and "A" and another one called a "seventh chord" which is too difficult to bother with. When you come to the part of the song that needs that chord, just buzz the strings lightly. Assume the above-mentioned thoughtful expression. This is known as "faking it," the first technique every amateur musician learns. "E" and "A" are easy to learn. Practice shifting back and forth between these two chords until your fingers bleed. While making chords with your left hand, it is necessary to strike the strings with your right hand. Many people prefer to use a pick for this, but you can use your knuckles for a folk-guitar effect. This soon gets blood all over the guitar.

Playing with only two chords limits your repertoire, but there are a few songs, like Clementine and Tom Dooley that can be played with only two chords. Unfortunately, they are not "E" and "A." —Dereck Williamson

1985 Mag Rag story, "Guitar Made Easy"

on the staff, I did not have the musical talent to participate.

The great people at GPI were wonderfully memorable and wonderfully easy to work with. Jim was without question the most laid-back CEO I've had the pleasure to work with, but he had clearly earned the respect of everyone on the staff and in the industry at large. Bonnie Schoenemann, Jim's secretary, kept Jim and his editorial team organized in an atmosphere of guitar riffs from various offices, and legendary musicians dropping in to visit or be interviewed for upcoming issues.

The actual legal challenges were few and far between, as the business was very much driven by respect for musicians and the music industry in general. My responsibilities seriously ramped up, however, when the decision was made to have the company acquired by a larger organization, but one that would respect the culture that had developed among a very dedicated team. It was a long hunt for the right fit and a long process to get it done, and though there were more twists after my gig was over, it is great to see that the *Guitar Player* brand and spirit lives on.

Tim Lundell (Penelope O'Neill)

It's great to see that the *Guitar Player* brand and spirit lives on.

1981 *GP* Christmas photo (Jon Sievert)

Behind-the-Scenes Photos

James Gurley and Jas Obrecht in 1978 (Clara Erickson)

Steve Rosen and Mick Ronson in 1976 (Brad Elterman)

Vern Ailee in 1975 crafting a *Guitar Player* Readers Poll Award (Jon Sievert)

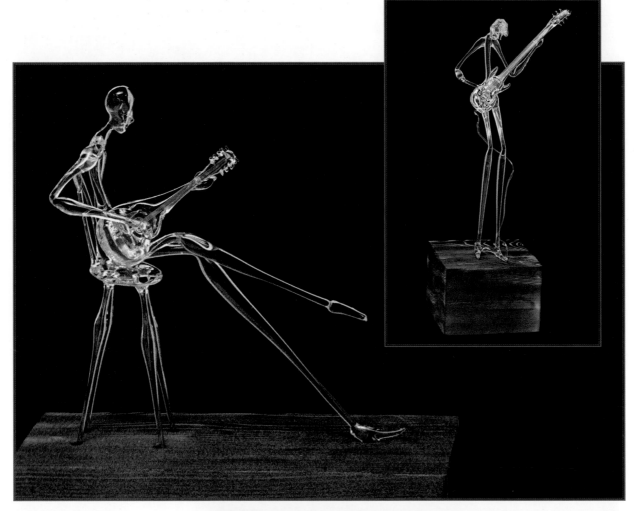

Two 1975 *Guitar Player* magazine Readers Poll Awards (Jon Sievert)

Dara, Jim, and Cordell Crockett at CNN Studios in 1986 (Jeffrey Mayer)

Jerry Garcia with Jon Sievert, taking a light reading (Jas Obrecht)

GPI ad directors Mattee Balin, Dennis Fullerton, and Jerry Martin (Jon Sievert)

Steve Caraway
packing GPI boxes
for the move to
Lazaneo Drive
(Jon Sievert)

Dan Forte and Barney
Kessel (Jon Sievert)

Don Menn, Eric Johnson, and Jas Obrecht in 1987

John Lescroart and Jas Obrecht in 1978 (Clara Erickson)

GPI groundbreaking ceremony for the Lazaneo Drive building in April 1977 (Jon Sievert)

Cordell Crockett
at a GPI jam

Jas Obrecht and
Pat Travers in 1979
(Terry Norman)

1980 *GP* Christmas photo (Jon Sievert)

B.B. King at a GPI Jam with Bob Doerschuk, Tom Darter, Jim Crockett, David Bromberg, Dennis Fullerton, and Tom Wheeler (Jon Sievert)

Dan Forte and James Jamerson (Jon Sievert)

Janine Cooper and
Billy Sheehan in 1986
(Jas Obrecht)

Jas Obrecht and Eddie Van
Halen in 1978 (Jon Sievert)

Janine Cooper,
Tom Wheeler,
and Lonni Elrod
in 1986 (Jas
Obrecht)

Jas Obrecht on guitar and Jim Hatlo on keyboard at a 1980 GPI jam (Jon Sievert)

Jas Obrecht and Dennis Fullerton jamming in the warehouse on Lazaneo in 1982 (Jon Sievert)

Dominic Milano doing paste-up in 1983 (Jon Sievert)

Steve Rosen, Tony Iommi, and a
crew member in 1974 (Paul Moran)

1987 *GP* staff photo (Jon Sievert)

Jas Obrecht and Tom Mulhern
in 1983 (Jon Sievert)

Jas Obrecht presenting Steve Morse with a *GP* Readers Poll Award in 1984 (Jon Sievert)

Yngwie Malmsteen
and Jas Obrecht in
1985 (Jon Sievert)

Jas Obrecht and
Jerry Garcia in 1985
(Jon Sievert)

Jeff Beck with Steve Rosen
in 1975 (Neil Zlozower)

FROM A "TYPICAL SUBSCRIBER" BY TOM WHEELER

Our Christmas parties are among my favorite memories. Once in a while, somebody would compose a song for the occasion. Here's one Tom Wheeler performed back in the day. We relied on the daily mail for story ideas and other valuable input, but this song was inspired by the occasional goofball letter. It references our address on Lazaneo; our town of Cupertino (which, until the arrival of Apple Computers, most people had never heard of); our founder, Bud (not Jim) Eastman; and our publisher, Jim (not Bud) Crockett. It's called "Typical Subscriber."

Dear *GP*:
I'm a typical subscriber and I love your magazine
I read the front, I read the back, and all that's in between
I own every single issue and I'm loyal to the core
I read 'em once, I read 'em twice, and then I read some more
I've memorized your masthead till I feel like fam-i-ly
but there's just one thing that I have got to know. . . .

Where's Cupertino? Are you out there near L.A.
I couldn't find you on my Triple-A map
and the phone book doesn't say
and what's a Lazaneo
Could you spell it fifty more times
Yeah I think I saw one once when I was drunk
Let's spend an hour on the telephone
And how do I fix my fuzztone
All I did was leave it in the rain
Say hi to Bud Crockett, we go back a long long way
signed, a typical subscriber USA

[*Spoken: Dear* GP, *I love your rag,*
that's magazine talk, ha ha!]

Can I have Eric Clapton's address
and Liona Boyd's phone number
and a picture of your office coordinator in her bathing suit
[Dear Lonni, Ah luv you,
signed, 019-951, State Correctional Facility
Camarillo, California]

Say hi to Bud Crockett, he's a close personal friend
signed, a typical subscriber, the end.

Craig Chaquico (second from left) and Mickey Thomas (far right) of Jefferson Starship with Jas Obrecht and Tom Wheeler at the GPI Offices in 1983 (Jon Sievert)

Jim Crockett in his office in the '70s (Jon Sievert)

Jerry Garcia at a GPI Jam with Tom Wheeler, Jim Crockett, and Rich Leeds (Jon Sievert)

Jim Ferguson and Jim Hall (Jon Sievert)

Jon Sievert and Rick Nielsen (Dennis Callahan)

Steve Rosen and Jimmy Page (Neal Preston)

Steve Rosen and John
Kaye (Jeffrey Mayer)

Steve Rosen and
Jimmy Page in 1977
(Neal Preston)

Peggy Shea and Jas
Obrecht with Van Halen
in 1986 (Ray Olson)

Steve Rosen and Jim Marshall
at the Marshall factory in New
Zealand in 1976

Ronnie Montrose and Steve
Rosen in 1976 (Neil Zlozower)

Ritchie Blackmore and Steve
Rosen in 1978 (Neil Zlozower)

CIGARS, ANYONE?

Don Menn got back from his trip to Jamaica wearing no tan. However, he did bring back cigars for Jim Crockett, Joe Pass, and Chet Atkins.
   —*Mag Rag*, Vol. 1, No. 2

Roger Siminoff, Chet Atkins, Don Menn, and Jim Crockett at NAMM (Jon Sievert)

Tom Wheeler and Claudia
Bennett in 1978 (Jas Obrecht)

Steve Rosen and Rory Gallagher in 1974 (Kevin Dubrow)

Tom Wheeler at a GPI warehouse jam (Jon Sievert)

B.B. King, Dennis Fullerton, Jim Crockett, Tom Wheeler, Cordell Crockett, and David Grisman in 1981 (Jon Sievert)

GPI jam with Bud Eastman,
Jim Crockett, and Jerry Martin

Dan Forte, Paul English, and Willie Nelson (Jon Sievert)

Randy California and Steve Rosen
in 1976 (Neil Zlozower)

Tom Mulhern, Tom Wheeler, Jennifer Batten, Joe Gore, and Matt Resnicoff at the 1989 NAMM show (Jon Sievert)

Tom Wheeler and Don Menn (Jon Sievert)

Steve Rosen with Wishbone Ash in 1974
(Kevin Dubrow)

Featured Artists and Monthly Columnists Look Back

We rarely—very, very rarely—ever had a player refuse an interview or a feature story. Some might not be available right away, or management might have needed reassurance that we were serious. And when we approached others about writing a monthly column for us, their gracious responses were virtually immediate.

Here, many of these players and authorities look back on their experiences with Guitar Player. —JC

Steve Morse

GP was the only guitar magazine I had ever seen, I think. The newsstand in town didn't have it, but I think the music store did. I believe it was Hendrix on the cover. Back in the '60s in a small town where I lived, for a young player to be able to read about the instrument was pretty rare.

My first interview was with Jas Obrecht. He said later that mine may have been his first interview, or one of the very first he did for the magazine. My band, the Dixie Dregs, had been around for years, but was aimed at an underground audience. It was a great surprise to be included in *Guitar Player*.

August '82 (Cover photo by Jon Sievert)

We were making albums and touring regularly. We probably swung through many major cities at least once a year.

It was really nice to have such a relaxing, knowledgeable guy to work with. Like most of my best interviews, it was heavily edited to make me seem intelligent. Seriously, it was a big deal to me, since I envisioned us totally missing the radar of any media whatsoever, because we were a totally instrumental band.

We were able to work before *GP* featured me, but I know for a fact it gave us more visibility. My theory was that *GP* awards couldn't make people like me, but they bestowed enough credibility on recipients that some people who were sitting on the fence before might come check out the show. *GP* did something special, by having an assortment of people like Chet Atkins, all the Guitar Gods, Christopher Parkening, and some way underground guys like me. I'll bet that if *GP* hadn't given me that credibility, I wouldn't have been seen in any other magazines, since I didn't have much in the way of a larger-than-life persona onstage or off. Music was all I cared about, and it was a huge deal to have the support of the *GP* readers on all those polls. I felt like it meant that I had to really work hard to make sure not to disappoint any of them that came to the shows. Recording-wise, I only saw one thing to do, and that was to make compositions that would be interesting, durable, but easy enough to listen to.

As I type this, I'm in Europe with Deep Purple, beginning my third decade of touring with my British brothers. Just heard that we're finally doing a U.S. tour. We all do side projects, from time to time, and I'm going to be finishing my second album with Flying Colors, and possibly working more on songs with Living Loud. Also hoping to do some more writing with my son, Kevin.

Thanks to Jim for his vision of having the magazine be so broad, and for encouraging readers to listen to more than one style!

Steve Morse

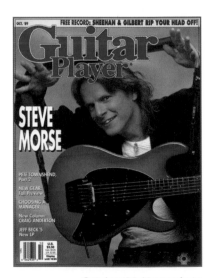

October '89 (Cover photo by Larry DiMarzio)

John McLaughlin
(Ina McLaughlin)

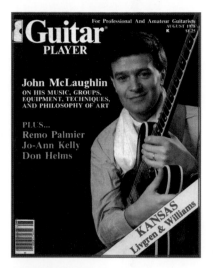

August '78 (Cover
photo by Jon Sievert)

March '81 (Cover
photo by Jon Sievert)

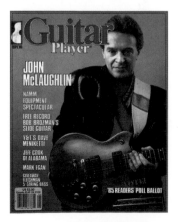

September '85 (Cover photo by
Paul Natkin/Photo Reserve)

John McLaughlin

Guitar Player and I go back so many years I don't even remember how many.

We all know everything's changed since the 1970s and '80s, but in those days, *Guitar Player* brought guitarists together in a single magazine. Today you can go online, type in any guitar player's name, and probably watch him or her play on YouTube. In the days before the collapse of the record industry, before the Internet, it was the printed word and photographs that kept us all up-to-date with who was doing what and where, It was wonderful. Let's face it, guitar players are one big family—actually, we are *all* one big family, but guitar players are special.

In any event, I've lost count of how many times I bought and read *Guitar Player* from cover to cover, and found out about new gadgets, guitars, amps, and all the rest of the guitar paraphernalia that we are so fond of. My thanks go to the editors and journalists.

Guitar Player forever!

Steve Howe (Glenn Gottlieb)

April '73 (Cover photo
by Neal Preston)

May '78 (Cover photo by
Neal Preston/Mirage)

September '86 (Cover photo
courtesy Arista Records)

Steve Howe

At the time of being contacted by *Guitar Player*, Yes was making waves in the U.S. The interviewers were very enthusiastic about everything.

By the late '70s, the importance of winning top guitarist in the *GP* Poll can't be over-emphasized. I had already won this in the UK in 1976, but then winning for five years straight in the U.S. was amazing!

Yes, then Asia, then GTR, then Anderson Bruford Wakeman Howe, then back to Yes has kept me busy, but I have continued to build my solo music and releases, including solo guitar playing, which is most important.

Michael Lorimer and Andrés Segovia in 1980 (Peter Klein)

Michael Lorimer (Irene Young)

Michael Lorimer

In 1976, *Guitar Player* magazine asked me to write a column on classical guitar, Master Class, shortly after *GP* published a feature article on my 1975 tour of the Soviet Union. The article, written by Alice Gilbert (excellent writer and wife of the great American guitar builder John Gilbert), was titled "Michael Lorimer—First American Classical Guitarist to Tour the USSR," and it was in the December '75 issue.

My first few columns were about my teacher Andrés Segovia—specifically, what it was like to study with him. For those columns, I contributed an article I had recently written at Segovia's request for a special booklet that Segovia and my manager Sol Hurok had planned to sell at Segovia's concerts. The booklet included articles on Segovia's impact on the guitar, Segovia's work with composers, Segovia's arrangements for guitar, Segovia's recordings, and—my article—Segovia's teaching. Before the booklet was printed, Hurok died and—too bad!—the project was never realized. The in-

Ernesto García de León
and Michael Lorimer in
2009 (Adam Wallace)

vitation from *GP* was perfect for bringing to light my article, an essay Segovia particularly liked and later reprinted in *American String Teachers Journal*.

After the Segovia articles, I addressed questions that players would ask me backstage or in master classes. I began with fundamentals:

• How to Sit with the Guitar
• The Importance of Attitudes and Beliefs in Guitar Study
• Tuning and Correcting Tuning Defects
• How I Approach Technique
• Right- and Left-Hand Positions
• Fingernail Shape, Length, and Polishing
• Nail Wear and Breakage
• Rest Strokes and Free Strokes
• Problems in Tone Production
• Tone Color, Harmonics, and Pizzicato

Along the way, I talked about master classes and workshops—their importance, how to prepare for them, and how to get the most out of them.

Michael Lorimer demonstrating a
hand position (Len DeLessio)

Classical
guitar
teachers still
use my *GP*
columns.

Next, I wrote columns on how to perform recitals, and how to make a career:

- Designing a Program That Works for You and Your Audience
- Program Notes
- Getting the Most Out of Your Practice Time
- Projection, Pacing, and Posture
- Clean Playing—Balance, Damping, and Eliminating Finger Squeaks
- Versatility in Right-Hand Position
- Making a Success of Your Concert—Publicity, Lights, Acoustics, Stage Requirements, etc.
- A Checklist for Polishing Your Playing
- The Day of Your Concert
- Performing—Showtime!
- Stage Fright
- After Your Concert—Reviewing the Concert and Renewing Your Study
- Making a Career—Repertoire, Determination, Managers, Contests, Recording, Teaching, etc.

For a special *GP* issue on Villa-Lobos, I wrote a column called, "Villa-Lobos's *Prelude*—How and Why Composers Could Profit by Analyzing Villa-Lobos's Guitar Music."

Finally, I addressed myriad issues in the art of guitar playing in several columns on a recently written, fifteen-minute guitar solo I had commissioned—William Bolcom's "Seasons." Bolcom went on to win the Pulitzer Prize in music; "Seasons" is still among the masterpieces of American classical guitar compositions.

I loved writing the monthly column. It gave me an opportunity to carefully consider and write about issues I felt were important to all guitar players. I also appreciated being able to refer players to published columns for detailed answers on particular topics. Writing the column, I got to read the magazine, learn more about the world of guitar playing beyond the classical niche, and meet writers and musicians I wouldn't have met had I not been a *GP* columnist.

I worked a lot with Jas Obrecht. Jas was great. I always appreciated his suggestions and support. I am still in touch with Jas. In 2013, Jas's online guitar magazine *Pure Guitar* published an extensive interview with me.

In the six years I wrote for *Guitar Player*, over 90 percent of my photographs were taken in one afternoon by the superb photographer Len DeLessio. Len had a "studio" (really just a closet) at 1700 Broadway—a skyscraper in the New York theater district, home of *Mad* magazine, near the famous Brill Building. The day of our shoot, Len set up a tripod and a few lights while I digested the smallness of Len's working space. Then we went for it. I had years of columns in my head, and in one session, I got Len to take all the photos I would need. You can see Len's shots of Alice Cooper, Smokey Robinson, and others at the Rock and Roll Hall of Fame Museum in Cleveland. As in all the photos Len shot for me, the clarity and level of detail here are outstanding.

Had I not written for *GP*, I am sure that my name would not have been particularly well-known in the guitar world outside of classical guitar. Classical guitar teachers still use my *GP* columns; I saw my *GP* column on stage fright posted on the bulletin board of the University of Michigan, Ann Arbor, School of Music; I still meet jazz, blues, country, and rock players who remember my columns.

I continue to study, practice, record, concertize, research, publish, and teach. To date, I have about fifty or so publications in print. I live in New York City and one especially exciting part of my teaching is my work with professional jazz guitarists—some of today's best. They study with me to refine their guitar technique in general and learn more about the classical guitar in particular.

The monthly column gave me an opportunity to write about issues I felt were important to all guitar players.

Larry Coryell

Larry Coryell (John Pierce Jr.)

Larry Coryell

Somebody from the magazine called me about writing a monthly column, Contemporary Guitar.

I loved being a columnist, although the deadline thing was always rough—no excuses on my part, my attitude and behaviors were sometimes a bit sporadic during those post-'60s years.

I can't recall my main guy there [Jim Ferguson], but he had the patience of Job and the demeanor of St. Francis—I was, at times, quite difficult.

Being a *GP* columnist was for me a great way of communicating with the guitar-loving public. Because we were reaching guitarists all over, I had worldwide contacts. It was an honor to be a part of this. *GP* became a means of bringing validation to the upgrading of the music that could be done on guitar. It wasn't just for cowboys and rockers anymore. We were showing the new things that we had learned, including new techniques—such guys as [Al] Di Meola, [Lenny] Breau, [Mike] Stern, [John] Scofield . . . were bringing new ways to express music on our instrument, and those ways became available to anyone who could read, both prose and music.

When I published my autobiography a few years ago, the publishers insisted on having a section where I reprinted some of my old *GP* columns, and I was surprised at how well they stood the test of time. I think that *GP* was the pioneer in modern guitar literature, in the sense that not only was there a respected place for classical guitar in the literary pantheon, but now other styles and stylists were able, through *GP*, to document their particular valuable ideas, especially in jazz and fusion, that have now become standard learning in music schools through the world.

Craig Chaquico

I first heard of the magazine at a couple of music stores where I would go in and drool over the guitars while I was still taking accordion lessons at Frank and Delores Music Studio on Fair Oaks Boulevard in Carmichael, California. I would go into music stores, not being able to afford a guitar, but I could almost always afford an issue of *Guitar Player* if my dad was in a good mood, which he usually was. Till my folks let me drop the accordion and pick up the guitar instead. Till I cut up my dad's driver's license to make a guitar pick once in the same shape as the Dunlop one I saw in *Guitar Player*.

I don't really remember who contacted me for an interview, except I had always seen Jas Obrecht and the photographer, Jon Sievert, around San Francisco and at concerts. Usually concerts by other people, and we would run into each other. I know the interview was already after four platinum albums for Jefferson Starship that had lots of guitar, but it was *right* after a song we did called "Jane" became a surprise hit that has one of my own favorite little guitar solos in it. I had to fight for every second. Our manager said it would never be a hit unless we shortened the solo, because long guitar solos were frowned upon and not popular at the time on radio. The band stuck by me, and we left it in. The song was a hit, so I smile whenever the solo comes on the radio. But our manager was right.

Years later, at an awards show in San Francisco, the Bammies, the guys in Metallica said it was their favorite song in high school because it was the only rockin' song with a long guitar solo on the radio at the time. So there ya go . . . twenty-eight seconds is "long" I guess? Not that long when you hear one of your guitar solos start up over the PA in the supermarket, and right when you start to play after the vocals are done somebody breaks in on the PA and says, ". . . Price check. Price check please? In produce? Price check please? Produce? Organic broccoli price, please."

There is at least ONE *Guitar Player* connection to that solo. I had read in *Guitar Player* that one of my favorite guitar players growing up would notch and etch his guitar picks with a razor blade to get a little more "tooth" or "bite" on the strings when he picks a note. You can actually hear that little "click" of the pick on the strings and almost see the speaker cone punching forward before the note is even heard.

My whole solo was done in just two takes, and we used bits from each take, mainly because the guitar pick broke from all those notch-

> I cut up my dad's driver's license to make a guitar pick once in the same shape as the Dunlop one I saw in *Guitar Player*.

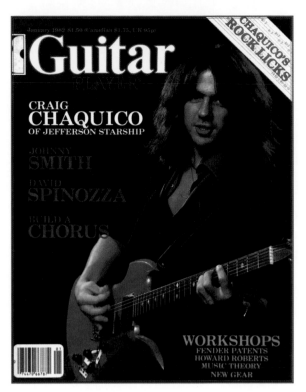

January '82 (Cover photo by Jon Sievert)

es and etches in it, and we listened back to the solos we had, and between the two lame ones there was one really good one. It helped that I actually had sort of "written" that particular solo and came in prepared.

I played all the guitar solos and much of the rhythm on all the Jefferson Starship/Starship albums, videos, and tours. So if it was a hit song or video or tour, that's me playing guitar, thanks to my dad's driver's license.

With Jas it was almost like I was interviewing him half the time, since we were both really huge fans of anything guitar in general. He had more interesting stories and things to say than I did. He told me a story about how he had this girlfriend who was apparently two-timing him and another musician without either knowing. But when they both showed up at the same girl's house and figured it out, with their guitars in the car, they actually wrote and played a song together and either left it on her answering machine or stuck a cassette in her home stereo player. Either way, freakin' great!!! Goodness gracious, great balls of fire. That's rock 'n' roll, baby. And the sense of humor and the blues of fellow guitar players.

Before the interview with Jas, we had just finished *Freedom at Point Zero* after just losing John Barbata on drums to a bad car accident. Grace Slick and Marty Balin both left as lead singers and songwriters right after a riot in Germany where we lost tons of gear including MY two '57 Goldtops, a '59 sunburst, a '58 dot inlay, an ES-335, a '60s Firebird, a double-neck, and four blonde Fender Bassmans. Ouch! But a riot in Germany led me to Carvin in California and I've been a happy, satisfied customer ever since.

At the time of the *GP* cover interview, we had also just performed one of my sci-fi songs called "Light the Sky on Fire" in the infamous *Star Wars Holiday Special*. The song was about ancient aliens, actually. UFOs, pyramids, legends, myths, star people who will return again someday and light the sky on fire. I liked the idea. I had just read *Chariots of the Gods* and seen *Star Wars*, so the holiday special sounded perfect! However, it isn't one of George Lucas's favorite historical moments in film (videotape) for some reason, as he doesn't want to ever release the video officially. That special may have been the reason why Marty Balin never came to any more band practices after that?

Once I appeared in *Guitar Player*, a lot of people I had always admired, having seen them in the magazine, actually had a better chance of knowing who I was when they saw me, and maybe I wouldn't get thrown out of as many gigs for not really being the guitar player in the band.

After *Guitar Player* more people recognized me, but I think a lot of that was the ads Carvin ran with me and the guys who were playing their stuff, too. MTV was just coming out, and we had a lot of videos with my guitars and amps in them that were also in *Guitar Player*, so there was a great connection there.

After the Starship broke up, and during all those subsequent reissues without me, I started playing acoustic guitar while my wife was pregnant with our son Kyle. The acoustic guitar was a lot more welcome around the house than the electric. Little did I know it would lead to working with Ozzie Ahlers, who was Jerry Garcia's keyboard player on tour, or that we would end up selling over a million CDs of acoustic guitar music, receiving a Grammy nomination, and having No. 1 songs and CDs in *Billboard*. Just like those guys in *Guitar Player* I had read about.

By the way, when I was twelve, I was in a very bad car crash. My dad and I survived, but we were pretty broken up for a while. The first thing I asked for when I came to was my acoustic guitar. My doctor encour-

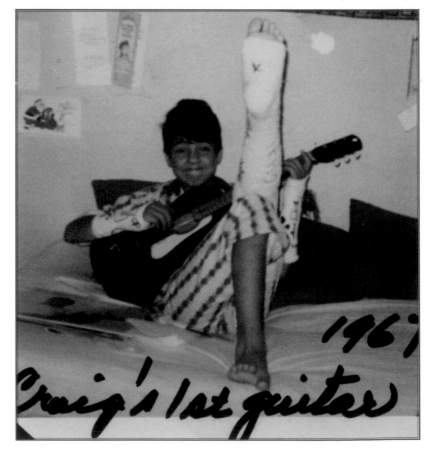

Craig Chaquico (Craig Chaquico Archives)

aged me to play, as she knew it would be good for my recovery, physically and spiritually. I was reading *Guitar Player* magazine with two broken arms, a broken leg, ankle, foot, wrist, and thumb in the hospital.

Dad told me about Les Paul, who was also in a car crash and had his arm set so he could still play guitar. He was brave through his physical recovery and became a great guitar player in spite of his injury and actually has a guitar called a Les Paul with his name on it. So Dad promised me if I was brave through my wheelchair, crutches, broken bones, and corrective shoes, he would buy me a Les Paul when I got better.

I wrote a song on the E string of my acoustic guitar while in the hospital, called "E-lizabeth's

Craig Chaquico
(Kaye Runner)

Song," named for my doctor, whose name was Elizabeth. The E string was the only string I could reach on the only guitar I owned with my little fingers sticking out only an inch. It was a song she heard over and over in the hospital whether she liked it or not. All on one string too. Ouch! She probably liked it more when I read *Guitar Player* in bed rather than actually trying to play a guitar with two broken arms, thumb, wrist, leg, ankle, and foot on one string without a pick or driver's license. Little did I know it would be on a Grammy-nominated solo CD thirty years later played on a guitar with my name on it, thanks to *Guitar Player* and my dad's keeping his word. And driver's license.

I still have a couple hundred *Guitar Player* issues in plastic boxes, some before I was ever in it. A bunch still have my name and address on 'em. Not exactly mint but hey, who is anymore?

I do want to add a quick thought to consider, if I may, the knowledge and insights into all the guitars, and the original guitar builders, and guitar heroes in the pages, and bigger-than-life imaginations the magazine often inspired. Also the real-life stories of real-life guitar players everywhere. Studio guys. Touring guys. Regional guys. Local guys. Part-time and full-time guys. Teachers. Repair guys. Inventors and innovators from all sides of the guitar that *Guitar Player* brought to our fingertips wherever we were. All the different styles and tunings and inspirations and tips for all us guys who play.

And what am I forgetting? Oh yes. And all those females who play guitar as well. Better even.

February '79 (Cover photo by Jon Sievert)

Lee Ritenour

I was still in high school when I first heard about *Guitar Player* magazine. For me, being totally absorbed in the guitar 24/7, the arrival of *GP* was a gift from the angels! It was the absolute coolest magazine on the planet! *GP* was obviously revolutionary and the first ever of its kind. Today, we take for granted all the magazines about the guitar in print and even more online, as if they were always there. But there was only one *GP* at the time, and it ruled!

As I started to work in the early '70s, I started to run into Jim Crockett at NAMM shows and other guitar-related events. I can't remember the exact time I met Jim, but I remember him being so excited and so passionate about the magazine. He was the creative force that grew *GP* along with the original founder, Bud Eastman. I'm pretty sure Jim was around the Monterey Jazz Festival in

Lee Ritenour (Rob Shanahan)

1974 when I debuted there, playing with Joe Pass, Jim Hall, and Mundell Lowe. Shortly after that, a review and pictures appeared in *GP*.

Around that time, I was also teaching part-time at USC and I remember being very interested in contributing to *GP*'s instructional pages. I started sending in columns, and Jim was very encouraging for me to contribute to *GP*. As I started coming up, the magazine started to feature me occasionally in their articles. Joe Bonamassa texted me a cover from the early '70s with Rick Derringer. Listed on the cover, it had my name with the caption "Watch for Him." Joe and I got a laugh out of that!

A few years later, when I won two Readers Poll awards for Best Studio Musician and Jazz Rock Musician, I was absolutely thrilled! It was one of the very first times I had won an award and it was in *GP*!

Today, *GP* still rules and continues the legacy. Even after some forty-five albums, thousands of sessions, and countless tours, which I am so grateful for, I can still read *GP* and learn something every time. In 2010, *GP* presented me with their Lifetime Achievement Award. Needless to say, I was thrilled to receive this award, and it meant even more because of my early connection with the beginnings of *Guitar Player* magazine and Jim Crockett's dream.

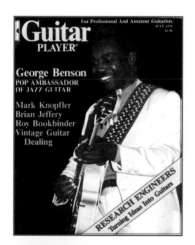

July '79 (Cover photo by Jon Sievert)

George Benson

People started to put out magazines about guitar. There was *Downbeat* and maybe a couple of other magazines dedicated to the jazz world, but *Guitar Player* magazine was the first one that dedicated itself to guitar players—or the first successful magazine dedicated to guitars that I can remember. Jimmy Boyd, my manager, would want to get his hands on this to feature his star. He discovered me, so anything that had my name on it, he would keep in his office. He would've called me and told me I was on the cover of *Guitar Player*.

My memories of that magazine are very nice. There were very interesting covers that really helped my career along and kept me in touch with the guitar world. When my vocal hits started coming, people thought

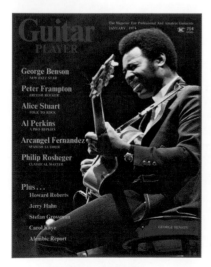

January '74 (Cover photo by Veryl Oakland)

George Benson (Courtesy Monster Music)

I had abandoned the guitar or they accused me of that, and it only takes one bad vibe to take things downhill, but *GP* kept me up front as a guitar player. One of my records had very little guitar on it, so this was very important to me.

There was a poll, too; and you had to have five wins in order to be in the Gallery of the Greats and we were on that list. I sure want to get that magazine because I forgot to tear that page out.

The one thing that would be sure is that, when I was interviewed by guys at *Guitar Player*, I would be talking to guitar aficionados, guitar lovers, and guitar players. That was big-time for us so that we could pass on guitar information to people in the few words that we had for the article that would get it straight or as straight as it could be to people, and that would be a help for me.

It was a more mature-based magazine—a mature *guitar*-based magazine. Nowadays, the guitar players are condensed down to a select few in the magazines. The superstar is in the magazines now, but we always remember our roots, you know? People like Django Reinhardt and Wes Montgomery and Barney Kessel being in the magazine back then were a good reminder to people of where guitar came from and we were being compared to those guys all the time. You would be reminded you got some practicing to do! The newcomers came in, but a format like that with reminders of where guitar had come from and where it should be and with all those great names, if you made it into that magazine it was saying something. I never took it for granted. I never said I belong here. I took it as an honor to be in that caliber of magazine. I didn't use it as bragging rights. I knew what it meant to my career and my association with guitar players. It was very, very important to me.

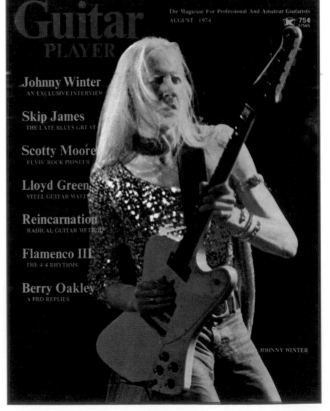

Johnny Winter

[Ed. Note: As we were in the final stages of preparing this book for our publisher, the world received word that Johnny Winter, seventy, had passed away in Zurich, Switzerland. The blues great will be missed by fans and guitar players everywhere.]

Myself and my peers were aware of *Guitar Player* magazine from the start and were big fans. I was thrilled at the opportunity to be interviewed for such a prestigious magazine. At the time, I was touring and recording the world over.

August '74 (Cover photo by Neil Zlozower)

August '83
(Cover photo by
Jon Sievert)

Johnny Winter
(Michael Weintrob)

Joan Armatrading
(C. Marco)

I always had great experiences with the publication. The interviewers were always very knowledgeable of my playing and of the blues in general. As with any prominent magazine like *Guitar Player*, any appearance in the magazine was a boost to my career.

Joan Armatrading

I knew about *Guitar Player* because of being a guitarist and being interested in guitars and other guitarists, and would look out for, and be told about, anything that had to do with guitars by friends. When I was asked to appear in the magazine, it made me feel like a proper guitarist. Even though I knew, and had many other people say to me, what a fine guitarist I was, it was when I was put in the magazine that I became really pumped up.

I know that at the time of doing one of the interviews for *Guitar Player* magazine I was rehearsing for a tour at the Ritz studio in Putney [UK]. When it was time for the interview, I gave the band a break and did the interview. I think the photos in that particular edition were taken at the rehearsal hall and I'm posing with my Ovation twelve-string.

I found the writers of *Guitar Player* to be really good and quite different to talking to interviewers of regular newspapers or magazines if I can put it like that. I had the feeling they, the *Guitar Player* interviewers, were either guitarists themselves or had a real deep interest in guitars and guitarists. That meant the conversations were not just about songwriting and performing, but about using the guitar to write songs to get textures and to enhance performances with the accessories used when playing the guitar in live shows. That gave one the opportunity to talk about what effect pedals had, what amps and what strings were used. These might be things that a non-guitarist might consider boring, but to me as a guitarist they are vital topics.

I have no idea if being in the magazine affected my career. I do know that I did well in certain readers' polls and of course appearing in *Guitar Player* helped. I know that it certainly made a difference to how I felt. Even though I was confident about my playing it was nevertheless a great boost to me and to my playing to be featured as a guitarist in a magazine that all guitarists regarded very highly.

Joan Armatrading (Joel Anderson)

Steve Vai

Guitar Player always seemed to be there in my life for as long as I can remember. The first issue came out when I was seven but I don't think I discovered it until I was eleven or twelve.

I think it was Tom Wheeler who first contacted me to do an interview. It was odd in a way, because before that it was rare to even see my name in any kind of print, and it was a bit surrealistic because the magazine was a monthly fix for me for years and its pages seemed so out of reach.

Perhaps in the beginning I was a little nervous, but the interviewers were good to me. I was so over the moon to be able to contribute to a magazine that meant so much to me as I was growing up.

It was a time in the magazine's history where everyone there was enthusiastic and passionate about contributing. It's still that way to a great degree, but when something is new and finding its

October '86 (Cover photo by Neil Zlozower)

Steve Vai (Larry DiMarzio)

audience, growing steadily and not really in direct competition with anything including recessions, lack of good content, etc., there is a different energy to it. It's fresh and exciting and all the people contributing felt that aliveness and the magazine carried the fragrance of their enthusiasm.

I believe the covers had a huge effect. From the day that "The Attitude Song" appeared in the magazine as a Soundpage, it changed the landscape of my career. It led to the part I played in the film *Crossroads*, helped to sell tons of *Flex-Able* records, and even helped to land me the gig with Dave Roth. Even if I had never appeared in the magazine it would have had a sizable effect on my career as a musician, because I used to read it all the time and there's so much stuff in there that is inspiring, educational, and just juicy!

Congratulations and deep thanks for such a vital magazine.

Tommy Tedesco
by Denny Tedesco

When my father was approached to write for *GP*, I think he may have been reluctant at first, because he wasn't that guy that could sit down and teach guitar. If my memory is correct, I think Jim Crockett suggested he write it from his point of view. So my father laid it out as straightforwardly, entertainingly, and bluntly as possible. He always started the Studio Log column with the answers to the questions he was always asked: Who do you work for? What kind of guitars do you play? How much do you make? I had heard that some of the older guys were pissed he was being too honest in the articles.

He would try to spread out the articles enough for every type of guitar player. There was always something to learn if you couldn't read music. So sometimes the music was an easy read, but maybe the situation had a learning experience. As they say, studio work is

> My father was a straight talker and a "deez, doze, and dem" kind of New York Italian.

Tommy Tedesco and Don Menn at *GP*'s Tenth Anniversary Party in 1977 (Jon Sievert)

90 percent boredom and 10 percent terror. Well, he made sure he put a few "terror" pieces of music in there. As he said, to scare the shit out of the few cocky ones.

The only person I ever saw that dreaded the article was my mother, Carmie. This was pre–home computer days. My Italian parents may have fought throughout their marriage, but the article meant a guaranteed fight. Like a high school student, my dad would wait until the last minute to write an article. Then he and my mother would sit down at the IBM typewriter and start. For those who remember the articles and knew him, he was a straight talker and, as he said, was a "deez, doze, and dem" kind of New York Italian.

So he would dictate his thoughts that sometimes were only clear to him and not to her. She would start to change it as she typed and he would say, "That's not what I said."

"Well it doesn't make sense how you're saying it," she would reply. The fighting would begin. Or he would be talking and she would be typing away when he decided to go a different route: "Let's change that . . . make it this way. . . ."

February '80 (Cover photo by Jon Sievert)

My mother used more correction tape on that IBM than a beginning typing student. That single "delete" key got lots of use, and she pounded on it harder toward the end of the article. In the end, he would always have her read it out loud. With his gruff voice he would say, "It's pretty good, hon." She would give her sarcastic "Yep," and we'd wait for another thirty days.

When he went to work at the studios, if there was something interesting about the date, he would take the music and fold it up and put it away in the guitar case. He would ask the composer if it was okay to write an article on it, and they were very accommodating and pleased. It didn't matter if it was John Williams or James Horner or maybe the newest composer on the block. Recently, I was told by a couple of copyists in the studios that when they went to collect music at the end of the date, my father's always seemed to be missing. Can you imagine what you would have to go through with the lawyers of today to write that article?

He got lots of comments from other studio players. To be named in the article was a badge of honor for the new guys. I think they loved it. There was nothing better or more fun than when he wrote about a session that the other guitar players were on. What I was most proud of, reading the articles recently, was his ability many times to talk about the guy next to him as being the hero of the date.

Now guitar players around the world started to learn who Tommy Tedesco was. This was the same time that he started doing seminars around the country and in Europe. He was with Yamaha, Gibson, and then, at the end, Fender. He loved doing the seminars. They were fun for him and fun for the audience. They were like the articles for those who attended. Just live! He was also at Musicians Institute at this point as well.

I've been traveling the country over the last few years with the film *The Wrecking Crew*, and it's amazing how many guitar players come up and tell me about how they loved the column and how he taught them things that they still use today as professional players. One guy was a drummer who was addicted to the article when his band was traveling. It was the only thing he read in the magazine. Another guy told me that he would read the whole magazine and leave that article for last. He called it dessert.

Nils Lofgren

I hit the road professionally in 1968, a year after *Guitar Player* magazine began. For decades, as the first independent magazine of its kind, it was a wonderful source of info and enjoyment for all musicians and anyone interested in music.

I was never one to regularly sample all the new musical inventions, and *Guitar Player* was always a helpful source of great, professional info and opinions on all the latest gear, pedals, amps, instruments, players, styles, techniques, everything I could possibly want to know about my musical field.

(I also enjoyed being featured

Nils Lofgren (Nils Lofgren Archives)

Nils Lofgren (Jan M. Lundahl)

December '85 (Cover photo by Jon Sievert)

a number of times in *Guitar Player*, and that was certainly fun and helpful to my own musical projects along the way.)

On the road constantly, I have fond memories of getting the latest *Guitar Player*, knowing every page would be a great read, interesting and informative. Something I could always rely on. It was written with passion and useful detail by people as excited and engaged by music as I was.

Whether music was your profession or hobby or both, in those early years, I could always count on the magazine for great info and exploration on every musical front.

I'm grateful for those years of the original, independent *Guitar Player* magazine. It was such a great source of discovery and enjoyment for me.

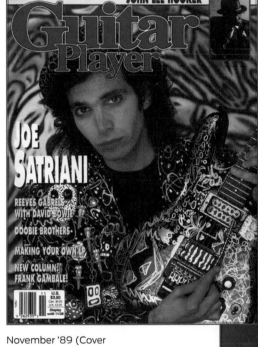

November '89 (Cover photo by Ray Olson)

Joe Satriani

Fun fact: To get started giving guitar lessons in Berkeley, California, I used to slip my own handwritten advertise-

Joe Satriani (Rubina Satriani)

ments on three-by-six-inch cards in *Guitar Player* magazines stacked at the local supermarket!

I think it was Jas Obrecht who first contacted me about doing an interview. I was still giving lessons at Second Hand Guitars in Berkeley, and recording solo guitar music at night. The interview experience was so exciting because the journalist asked all the cool questions. They don't do that anymore.

When *GP* put me on the cover, and had my new song "The Crush of Love" inside on the Soundpage, it had an enormously positive effect on my career. The song went on to become a radio hit for me, and *GP* can take the credit for "breaking it"!

As I write this, I just finished writing a book, *Strange Beautiful Music: A Musical Memoir*. It's been published by BenBella Books to coincide with a very special box set of my entire musical catalog. We remastered all the studio recordings and added bonus tracks as well.

Country Joe McDonald

I am not sure how I heard about *Guitar Player*. Of course, at that time there were not a lot of magazines talking about guitars. Probably from friends. Maybe it was Jon Sievert, who took photos for the magazine, who told me. Somehow I got to a few jams. I lived in Berkeley, so it

Country Joe McDonald (right) with Lachlan Throndson and Roger Siminoff at a GPI jam (Jon Sievert)

Country Joe McDonald (Tom Weller)

was local. At the time I was working as a traveling musician. I don't think that they ever interviewed me as a guitar player, but that is not surprising, as I am a singer/songwriter who plays and writes on the guitar, but not a lead guitar player. I remember that *GP* allowed me to do a little article on Jon Lundberg, who owned Fretted Instruments shop in Berkeley, and I worked in the shop in 1965. He and the shop were very important to the acoustic guitar renaissance that was happening at the time, and he was an expert on pre-WW2 Martin guitars. I had interviewed him about the story of how he started the shop and his experience with guitars. As far as I know, this is the only exposure he ever received as a pioneer in that field.

I remember hearing B.B. King play at one of the jams and am told that I brought my trombone down once and played it! I am not really a jam session kind of guy. I had inherited a collection of the magazine *Broadside*, published in NYC by Sis Cunningham, that was so important in the protest-song-writing movement of the '60s, and Jim Crockett had a collection and allowed me to copy the missing ones for my collection. That collection now lives in the Cleveland Rock and Roll Hall of Fame, and Jim donated his to a local library. I am semiretired now and working on an autobiography and doing occasional performances solo with acoustic guitar.

One last thought: In my archives there are no *GP* magazines, but there is a Jon Sievert pullout of the guitar of the month! I am sure it is the only magazine in the world that featured guitar centerfolds!! Beautiful.

Pat Metheny

My parents had a college friend, Warren Manley, who relatively late in life had gotten interested in the guitar. He had a Gibson LG-0, and that was one of the first real guitars I had ever seen up close. I would have been around eleven or so at the time and had just gotten interested in guitar and finally talked my parents into letting me use my paper route money to buy my first guitar. Mr. Manley said, "You should check out *Guitar Player* magazine—they have everything in there, it is all about the guitar." So, along with my first guitar, I got a subscription to *Guitar Player*. I don't think I missed an issue from 1967 until the mid-'80s one way or another.

I can't remember exactly when the first time was that I was in the magazine. I think I kind of remember that it was a kind of introductory thing that also included Neal Schon, who was about my age, as another new guy. But I might be wrong about that. I do remember the first cover I was on, though, which was the December 1981 issue— that was a pretty big deal for me, since I had been reading *GP* since I was a kid. By the time I was on the cover, I had started my own band

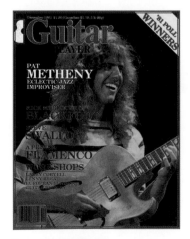

December '81 (Cover photo by Neil Zlozower)

and was touring all over the world two hundred–plus days a year playing everywhere I could possibly get us a gig.

I think it was the writer Dan Forte who covered me during those years. He was a great guy who seemed to really understand my thing—I always enjoyed talking to him. And of course he went on to adopt the name "Teisco Del Rey," which I always thought was hilarious.

In a way, and especially during those years, I was always a little bit outside of the "guitar" thing that was popular then. I have never put too much emphasis on the guitar-playing aspect of things, and I honestly think a lot of what I was doing and was interested in at that time was kind of lost on a certain part of the "guitar" audience. I never really played fast just to play fast. I was more into playing with lots of dynamics and not that loud all the time, really invoking detailed harmony in the lines and a more narrative kind of improvising that was connected to a tradition that was not that much in style then. Over time, people seemed to get my thing a little bit more, but I was kind of a reactionary to the kinds of things that gui-

Pat Metheny (Jimmy Katz)

tar players were doing in the '70s and '80s in terms of chops, etc.

I think my being on the cover a few times made guitar players a little more curious about what I was up to in a good way. I was always grateful to be included.

I feel very privileged to be able to continue to do the kinds of things that I was doing back then—playing lots of concerts around the world and most importantly, to continue to research music by being in-

January '80 (Cover photo by Steve Joester)

volved in it on a near constant basis by playing with really great musicians. I am really still just trying to get better more than anything.

Pat Travers

I can't really remember when I saw my first copy of *Guitar Player*, but I do remember getting every issue while I was in London, England, from 1975 to 1978. There were a lot of other guitar magazines on the newsstand, but *Guitar Player* always stood out to me because of two things: first, the magazine just looked better than any of the other ones, and second, the articles and interviews had credibility for me.

Pat Travers (Thomas Swanson/Rock Image Photography)

If there was an interview with a major player like Jeff Beck, then you knew the interviewer would have done his homework and always seemed to have created a personal bond with the artist. It seemed like *Guitar Player* was not just another stop on a PR tour for a new release.

When I moved to the U.S. in 1978 and my career was taking off, I would eye the new *Guitar Player* each month and dream of actually being on the cover. Well, this finally happened with the January 1980 issue. Wow! I had made it! I still have people coming to shows with copies of that issue that they would like me to autograph. I still get a little puffed up when I see one.

Guitar Player magazine was the most respected publication of its kind, and I think the reason why was because of the people that worked for it. Genuine and sincere lovers of the art of making music on the six-stringed instrument that changed the world.

Cordell Crockett

I grew up a very privileged kid. I remember when dad first got the *Guitar Player* gig, because I got to play with the art supplies when I'd visit the office. He would take me and my sisters to concerts like Barney Kessel, Gladys Knight, Mel Tormé, Ron Carter, Ray Charles, and of course B.B. King.

When he was producing the first *GP* album, I was invited to watch B.B. track two songs in the studio. I got to hold "Lucille." I got a B.B. King pick. I was eleven years old. Needless to say, by age twelve I was ready to join in. Upon hearing my sisters' Ohio Players'

"Love Rollercoaster" record, I asked my mom what that sound was. She said it was the bass. She called Pops up, and within days I had my first Aspen bass, with a Marlboro amp. Dad suggested bass lessons with one of his writers from *Keyboard* magazine, Jim Aikin, who also played cello and bass guitar. My mom would drive me to Jim's place once a week. The first lessons were ear training, and the twelve-bar blues. He was a great teacher. I'd watch him play at the GPI jams every month. Then one day, B.B. King, Tom Coster, Country Joe McDonald, Dave Grisman, and Darol Anger came to play. Somehow, I was asked to play with B.B.! I was now fourteen or fifteen. He called out "The Thrill Is Gone" in A. I was so nervous! Playing the fretless P-Bass with no markers didn't help. Dad started the count, we hit the downbeat, and I began playing in A . . . MAJOR!! In DOUBLE TIME!!! I am one of the few musicians to survive the stare of B.B. while making a blunderous mistake. "Half time on the bass!! . . . Half time on the bass!!" Fortunately for me, Tom Wheeler leaned over and sang the groove in my ear, and by the 6, 5, turnaround I was cool. Whew! Then B.B. calls out the next jam, "3/4 blues in D minor!"

The lessons from my second teacher, the great Carol Kaye, about arpeggios, kicked in! I just kept my eye on dad's right foot, count-

GPI jam in 1981 with B.B. King and Dennis Fullerton, Jim Crockett, Tom Wheeler, Cordell Crockett, and David Grisman (Jon Sievert)

Cordell Crockett (Karina Kohl)

ed 1-2-3 and played arpeggios! And I killed it! Years later, I still tell that story.

I also worked at GPI in the mid-'80s. I tell you, that place was *all* about the music. You'd have guys like Stanley Jordan walk in with a chorus pedal, practice amp, and guitar, and change the whole game. I would go to every NAMM show with Pops, meet artists, manufacturers, and journalists. Now, in the midst of my own professional career as bassist of Ugly Kid Joe, and guitarist of Hear Kitty Kitty, I draw upon all of those experiences.

Like I said, I was a very privileged kid!

Liona Boyd

I first heard about *Guitar Player* magazine back in the early '70s when I started to play small guitar societies across Canada and the U.S. As I recall, many of the guitar teachers had the magazine in their studios, and I devoured every issue I could lay my hands on as I wanted to learn more about the intriguing guitar world and its colorful, talented characters who usually played different styles to mine, but with whom I shared a great passion . . . guitar! And what an eye-opener it all was for me, who had just completed a four-year degree in classical music, had returned from two years in Paris studying with Alexandre Lagoya, and had basically been brought up in the classical world. Although I had been a huge fan of the music of Bob Dylan, the Rolling Stones, the Beatles, Joni Mitchell . . . I was no expert on any of their guitar styles, and now in this magazine I subscribed to I loved reading the fascinating interviews that gave behind-the-scenes glimpses into the lives and careers of players and composers, musical tips, new tuners, cases, gadgets, gizmos and everything I could ever want to know about guitars.

July '87 (Cover photo by Deborah Samuel)

I think it was probably Jim Crockett himself who first approached me about doing a story, as I was everywhere back then, touring as the opening act for Gordon Lightfoot and playing to many thousands every night, introducing the pop and folk fans to my classical guitar repertoire. I was also doing dozens of international tours, recording for CBS Masterworks, and making regular appearances on *The Tonight Show Starring Johnny Carson*, the *Today* show, Mike Douglas, and Merv Griffin. Looking back, I believe I was a somewhat of a pio-

Liona Boyd (Don Dixon)

neer, expanding the classical guitar's reach by doing nontraditional things such as recording an album with one of my guitar heroes, Chet Atkins. And let's face it, there were very few women back then in the guitar world, so I probably received more than my fair share of attention for my adventurous spirit and desire to experiment, even posing on a white stallion in the poppy fields of Andalusia for my "Best of" cover! I was very proud when I would later discover that I had been a role model to many young women players.

In 1987 I was thrilled when GPM featured me on the cover along with Alex Lifeson, Rik Emmett, and Ed Bickert, but to this day I cringe when I see that rat's nest '80s hairstyle! Fans still bring that particular cover after shows to have me sign it, and I suppose it's now become a collector's item. The instrumental we four Canadians did together for that issue, "Beyond Borders," was great fun to record . . . all thanks to *Guitar Player* magazine!

When I started to win the Readers Poll for Classical Guitar I was absolutely thrilled, as being appreciated by my peers and fellow guitarists was the best feeling in the world! When, after five wins, I was inducted into their Gallery of the Greats, I was over the moon about it, and from that moment have always included this accomplishment in my publicity bios. Three of the awards reside in my Toronto condo, and the other two are displayed in my Palm Beach, Florida, house.

Guitar Player magazine was always been my favorite magazine, as it dealt with my world of guitar and all the wonderfully talented, eccentric, crazy, and delightfully obsessive characters with whom I felt a common bond. I loved that it ranged from articles and interviews with serious classical composers such as Jack Duarte to unique stylists such as my dear late friend Lenny Breau, plus Pat Metheny, Muddy Waters, Eric Clapton and David Gilmour (both of whom I recorded with). It was so wide and inclusive in its scope, and I so enjoyed being interviewed by great writers such as Jim Ferguson! I remember penning the odd technical article and letter to the editor, usually expressing my thanks for a well-written piece in the magazine.

Around 2003 I developed in my right-hand fingers something called "musician's focal dystonia," a condition brought on by over-practice, which forced me to leave the concert stage for six years. While there was never anything physically wrong with my fingers at all, the brain maps had undergone subtle changes and this wreaked havoc with my finger coordination. I reinvented my technique, even playing with a pick for a year, but slowly retrained my fingers and reemerged in 2009 having added singing to my new musical style. I wanted to warn fellow musicians about the dangers of too much playing, as this is quite a common affliction. The experience inspired an entirely different chapter in my life, made me single again, and gave me a style of music that I now realize had been my destiny all along . . . to be a singer/songwriter/guitarist. My new songs have been described by one critic as "Enya meets Leonard Cohen, meets the beautiful guitar tones that could only come from Liona Boyd."

I am still as much in love with the guitar as ever, play it every day, and am constantly writing new music. I released a very ambitious fifteen-song album called *The Return* in September 2013, which I count amongst my best work, and am presently recording my twenty-fourth album, called *Christmas Fantasy*, which is mostly instrumentals. I look forward to sharing much more of my unusual journey in music with readers of *Guitar Player* magazine.

I am truly thankful for all the great support *Guitar Player* has giv-

I am positive that *Guitar Player* inspired thousands, if not millions, to pursue the guitar.

en me over the course of my career. I'll never forget sitting next to a young man on a flight from Lima to Mexico City and to my amazement seeing him flipping through an issue that featured one of my interviews. When he got to my page I couldn't stand it anymore, and when I told him who I was, the guy almost jumped out of his seat! Thank you, dear Jim Crockett, for having the vision to expand such a wonderful magazine and for all the pleasure you have given to the guitar world. I am also positive that your magazine inspired thousands, if not millions, to pursue the guitar as a both a hobby and a career. We in the guitar world all owe you a huge debt of gratitude.

June '74 (Cover photo by Wendi Lombardi)

Andy Powell

I believe I first heard about *Guitar Player* when Wishbone Ash started to travel extensively in the U.S. We'd always be at airports and would see *Guitar Player* at the newsstands. Of course, the UK was more print-based than the U.S., which also heavily depended on radio for promotion of rock artists and bands. It was natural that our interest would turn toward the magazines that catered to the more serious side of popular music, which was what we considered rock to be at the time.

We would have been at the end of the initial phase of our career, which had seen us break big in Europe after the release of our third album, *Argus*, and then embark on trying to conquer the United States—every British band's goal at the time. We'd been a band for almost four years by the time we were featured on the cover of *Guitar Player*, and *Argus* definitely made it into the *Billboard* charts. For my guitar partner Ted Turner, sadly, it all proved too much, and he decided to quit the band not long after that *Guitar Player* cover. So, unfortunately, that image of us two twin guitar players, in what was Europe's premier twin lead band, proved to be short lived. The original band lineup really was poised to break the U.S. in a big way at that time. We did in fact move to the U.S., where I still make my home and spent some intense years touring all over, playing all the major venues.

Andy Powell (Alan Barnes/ C4Miles Photography)

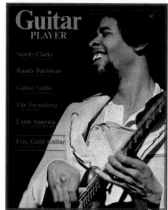

July '75 (Cover photo by Howard Brainen)

Stanley Clarke (Steven Parke)

My experiences with *GP*'s writers were that they were very respectful and very interested in all things British. Don't forget, the UK was spearheading the whole lead guitarist thing in a big way. We were the natural heirs to all the work done by Clapton, Beck, and Page before us. If you played guitar well, in a British band—especially one like ours, which was bringing a whole new concept to the table—the world was your oyster. We had an American manager, Miles Copeland, and also a U.S. label, MCA/Decca, so our whole thrust was toward America.

I think these *GP* covers and poll awards gave artists like us serious credibility. Fans and other writers and the labels all took notice of these accolades. A lot of labels needed educating about the world of rock and the artists they were, by now, beginning to sign, and so magazines like *Guitar Player* had serious clout.

I still play in Wishbone Ash. I'm the last man standing, so to speak. I simply never quit. I love the band and the life. The original members all left the band over time. Wishbone Ash plays about 150 tour dates annually worldwide these days, and we regularly release albums and DVDs.

Stanley Clarke

Back then there were very few magazines that dealt specifically with instruments, so *Guitar Player* stood out and was the go-to for guitar musicians. Now there are tons of magazines dedicated to just about any instrument out there as well as its variations. Then, there was only *Guitar Player* for *all* guitar players.

I don't remember who contacted me. I did various interviews with *Guitar Player* over the years and was on the cover twice during that era, 1975 and 1980. I believe I may have been the first bass player to be featured on the magazine's cover. [*Ed. Note: While* GP *had started including bass guitarists from the April '72 issue, even mentioning some on the cover, Stanley is right—his July '75 cover was* GP's *first that featured a bassist.*]

In 1975, I was touring on my breakout album, *School Days*. It was a very thrilling time for me. The bass was finally out of the closet, going from a background instrument in the band to a lead instrument, which is where I wanted it to go. The tour was extensive. At the time, that was critical for the bass. In L.A. there were billboards on Sunset Boulevard, twelve sold-out shows at the Roxy, album covers featured on the then famous Tower Records, and more . . . a cover on *Guitar Player*. In 1980, I was coming off the successful Return to Forever tours and album projects and moving into my work with George Duke and the Clarke/Duke Project. All of this was also very exciting.

I don't specifically remember the writer [Jim Crockett], but in 1975 I was still very young and quite inexperienced with media attention. I know it must have been exciting to be interviewed by a major magazine that I respected and knew all my friends would be reading. Never in a million years would I have expected to see myself on the cover of a magazine. It was surreal to walk down the street in New York at the time and see my face on newsstands. It felt great! *Guitar Player* was the cutting edge for guitar players and other musicians. It also began expanding to the general public of music lovers interested in rock music. Being featured in the magazine made one a "musician's musician" among his peers and the public. It legitimized me and, more importantly to me, the bass. It made playing the electric bass fashionable.

Today, I'm as busy as ever. I've won three Grammy Awards over the past few years, one of my own for *The Stanley Clarke Band* and two with Return to Forever for *Forever*. I'm still out on the road performing much of the time. I'm still producing and am composing film and television scores. In 2011 I was honored at the Montreal Jazz Festival with the Miles Davis Award for my career body of work. And I'm still considered by *DownBeat* magazine's 2013 Critics and Readers polls their Best Electric Bass Guitarist.

I'm extremely fortunate doing what I love and it's still very exciting.

May '80 (Cover photo by Darryl Pitt)

May '86 (Cover photo by Mary Beth Greenwood)

Eric Johnson

I remember being in tenth grade and walking into the high school library one day and there on the magazine stand was *Guitar Player* magazine. Never heard of it before; there was no guitar magazine until *GP* came out. To make it even more astounding, Jimi Hendrix was on the front cover. I read it front-to-back and ever since have been an avid fan.

Those were the glory days, much more about music than gear; more open-minded and seemingly less judgmental and edgy for sake of "preferred polarization."

Eric Johnson
(Max Crace)

Probably one of the biggest breaks to start my career was Steve Morse mentioning me in a *Guitar Player* article on him. What followed were a couple of articles on me, including a cover story. Jas Obrecht and *GP* stuck their neck out for me when I couldn't get arrested. I will always remember that and be grateful to all those great guys who started *Guitar Player* magazine.

Rusty Young

My Steel Symposium was a column that provided readers with tips on playing pedal steel guitar. As a result, it could only run until I ran out of tips. Toward the end I think I had to resort to tips on what to wear when playing pedal steel and why manicures were essential to good hygiene, as well as good technique.

I think Jim Crockett asked me to contribute a column and since I'd taught steel guitar since I was fourteen years old, I thought it was something I'd enjoy. When Jim made the effort to fly to Denver to do my first *GP* interview, we quickly became friends and we thought my column might influence other musicians and I'd have the chance to pass on some of what I'd learned.

Rusty Young (Jim Crockett)

It was a thrill to contribute to such an iconic magazine, and I did my best to write columns that people would want to read. It really made me a hero to the guys I used to play with and the folks at the guitar store I worked at back home. But because I had such a heavy touring schedule with Poco, it was hard for me to make the deadline every month and, as I said, I eventually just ran out of tips.

I don't remember working with anyone directly other than talking to Jim occasionally, and he was really annoying—ha!

The column did bring a certain amount of respect among steel players and guitar manufacturers. I still have people at concerts come up and say they used to read the column and how much they enjoyed it. That's pretty cool!

I was just inducted into the Pedal Steel Hall of Fame, and after forty-six years I still play concerts with Poco and concerts on my own. But these days my focus is on finishing a book I'm writing about those forty-six years, the people I've met, the experiences I've had, and the lessons I've learned.

Rusty Young (Rusty Young Archives)

Rusty Young (Rick Malkin)

Happy Traum

I have been a guitar teacher almost as long as I've been playing the instrument. I started teaching to make a little spending money while I was still a student at New York University. It was a natural progression for me to continue this trend after I graduated and needed to make a living. Aside from teaching community group classes and at numerous summer camps and music schools, I started writing the Teach-In column in *Sing Out!* magazine, which resulted in my first book, *Fingerpicking Styles for Guitar* (Oak Publications, 1965).

When *Guitar Player* started, I saw it as a new and bigger venue for my interest in documenting and teaching the traditional playing styles that had captivated me: country blues, Piedmont-style fingerpicking, bluegrass flatpicking and folk song accompaniment. My wife Jane and I met with Jim Crockett and, with his encouragement,

Happy Traum in 1968 (Diana Davies)

Happy Traum (Dion Ogust)

I grabbed that side of guitar instruction in the magazine with my column Strictly Folk. Jim was open to anything I thought was worthy of passing along to readers, and my involvement blossomed into several years of instructional pieces ranging from easy techniques for beginners to more advanced instrumentals for aspiring pickers. As the magazine grew and expanded its scope, I always appreciated that Jim allowed that island of acoustic styles, among the rock, electric blues, jazz, classical, and other guitar forms, to be prominently represented in its pages.

The most satisfying result of writing these columns is that, to this day, players and enthusiasts remember me as a contributor to *Guitar Player*, and they tell me how much they learned from my work. I continue to be proud of my association with Jim and the wonderful editorial staff he assembled from the start of the magazine's run.

Another important development in my writing arose when Jim approached me with an idea for a book about the steps an aspiring folk singer needs to take to make his or her way in the music world. The result, *Folk Guitar as a Profession*, was the first in a Guitar Player Career Guide Series, and my first book without guitar transcriptions or playing instructions. It was published in 1977 with an introduction by my lifelong friend John Sebastian (John's wife, Catherine, took the cover photo) and it was well received although, sadly, it is long out of print now.

As I have said elsewhere, *Guitar Player* and Homespun Tapes were born in the same year, so the trajectories of our companies intersected very comfortably, especially in the early years. I like to think that the symbiosis of our two ventures helped us both. We provided advertising and I contributed my teaching columns. *GP* gave us a great platform to reach the musicians who would benefit from our growing list of instructional products.

Today, more than fifty years later, I continue to play my music—still mostly, if not "strictly," folk—and Jane and I continue to produce numerous music instruction DVDs and digital downloads for Homespun each year. All in all, I have had a long and very satisfying life in music, with many strands making up the total fabric of my career. *Guitar Player* magazine has been one strand of which I've been particularly proud.

Mick Jones

Guitar Player's writers were always very professional and approached my interview for the February '79 issue very seriously. They always asked very educated questions and knew a lot about me. They knew about my past and my history as a musician, and I always appreciated that during my interviews.

Mick Jones

It brought attention and prestige to what I was doing; not just as a songwriter, but as a guitar player. It was great to be recognized for both aspects of my musicianship, the writing and the playing.

I re-formed Foreigner in 2004 and we've been traveling around the world. It's been an incredible experience. Almost like starting all over again.

Mick Jones (Bill Bernstein)

George Gruhn

George Gruhn

When I first opened my shop in January 1970, *Guitar Player* and *Bluegrass Unlimited*, two very different publications, were virtually the only periodicals offering information about guitars. Not only was I interested in reading the articles in both magazines, but as the owner of a new business wanting to reach out to the public, I was interested in advertising.

Bluegrass Unlimited offered classified ads as well as display ads, while *Guitar Player* did not accept any ads smaller than a 2.25" x 2.25" display, and did not print classifieds until many years later. While the classified ads in *Bluegrass Unlimited* were inexpensive, the smallest display ads in *Guitar Player* cost $250, which, in the early 1970s inflation-adjusted, was far more expensive than that amount would be today. By contrast, the monthly rent for my first building, which measured twenty by sixty feet—twelve hundred square feet total—was only $200 a month. However, the return on my advertising investment in *GP* justified the expense. At that time there simply was no other magazine capable of providing the same return on investment for my purposes. *Guitar Player* had virtually no competition in the field. When I started advertising there, my ad was the only one in the magazine representing an independent music store—all the others were from manufacturers and distributors of new products—but my small ad generated as many as twenty calls a day from people worldwide who were keenly interested in the vintage instruments I had to offer.

In the mid-1970s I wrote a few articles for *Guitar Player* that were very well received. Shortly afterward, Tom Wheeler, the magazine's editor at that time, invited me to become a monthly columnist, which I happily accepted. My articles and columns, called American Guitar, were some of the earliest published information available on vintage guitars and other fretted instruments as well as published commentary regarding the vintage guitar market. *Guitar Player* played a pivotal role in the rapidly expanding guitar market.

Tom Wheeler and the staff working with him were enthusiastic as well as highly skilled, knowledgeable, and creative. It was a pleasure and privilege to work with Tom and the magazine staff. The relationship was mutually beneficial for my business and the magazine. My columns not only provided information about the instruments, but they helped to stimulate demand for vintage instruments, and my relationship with the magazine as a monthly columnist enhanced the reputation of my shop.

Shortly after assuming the role as a columnist for *GP*, I also started writing the "Technical Reference Manual" column in May '78 for *Pickin'* (which later blended into *Frets,* which was acquired by GPI Publications). I started writing the Looking Back column for *Frets* from March '79 until that magazine ceased publication. *Gruhn's Guide to Vintage Guitars* and two other books I coauthored were initially published and distributed by GPI Publications.

I continued my work with *Guitar Player* as a columnist until late 1986, shortly after I was involved with a group that acquired the Guild guitar company. After I assumed the role of executive vice president of research and development and artist relations, as well as a position on the board of directors of Guild, I was informed that in spite of the fact that my column covered exclusively vintage rather than new instruments, the magazine felt it to be in their best interest to avoid any appearance of conflict having me as a columnist.

My relationship with Guild was over by late 1988, leaving very few fond memories, but to this day I feel privileged to have been able

Regarding the vintage guitar market, *Guitar Player* played a pivotal role.

George Gruhn (Vincent Ricardel)

to work with Tom Wheeler and the inspired and creative *Guitar Player* team of the mid-1970s through mid-1980s. There are numerous publications devoted to guitars today; however, in my opinion, none have had a deeper or more long-lasting worldwide impact than *Guitar Player* under its inspired leadership of the 1970s and '80s.

The mid-1970s through mid-1980s were indeed a very different time from today. Tom Wheeler had not yet written his book *American Guitars*, no other books covering vintage American fretted instruments were on the market, reprints of vintage instrument catalogs were not yet available, but the guitar market was rapidly expanding and there was a thirst for knowledge. Nobody I knew had a home computer, there were no websites offering information because the Internet did not yet exist, and desktop publishing was still years in the future, so producing a magazine was far more time-consuming and expensive than it would be later. *Guitar Player* had a virtual monopoly on the market coupled with a rapidly expanding number of guitar players who were literate and hungry for information.

When I was writing for *GP* I was a baby boomer writing for a baby boomer audience. The market seemed far more focused at that time compared to the very fragmented market we have today. I was writing for one generation, whereas today it is necessary to try to reach out to baby boomers and to Generations X and Y, who do not necessarily share the same interests or background.

When I wrote articles and columns for *Guitar Player* and *Frets*, I received considerable reader feedback, and it was very clear to me that being a columnist for *Guitar Player* and *Frets* provided a strong boost to my business and impacted the market as a whole. Tom Wheeler's book and other early books on the market by me and other authors sold well and generated significant royalty payments. It is ironic that today, when so much information is readily available, often free, the public appears to be far less excited. If book royalties are any indication, the public today is certainly far less willing to pay for information. It is easy for me to lapse into nostalgia thinking about the great times I shared from the mid-1970s through mid-'80s with the staff at *Guitar Player*.

While I wax nostalgic about my tenure at *Guitar Player* and *Frets*, I also recall that the generational and economic dynamics of the market shifted dramatically during my tenure as a columnist. I grew up during the great folk music boom of the late 1950s through 1963. I knew Mike Bloomfield before he started to play electric guitar and witnessed his involvement with the Butterfield Blues Band in the mid-'60s. I experienced the Beatles' and the Rolling Stones' rock invasion of 1964 through the late 1960s. When I started writing for *Guitar Player*, folk rock as epitomized by bands like Crosby, Stills, Nash & Young was still at the top of the charts and the guitar market was very much driven by the baby-boom generation.

By the late 1970s a very high percentage of the baby boomers had dropped out of the market. They were working their fingers to the bone supporting an expensive home, a car, a wife, and children. They did not reenter the guitar market until they had midlife crises in the late '80s.

During the mid- to late 1960s, many guitar companies had been acquired by large holding corporations—Fender was bought by CBS in 1965; Guild was purchased by Avnet in 1967; and Gibson, which had been owned by Chicago Musical Instrument company, CMI, since 1944, negotiated a sale in 1969 that was completed in early 1970 to Norlin. By the early '80s, a high percentage of popular music was no longer guitar-centric, with the exception of heavy metal music as exemplified by Eddie Van Halen and other players who would not touch a guitar that did not have a dive bomb locking nut tremolo system. During the early 1980s the economy was in deep recession and prime rate interest was over 20 percent, making it impractical for businesses to borrow money to sustain their operations, or for customers to finance the purchase of instruments. The holding companies were no longer making money on the guitar companies they had acquired. CBS sold Fender in 1985, Norlin sold Gibson in early 1986, and Avnet sold Guild in August of the same year. But shortly after the holding companies divested themselves of

> More than two thirds of guitars in U.S. history have been made since 1990. These can last well over 200 years with proper care.

their guitar holdings the baby boomers started to reenter the guitar market. Martin, Gibson, and Fender have tremendously expanded production since the mid-1980s, and new manufacturers such as Taylor, PRS, and Collings entered the market and have been extremely successful. Today there are vastly more guitars being made annually in the U.S. than there were during the mid-1980s, but, still, the market is under stress.

More than two thirds of the guitars made in the history of the U.S. have been made since 1990. These instruments can last well over two hundred years with proper care, and in the past half century no new models have been introduced which render vintage and used instruments obsolete. The market is highly saturated and the number of used instruments available for resale grows every year. The baby boomers have aged and are no longer buying nearly as many guitars, and cannot be counted upon to buy more in the future. Generations X and Y were not nearly as interested in high-dollar vintage guitars or even guitars in general in their formative years as were the baby boomers and cannot be depended upon now or in the future to support the market in the same manner as the baby boomers did.

Older generations have criticized upcoming younger generations as long as written records going back to ancient Egypt have been discovered, but it is clear that "the times they are a-changing."

Buddy Emmons

I first heard about *Guitar Player* through guitar player friends of mine. To the best of my recollection, Bud Eastman contacted me by phone around 1970 when I was living in Downey, California. I had taken a job with Roger Miller in 1968 as a bass player and, thanks to the success of a Judy Collins album I had played pedal steel guitar on, was starting to establish myself as a studio musician.

My only interview experience was with Bud Eastman. When he asked if I'd be interested in a column regarding pedal steel, called Steel Guitar Workshop, and perhaps tablature, I almost turned him down. To me, the prestige of *Guitar Player* was such that I felt like the steel guitar and I would fit like a square peg in a round hole. When Bud told me he played steel guitar I was completely blown away, and for that reason I accepted his offer.

Buddy Emmons (Ernie Renn)

Buddy Emmons
(Ernie Renn)

From the mid-'70s into the '80s, I recorded several albums on the Flying Fish label, which led to my receiving the Readers Poll awards and a few awards from the Academy of Country Music in California, which I felt my experience with *Guitar Player* had much to do with.

I retired in 2007 after the passing of my wife, Peggy. My interest in playing was leading to a few steel shows throughout the year that would allow Peggy and I to take a break from our home activities, keep in touch with our friends across the country, and pick up a little Walmart money on the side. When Peggy left, she took my interest in doing it with her.

Billy Sheehan

I remember my family subscribed to several magazines in the '60s—*Look*, *Life*, and a few others. I saw a small ad way in the back of one of them about a magazine for guitar players. I sent away and subscribed. It changed everything for me! It opened up a whole new world about guitar and bass playing that could be gotten nowhere else. There was *DownBeat* at the time—but that was exclusively jazz. *Guitar Player* was for everyone. By covering artists in so many genres, it served a great pur-

December '86 (Neil Zlozower)

Billy Sheehan (John Zocco)

pose in spreading influences across stylistic boundaries. Something we need more of today.

Mike Varney [a columnist focusing on new talent] and I spoke on the phone a lot—I felt it was inappropriate to ask him to put me in his Spotlight on New Talent column, so thankfully he asked *me* if I wanted to be in it. It was a dream come true to see my name mentioned anywhere in the magazine, and it was a huge boost in my career at the time.

I was playing in Talas—my band from Buffalo, New York. No record deal, but we played constantly all over the East Coast. After I was in the magazine, we saw a big increase in interest and a surge in attendance for all of our shows.

I interviewed with Mike Varney— he is still one of my favorite people in the world, and speaking with him was entertaining to say the least! All the other journalists there who spoke with me over the years had a depth of knowledge and understanding of guitar-/bass-oriented music like nobody else. Always an absolute pleasure.

It was the realization of a lifetime dream and goal to be on the cover—when I was first on, it was also the issue where I won the Readers Poll for the first time. The day I found out, I was in Buffalo, on tour with David Lee Roth. We were headlining the same auditorium where I saw my first concert—Jimi Hendrix—many years earlier. If that wasn't enough, the mayor of Buffalo issued a proclamation declaring the day "Billy Sheehan Day"—and then they slid the magazine under the door of my hotel and I saw it for the first time. Pretty tough to top that day! I'm so thankful for everything that happened, and *Guitar Player* played a *huge* part in it all.

I have a new band with Richie Kotzen and Mike Portnoy called the Winery Dogs; still tour with Mr. Big every few years; play in another band with Tony MacAlpine, Mike Portnoy, and Derek Sherinian called PSMS; and have a Hammond B3 trio with Dennis Chambers on drums called Niacin. It's a busy time!

Mitch Holder at a recording session in 1975

Mitch Holder (Robb Lawrence)

Mitch Holder

I was a high school student, taking guitar lessons after school, and I saw a small magazine ad where there was a box to cut and fill out. I sent it in, got *Guitar Player*'s first issue in 1967, and have continued since then. I have every issue.

For the October '78 issue, I had a very nice time talking with Tom Mulhern. He led the interview in a way that made it flow very well. I was playing—mostly studio work, movies, TV, records and TV/radio jingles. I had a few students, and played live when time allowed.

There were many positive comments to me about the piece from various people, both in and out of the studio business. It was very beneficial from a public relations/publicity standpoint.

I'm still playing guitar professionally and teaching. I wrote a book several years ago on the subject of a former *GP* columnist, Howard Roberts.

Robb Lawrence

My affiliation with *Guitar Player* magazine began in roundabout fashion from a visit to Arizona buying my first Les Paul sunburst guitar . . . that led to a birthday party for *GP* founder Bud Eastman! I started playing surf and R&B music in late 1963 and also took up photography, so taking pictures of interesting guitars I found went hand in hand with drawing gear/band setups in school—and collecting those colorful Fender catalogs!

In 1970, I met John Dopyera, the inventor of the National and Dobro guitars, at the Fiddle-Fret shop in Escondido, California. Upon hearing his incredible depictions of the wild '20s and '30s escapades of musicians and craftsmen, of brawls and target practice . . . it became a novel and virtual movie in my mind. Thus I was inspired to write the untold story of America's rich history of guitars and guitarists, coupled with the lives of those who created them.

An older jazz guitar buff was visiting my girlfriend's parents in Arizona and turned me on to some hip Johnny Smith recordings. I mentioned a project I had recently started, amassing photographs of various older guitars I had been finding around California and interviewing people. Having enjoyed a '36 L-5 (with an Oscar Moore pickup and custom Owens bridge) led me to Hollywood and friendships with Barney Kessel and veteran Hollywood repairman to the stars, Milt Owens. This jazzer mentioned I should meet his friend steel guitarist Bud Eastman, who had started *Guitar Player* magazine a few years earlier. The next day I had to buy a seat for my bright tangerine sunburst, tiger-top Les Paul Standard guitar.

I soon rang Bud upon my arrival home in San Diego and it turned out to be his birthday. He invited me to swing by to celebrate and jam. I zipped over and had a great time visiting and playing some fun tunes. His steel playing was sweet! After sharing some of my guitar photography and ideas for a book, Bud said I should visit his editor, Jim Crockett, in Los Gatos about writing for them.

Since my plans were coming together for an American guitar safari, Bud said to definitely visit Les Paul while on the East Coast. Drummer Steve Rodriguez and I set out in a Dodge van from San Diego for a grand, cross-country trip visiting with George Gruhn in Nashville; Christian Frederick Martin III in Nazareth, Pennsylvania; Jimmy D'Aquisto in Long Island; and Les Paul in Mahwah, New Jersey, leading to Lyon & Healy in Chicago and a visit with Julius Bellson and Ted McCarty in Kalamazoo, Michigan.

Shortly thereafter I was doing some sessions in Hollywood with bassist Lonnie Turner (Steve Miller/Dave Mason) and we put the National/Dobro archives in order. We were en route to Mill Valley

I soon rang Bud and it turned out to be his birthday. He invited me to swing by to celebrate and jam. His steel playing was sweet!

in Northern California and made a point to swing by Los Gatos to visit with Jim. He liked what I was doing and thought I could start the original byline for a new column they had just begun about guitar history—Rare Bird. What a great day that was!

The first choice to write about was the sensational, futuristic Explorer Gibson guitar! My fellow bandmate Michael Sterling had a '59 Flying V, and Don Preston had let me play his '58 Explorer backstage at a Leon Russell/Pink Floyd concert in Southern California's La Jolla. I instantly saw the correlation to the original Firebird's inspiration. It was my current, most exciting rare find in our guitar collector/player circle and fitting for a debut in the literary world of guitars.

I sat on the living room floor, in the sunshine, penning the first exposé of the rarest and most coveted of korina-wood Gibson guitars. My thanks to Don Preston and Willie Spears, Eric Clapton's guitar tech for the inspiration and opportunity to photograph this most Holy of Rare Birds. It came out in the April '73 issue featuring Steve Howe of Yes, opening a lot of eyes in the guitar community and spawning the first Explorer reissue in '76. I later bought a '58/'63 and recorded with Jim Keltner at the Record Plant in 1973. What a distinctive tone came from that big korina-wood guitar!

Since my guitar playing and collecting tastes are so diverse (acoustic, bass, archtop, etc.), I chose to do my May article on Martin's original Ditson DM-111 dreadnought (thanks to George Gruhn). This instrument became what has become the most famous icon of all acoustic flattops. I went through a dozen vintage D-28s to find a superlative 1956 recording guitar. That very issue included Les Paul's first article, "Its Beginnings," featuring the original portrait I took of Les with the '60 Les Paul.

The July '73 issue featured Wes Montgomery and a '58 mint Precision Bass I played, along with a portrait of Leo Fender with my '52 P-Bass. Doc Kauffman and I had just spent a terrific afternoon reminiscing with Leo about their 1940s adventures. That sunburst '58 went on to record "Rikki Don't Lose That Number" with Walter Becker and Steely Dan.

September's issue featured the '58–'60 sunburst Les Paul Standard models that have become the Stradivarius of solid-body guitars. That fancy '60 tiger-top flame maple was exposed up close here. It had just flown the coop to England with guitarist Clem Clempson after a great jam with Stevie Marriott and Humble Pie at the A&M Chaplin stage. I'll say, they were certainly smokin' on that tour!

Being a steady Fender player, I had learned about the Broadcaster guitar from my first trip to Fenderland in 1968 with a '54 Stratocaster in tow. I logically went to the Fender Sales building listed in my '64 catalog, finding they had relocated to the new CBS building near

> A sunburst '58 I played went on to record "Rikki Don't Lose That Number" with Walter Becker and Steely Dan.

Robb Lawrence in La Jolla, California, in '73 (Paul Cowie)

the '53 factory. Later that day a savvy repairman out in the orange fields told me about the late-1950, early-1951 version of the famous Telecaster guitar. After my interviews with Leo, George Fullerton, and Freddie Tavares, I was anxious to share the Broadcaster story with the world via Rare Bird number five. About this time, the term *vintage* was finally adopted, due to our fascination with older, used guitars and their intrinsic high-quality, great tonality, newfound panache, and beautiful patina-like furniture aging.

My in-depth interviews with the Dopyeras, Paul Barth (with Steve Soest), Nolan and Jess Beauchamp, and Adolph Rickenbacker resulted in the first Dobro column with Emile Dopyera's portrait (October's 1973 issue) and the first Electric column with Mr. Rickenbacker holding the wooden prototype of the Ro-Pat-In "frying pan" Electro guitar. Sol Hoopii and Alvino Rey helped pioneer this historic instrument, launching a true revolution in music that resounds loudly today.

Robb Lawrence (Brad Smith)

The Jeff Beck issue in December of that year had my story of Gibson's illustrious engineer/musician Lloyd Loar developing the famous tap-tuned, f-hole design breakthrough for the L-5 Master Model. This instrument changed the archtop jazz world forever with "cutting power" that could be heard to the back of the hall, enabling the guitarist to be heard with the popular big bands of the day before electric amplification.

While I was visiting with Jeff Beck at the Continental "riot" Hyatt in Hollywood, an interviewer named Steve Rosen came up to Jeff's room. As he conducted his interview there was a lapse and I asked, "Do you consider yourself a flash guitarist?" Jeff's reply was, "Certainly, always have!" He told me in 1973 he wanted to meet his

A few friends told me, "You're responsible for this [vintage guitar] craze!" I replied, "It would have happened anyway, so I just nudged it along!"

idol Les Paul, the original flashy guitarist. That finally happened in 1975 on the Blow by Blow tour, when we visited at the Avery Fisher Hall in NYC.

In 1974, I wrote an article on John McLaughlin's Double Rainbow twin-neck guitar by Rex Bogue and Ren Ferguson. After an interview with John at a Mahavishnu concert, visiting with Rex and taking numerous photos, I turned in an article similar to my Rare Bird efforts. It was made into a feature article and was added to somewhat. One highlight of that encounter was riding with both Rex and John in a Mercedes 300SL roadster painted psychedelic!

After a year of articles for *GP*, Les advised me I should hold on to my invaluable materials and wait to get a book deal. I lived with Les, his son Bobby, and bassist Wally Kamin in 1975 and we visited various book publishers who all loved the idea—but wouldn't do full-color books. So we waited. Meanwhile, Tom Wheeler came to visit me in San Diego when his exciting *American Guitars* book helped launched his career. He signed my copy saying, "Robb, you were there first! Thanks for the great input and inspiration!"

Leo Fender's first partner, Doc Kauffman, told me during our interviews, "Robby, you put everything that's interesting you discover into your books, and the world will thank you for the insights you share." Funny thing, once the vintage guitar shows got going, a few friends told me, "You're responsible for this craze!" I replied, "It would have happened anyway, so I just nudged it along!"

During the mid-'70s I had the great pleasure of meeting Kitty Salvatore Lang Good, a real Ziegfeld gal and widow to the late, great guitarist Eddie Lang. We met through my dear friend Mitch Holder, protégé of the late Howard Roberts and staff guitarist for *The Tonight Show Starring Johnny Carson*. He told me to call Kitty since she was selling Eddie's favorite Gibson L-5. I called Les Paul and he said, "Robby you go get that guitar of Eddie's!" We visited and did some memorable interviews about Eddie and his pioneering jazz guitar playing with Joe Venuti, Paul Whiteman, Lonnie Johnson, Louis Armstrong, and Bing Crosby.

Kitty entrusted me to take care of Eddie's special 1929 L-5 Gibson. He had picked it out of five unfinished L-5 guitars in Kalamazoo and used it on many famous recordings and movies. In 1983, I wrote a feature article on the instrument to coincide with other articles on the jazz guitar giant. I included quotes from Kitty, Les, and Milt Owens, who set up the instrument in Hollywood during the filming of *The Big Broadcast*. The portrait of the guitar I took with my grandfather's 1954 Leica M1 camera instead of my trusty Nikon F2. Over the years many guitarists have played the guitar, including Tony Romano, Eddie Arnold, Tommy Bolin, Joe Pass, Carlos Santana, Bob

Bain, Tommy Emmanuel, and Martin Taylor and others who have made a trip to see the maestro's treasured instrument.

After selling a few outtake photos of Clapton, Beck, and Roy Buchanan for Fender's *Classic Moments* book, I made a pitch to Brad Smith, marketing director of Hal Leonard publishing. They loved my Fender and Les Paul book layouts. I finally had the opportunity to do full-color, boxed sets, starting with *The Les Paul Legacy*, a two-volume history of Les Paul's career and the famous Gibson guitar that bears his name.

Editor-at-large Barry Cleveland favorably reviewed my 2008 Hal Leonard release, *The Early Years of the Les Paul Legacy*, bringing me back into the *GP* fold. In recent years I've written stories about the first National guitar, early versions of the first electric solid-body guitars, Tony Iommi's SG collection, and memorial articles on dearly departed friends including Dan Armstrong, George Fullerton, and Bill Lawrence.

It's been a great pleasure and a true privilege to write for such a prestigious and prolific magazine profiling America's finest instruments and guitarists' heartfelt impressions (five *p*'s!). My sincere thanks to Bud Eastman and Jim Crockett for my start in the literary field, fellow RB columnists Tom Wheeler, George Gruhn, and Richard Smith for their inspiration and friendship—and all the fans of the guitars and people that shaped our musical history of heart-stirring songs! My writing could not have been what it is today without these humble beginnings at *Guitar Player* magazine. Thank you, Bud Eastman, for the gracious invitation!

Mike Varney

As a young reader of *Guitar Player* at age twenty-three, I felt that there should be a place in the magazine for unknown guitarists to be featured. In some of the rock magazines of the era they would review demos or feature photos and little stories about artists on the way up who had not yet made their mark on rock 'n' roll history. I started Shrapnel Records in 1980 as a niche label for heavy metal guitarists of extraordinary ability. As a guitar fan, I knew there had to be a lot of unknown players who were as good as the best-known players, and I was determined to find them.

In 1980, I contacted all of the "local" music magazines that I could find around the United States and told them that I was compiling a record of the best unknown guitarists from the U.S. I asked the editors if they felt that someone in their area might have a shot at being one of the ten best unknown players in the States. The response was amazing, and most of the regional publications ran a story about my quest to find

It was always an honor to write for *GP*, especially at the age of twenty-four.

Mike Varney in 1982 with
Iron Maiden (Jon Sievert)

the best unknown guitarists. I even wrote a letter to *Guitar Player* and it was printed in the letters section. Jas Obrecht read about me in *BAM Magazine* and sent me a note that said if I ever found anyone noteworthy that he'd like he'd appreciate hearing about them. We got in touch and at the time I had finished a record for EMI records, which was a rock opera called *Rock Justice* that I had written with Jefferson Airplane/Starship singer Marty Balin and attorney/writer Bob Heyman. Jeff Pilson, pre-Dokken/Foreigner, was on the record with a lot of other cool players, and Jas was kind enough to review the record in *GP*. When I told him of some of the great guitarists that I was finding, he decided to write a feature about my search for the greatest unknown American guitarists, and it ran in *GP*. At about this same time, Jas invited me to a Halloween party/jam at *GP* in 1981, and I went down there with a couple of the young hotshots I'd found and we jammed and had a great time. I met Tom Wheeler at the party and saw an opportunity to pitch him on my idea for the column, and he asked me to write a sample column, and the rest, as they say . . . is history.

It was always an honor for me to write for *GP*, especially at the age of twenty-four. I was the new kid on the block and had the opportunity to work with people whom I had looked up to for years. I remember going to the NAMM show and hanging out in the *GP* booth and I was happily surprised to see how many people had been enjoying the column. Based on the success of the Spotlight column, I had offers to write a similar column from *Guitar for the Practicing Musician* and *Guitar World* in the '80s, but I was loyal to *GP*.

GP also asked me to write some features for the magazine, and those were a lot of fun too. Before the magazine, I had been receiving a lot of demos, but for

Mike Varney
(Chris Logan)

a few years, in the heyday of the column, I received an unbelievable amount of material from all over the world. It was staggering. Most of my time went into picking up, opening, and listening to all of those demos. Writing the column was the easy part. Through the column, artists such as Billy Sheehan, Scott Henderson, Yngwie Malmsteen, Paul Gilbert, Vinnie Moore, Jason Becker, Tony MacAlpine, Richie Kotzen, Greg Howe, Shawn Lane, and many others, received their first pieces of mainstream international press.

Jas Obrecht was my main contact, and he was very encouraging. It was Jas who saw a talent in me as I saw the talent in unknown guitar players, only my talent was a lot less. :) Jas was a lot of fun to work with, and he taught me a lot of things, as I had never written professionally prior to writing the Spotlight column. Tom Wheeler was also an inspiration. Both Jas and Tom were true journalists. Nothing would have happened without Jim Crockett seeing the vision, too. The idea for the column was to bridge the gap between the platinum rock stars and the guys grinding it out in the clubs by providing a platform for the latter to be recognized in the world's greatest guitar-oriented publication.

Before the column, I was a songwriter, musician, record producer, and record company owner. The column expanded public awareness of some of my company's artists and productions, and I recruited some of my artists after hearing their submissions for the column. After *GP* decided to have the Spotlight column written in-house in 1990, *Guitar World* once again offered to have me write their Hometown Heroes column, which I did for a couple of years, but it never seemed to have the panache of the original column in *GP*.

I still am running the Shrapnel Label Group, which encompasses Shrapnel Records, Blues Bureau International, and Tone Center. I am also the co-owner of Magna Carta, a New York record company run by music business veteran Peter Morticelli. I am still active in producing records and do a lot of cowriting with some of my artists, which I have always enjoyed doing. Through the years, the various labels have made recordings with artists such as Frank Gambale, Marty Friedman, Pat Travers, George Lynch, Michael Schenker, Rick Derringer, Greg Howe, John Five, Jacky Vincent, Dario Lorina, David Lee Roth, Kansas, Bozzio Levin Stevens, Michael Landau, Liquid Tension Experiment, Johnny Hiland, Eric Gale, Chris Duarte, Stoney Curtis, Craig Erickson, Jake E. Lee, John Norum, Joey Tafolla, Jon Butcher, Glenn Hughes, Victor Wooten, Jimmy Herring, Jeff Watson, Mato Nanji/Indigenous, Joe Lynn Turner, Doug Pinnick, Stu Hamm, Steve Smith, Billy Sheehan, Scott Henderson, Yngwie Malmsteen, Paul Gilbert, Vinnie Moore, Jason Becker, Tony MacAlpine, Richie Kotzen, and many other incredible musicians, some of whom should have been first on the list, but my memory is not as sharp as it used to be, and for that I apologize.

Sharon Isbin (Alix Jeffry)

Sharon Isbin

Guitar Player was the go-to magazine when I was starting a career in the '70s, and one of the few that embraced all genres of playing.

My first feature ran in May 1980, when Tom Wheeler was associate editor. I had just made my New York debut the year before at Lincoln Center's Alice Tully Hall, won several major competitions, and premiered my first concerto commission. I was touring throughout the US, Europe, and Asia and was about to release my second album. It was an exciting time for a young guitarist in her early twenties, and *Guitar Player* was on it!

As time went on, however, I forgot about that feature—until twenty-four years later, when a bizarre airport experience brought it all back. I was stuck in a funky-looking AirTran terminal in New York, trying to get through security. After the guitar passed through their X-ray machine, the inspector asked if I knew who Stanley Clarke was. I said no, but that I knew Stanley Jordan and that he was great. Displeased, they tore through the entire case, rolled it through the machine, and grilled me again about Clarke. This continued at least five more times. They couldn't believe I was a guitarist and didn't know who Stanley Clarke was. I had to be an imposter, or worse. Finally, after I flunked Guitar 101, they gave up and let me pass. When I asked why all this nonsense, they explained that at AirTran, they believed the next terrorist would come toting a guitar case, and Clarke was their litmus test! A few days after I told this strange story to a friend, she sent me a copy of the May 1980 *Guitar Player*. There on the cover was Stanley Clarke, with my name just below!

The next interview was in February 1985. This was timely, as I was about to present my weeklong Guitarstream '85 festival at Carnegie Hall. Michael Hedges was on the cover. I could never have guessed that two and a half years later we would be playing his last tour together, a month before his tragic death in a car crash.

Early *GP* press proved to be a wonderful means of access to the non-classical guitar world. It led to multiple Readers Poll awards in the '90s and beyond, and to future *GP* features, including in 2011. Reading *GP* in those early days helped to educate me on the rock and jazz stars of the time, and paved the way for my later collaborations with such guitarists as Steve Vai, Steve Morse, Larry Coryell, Herb Ellis, Laurindo Almeida, Michael Hedges, and Stanley Jordan.

Today, I'm the founding director of the guitar department at the Juilliard School, and recently received another Grammy, for my CD *Journey to the New World*, with guests Joan Baez and Mark O'Connor. My Sony CD, *Sharon Isbin & Friends: Guitar Passions*, includes guests Steve Vai, Stanley Jordan, Steve Morse, and Heart's Nancy Wilson. A documentary titled *Sharon Isbin: Troubadour* premiered in film festivals and was broadcast nationally on public television stations with a release as well on DVD and Blu-ray. The trailer includes Steve Vai, Janis Ian, Garrison Keillor, Martina Navratilova, and the Obamas.

Sharon Isbin (J. Henry Fair)

Arlen Roth

Even before I had ever become involved in writing Hot Guitar for, or being a part of, *Guitar Player* magazine, it already held a very important place in my heart and in my psyche. After all, back in the days of the '70s and early '80s, there was nobody who could hold a candle to the excellence this publication put forth, and the way it single-handedly satisfied all those guitar-hungry fanatics out there who just couldn't get enough "guitar!" We were players, collectors, and, most of all, *fans* who simply wanted to learn all we could about our favorite instrument and the world it occupied!

It was *Guitar Player* that was the first to really publish any in-depth articles about me, such as Happy Traum's piece on me back in 1979 (with Bad Company's Mick Ralphs on the cover). Funny coincidence about that issue was I recall being so excited that there was a big article about me in it that in the Madison Square Garden train station in NYC I noticed that there was a whole pile of them. Before getting on the subway to go home, I grabbed as many as I could, probably a dozen, paid for them, and went home. When I finally looked at them, I noticed one had been signed in the *Guitar Player* logo by Mick Ralphs himself! Apparently, Bad Company had just performed at the Garden, and he had left his mark. Truly an amazing coincidence for *me*, of all people, to be finding!

Soon afterward, when my second album, *Hot Pickups*, was released, *Guitar Player* quickly gave it the featured review of that month, and Tom Wheeler called my version of "When a Man Loves a Woman" "likely one of the most intense workouts ever recorded on a Telecaster!" I had no idea of the extreme reach this kind of review could have until one day during the following year, when I was sitting and playing a guitar in a little shop on Forty-Eighth Street in Manhattan, and a young kid walked in, watched me play, and then said "Hey, your version of 'When a Man Loves a Woman . . .'" (Needless to say, he pretty much quoted the entire album review word for word and totally blew my mind!) I can recall Tom Wheeler calling me up as he was planning to write that review, making sure I was not using a B-bender or any other pulling devices on the guitar, saying, "This is just unbelievable!" It was sure exciting to me, as he sounded like a true writer caught up in the moment of simply being excited about, and enjoying, my music!

Later, in 1979, when my touring over the previous two years with Art Garfunkel and Phoebe Snow had ended, and there seemed like little gigging or work on the horizon, I decided that with our last $2,000, my wife Deborah and I were going to start a taped musical instruction company called Hot Licks. I had long since had the idea to

It was *Guitar Player* that was the first to publish any in-depth articles about me.

do lessons on cassette, since my students as far back as 1972 used to tape their lessons as a way of really getting *all* the info that was sometimes passing them by during the course of one of my classes with them! One day, a student moved away to Colorado and told me he "sure missed those lessons on tape," and that was all I needed to store away in the back of my mind for future use in case I should ever decide to start a new business all my own! That day finally came, and in 1979 the $2,000 we had left bought me a half-page black-and-white ad in *Guitar Player*, and $500 got me a used Teac tape deck in the electronics store across the street. (At this point, we were living in a loft just two blocks north of the World Trade Center!) I started to feverishly record my initial forty-eight audio lessons, which were about to be announced in our first February 1979 ad in *GP*, and lo and behold, not realizing that the *cover* date was about two months later than the actual publishing date, the orders started filling the mailbox at 46 Warren Street in Manhattan before I was even done recording the lessons themselves!! I always knew that repeat customers were going to be the backbone of the business, and I knew that *Guitar Player* magazine readers were of such a dedicated and voracious variety, I needed to offer them a full palette of styles and techniques to sink their teeth into. It sure paid off, as that very first ad, and the investment of all $2,000 I had at the time, turned into over $18,000 in responses just for that February 1979 issue alone! My trust in the *GP* readership had paid off, and I knew that I could count on their knowledge of me, through the articles and reviews giving them enough familiarity with me to *trust* my new Hot Licks product!

Guitar Player always felt like a close and trusted friend to us in those early years, and it was a logical stop on the California coastal trip Deborah and I had planned when we got married in July of 1981 and went on our honeymoon! Cupertino was a location we just *had* to see, and everyone there was so friendly and welcoming to us! It was amazing for me to finally meet, in *person*, folks like Dennis Fullerton, Tom Wheeler, Jas Obrecht, Tom Mulhern, and of course Jim Crockett. It was a time we never forgot, and it was an important step in those early, formative years for me as a writer, and also as an entrepreneur starting my own business.

The next big and very important step occurred soon after this, in 1982, when I had started writing guitar-instruction-oriented columns for both *Circus* magazine as well as *Guitar World*. I received a no-frills, all-business kind of call from Tom Wheeler, asking me to come onboard with *GP* as an "exclusive" monthly columnist for them. At this point I had already written some features for *GP*, such as the one on Duane Allman in 1981 and a few others, so they must've been confident in my writing abilities by this point, not to mention that I had

Deborah and Arlen Roth in NYC in 1979 (Chuck Horan)

I knew that *GP* readers were dedicated and voracious, and I needed to offer them a full palette of styles and techniques to sink their teeth into.

already published three best-selling books as well. I also figured that with Hot Licks being advertised by us in nearly every issue, a full-page monthly column by myself would only help to act as yet *another* piece of advertising that would translate into more public *trust* and therefore more *sales*! I felt a little trepidation about giving up writing for two other magazines, but to be onboard with *GP* was truly to be recognized as one of the best at what I did, and it felt so good to have Jim Crockett write a truly warm and heartfelt welcome to me in his publisher's column on the opening pages of that 1982 issue that ushered in the next ten years of my Hot Guitar column! I can recall arriving at the NAMM show that winter in Anaheim, running into Noe Goldwasser of *Guitar World*, and with me being full of anticipation knowing I had just *left* that magazine, and all he simply said to me was, "Hey, you can't beat what Jim Crockett had to say about you!" It felt really good, and it was obvious he had no hard feelings, and even more so, sent me off to *GP* with his blessings.

Arlen and Lexie Roth
(Arlen Roth Collection)

Of course, there were the seemingly endless NAMM shows that I attended throughout the '80s and '90s and the *Guitar Player* breakfasts were always something not to miss! Ever fueled by the good cheer and presence of folks like Don Menn, Dominic Milano, Tom Wheeler, and Jim Crockett, this was the place to be on any given morning in Anaheim or wherever else the NAMM show might be that year, and it was always fun showing up with a cassette so I could play Tom Wheeler my latest album in the works, and it was a gathering that always got you set for a good and long day at NAMM! Was always proud to be there!

One memorable (and funny) time was at the New Orleans NAMM show, either in '84 or '85, when I got the chance to hit the stage with my friend John Entwistle of the Who, and others such as Eddie Van Halen and Brian May. We really tore the house down, and I was flying across the stage in a white suit jacket, with Hawaiian printed swimming trunks down below, which I thought was a totally normal and cool outfit for such a show. I think I wore the same thing the next day, because I remember standing at the *GP* booth and Jim Crockett suddenly and very candidly saying to me, "Arlen, what are you WEARING?!" It was just one of those moments in time that to this day still cracks me up when I think of it!

Another thing about that moment and all the other moments with my days at *Guitar Player* was just what a *family* it really always felt like. Yes, I was on the East Coast, and the only time I was ever at their offices was when Deborah and I were on our honeymoon, but the communication was always great, and the sense that you were really a *part* of something very special was always felt. I was so happy to see that *Guitar Player* had released my ten years of Hot Guitar columns (1982–1992) as a book, and I am always turning everyone on to it. After all, I can still barely ever run into a fan or fellow guitarist who doesn't immediately bring up how they loved and always followed my columns in *Guitar Player* during those "golden years"! Great years they were, indeed, and here's to the legacy that the entire staff at *Guitar Player* has left forever for all those who really love this incredible instrument, and the players and the world around it!

Guitar Player always felt like a close personal friend.

John Carruthers

Tom Wheeler had told me about an opening at *GP* to write a column about guitar repair and maintenance. I thought that this was an excellent opportunity and agreed to take the position. Tom and myself met and worked at Westwood Music. Tom was giving guitar lessons and I was doing guitar repair work. I helped him write his first book. I was doing a lot of work for many of the popular artists and bands at the time. I did work for the Rolling Stones, Eagles, Fleetwood

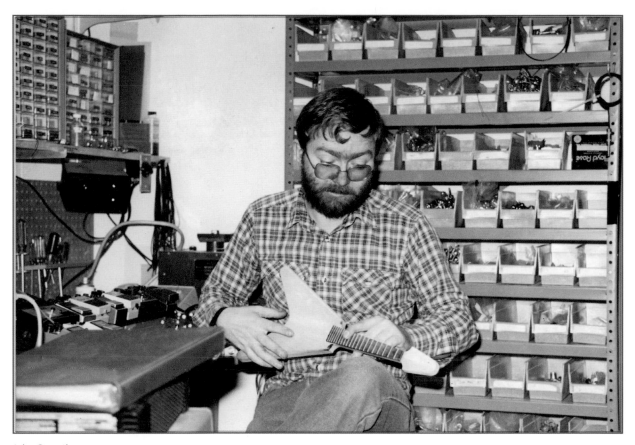

John Carruthers

John Carruthers (Darryl Jones)

Mac, Steely Dan, Kenny Loggins, the Byrds, Grateful Dead, Frank Zappa, the Band, Eric Clapton, Bonnie Raitt, Linda Ronstadt, and Albert Collins, including many studio musicians like Lee Ritenour, Larry Carlton, Dean Parks, David Cohen, Jay Graydon, Leland Sklar, Chuck Rainey, and many more, some of whom were featured in *GP* articles. My first column, Guitar Workshop, appeared in the January 1977 issue that featured Frank Zappa on the front cover holding a Strat that I had worked on that was given to him by Jimi Hendrix, and continued for nearly ten years.

My column was a way to educate players about proper setup, adjustment, and maintenance of their guitars. Occasionally, I would do an article on modifications. I found the job to be quite challenging. We would have deadlines usually about three months in advance of publication, and any drawings or photos that were needed were our responsibility. I felt that it was very important to make all the technical aspects very clear to the reader.

I found myself to be in great company with the many famous players who did interviews or who were also staff writers. The editorial staff were exceptional people and worked hard to further the success of the magazine while helping the columnists. It was an honor for me to work with Jim Crockett, Tom Mulhern, Dan Forte, and Tom Wheeler. They were very professional and great friends.

I found that the column gave me a lot of exposure and helped me expand my business, Carruthers Guitars. Companies like Yamaha, Fender, Music Man (Leo Fender), and Ibanez hired me to do consulting work. I was able to have a direct hand in designing, manufacturing, and marketing guitars for these companies.

Jerry Silverman

When I was contacted by *GP* in 1978 to write an open-ended series of columns about the joys and sorrows of playing and teaching "easy" guitar, I felt as if I had been slipped a passkey to a candy store or an ice cream parlor. Just imagine: Come any time (well, once a month), stay as long as you like (please keep it to one page), and write whatever you like (just don't break any dishes). So much to say for posterity. So many eager neophytes anxiously awaiting my words of wisdom. No frustrated students: "It's too hard. . . . My fingers hurt. . . ." No annoyed and annoying parents breathing down my neck: "He (she) didn't practice once all week .. . . It's costing me MONEY!"

Jerry Silverman in 1980 (Jon Sievert)

What a deal! It was an offer I couldn't refuse.

So I set to work typing (remember typewriters? Or was it with a quill pen?) my first Easy Guitar Workshop column, for the April 1978 issue, titled "Your First Guitar: A Big Decision." The inside scoop on the burning question of nylon versus steel-string guitars. Of course I was talking about *acoustic* guitars. Remember folksingers? Hey! Remember *me*?

From that point on it was easy going with captivating columns with subtitles such as: "Accessories After the Fact" (capos, picks, music stands . . .); "How to Study the Guitar" (finding a teacher, on your own, books . . .); "Bass Runs, Arpeggios, Hammering On and Pulling Off"; "Blues" (lots of stuff here); "7/8 Time" (what's that?); "Calypso"; "Ragtime"; "Movable Chord Shapes"; "Hemiola" (you could look it up); "How to Teach Guitar and Still Make an Honest Living" . . . I could go on and on. As a matter of fact, I did.

Jerry Silverman (Osni Omena)

Many of these subjects found their way into my method books, songbooks, and anthologies. Legitimate music publishers (as opposed to the other kind) such as Mel Bay, Hal Leonard, Alfred, Cherry Lane, Warner Brothers, Schirmer, and others were receptive to the approach to music that formed the basis—before, during, and after—of my *GP* columns.

As I write these words (no more quill pen and typewriter), it suddenly has dawned on me that over forty years have flown by since my last column appeared in the pages of *Guitar Player*. Dear reader, is it possible? Let me count the decades: 1980s, 1990s, 2000s, 2010s . . . No doubt about it; the numbers don't lie. So what else is new? Quite a bit, as a matter of fact.

In 2002 Syracuse University Press published my book and CD *The Undying Flame: Ballads and Songs of the Holocaust*. Since then, among other things I've been doing, I've been touring the U.S. with a lecture/concert program based on readings and songs from the book. I've also presented the program in Italy and England and at the Shanghai Jewish Refugees Museum.

So thanks for all that good pickin' and singin'.

Take it easy—but take it!

Stefan Grossman (Guido Harari)

Stefan Grossman

Writing the *GP* column Acoustic Set was a great experience because I was able to bring acoustic finger-style blues and ragtime playing to the magazine.

Being a *GP* columnist gave me a certain respectability in the guitar playing community. There were not many magazines like *GP*, and it was an important monthly gathering of interviews, reviews and teaching columns.

I was given a *totally* free hand as to what I would write—i.e., what material the column would cover. The only compromise was to the type of tablature to be used. I preferred a tab that used the spaces, while the magazine wanted to standardize all the tab to be on the lines.

My *GP* column got my name and music recognition far beyond the world I traveled in. Even today I meet folks at concerts that tell me their first contact with my music was from my *GP* columns.

Stefan Grossman (Sergio Kurhajek)

Forty years after my *GP* columns I find myself still doing the same things! I write instructional books on guitar playing; do concerts and workshops worldwide; and, perhaps most importantly, run Stefan Grossman's Guitar Workshop, where I produce historical video collections on our Vestapol DVD line and instructional videos on our Guitar Workshop line of myself and other guitarists like Chet Atkins, Larry Coryell, John Renbourn, Duck Baker, John Fahey, Pat Donohue, Buster B. Jones, Marcel Dadi, Tom Feldmann, John Miller, and many others. Guitar is still my life!

Richard Smith (Tom Davies)

The chance to work with pro editors at *GP* was an invaluable opportunity.

Richard Smith at Leo Fender Gallery in Fullerton, California (Bob Hewitt)

Richard Smith

Leo Fender once told me, as he tried to remember a name, "You can't keep everything in the top drawer with your socks." That truism sizes up my memory of *Guitar Player*'s Rare Bird column from 1986 to 1995—I simply forget a lot that happened and how it started. I do know that I met George Gruhn over the phone in the late 1970s while I chased after vintage guitars. When he got too busy to contribute monthly to *GP*, he put my name on a list of possible replacements he recommended to Tom Wheeler.

After talking with Tom, I agreed to submit a sample Rare Bird with photos. Tom's idea at this point was to pick a handful of guys with different areas of expertise to rotate as writers. I was doing research for what would become my Rickenbacker and Fender books. I lived in

Southern California and played a good dose of surf music and country western. My place in the RB rotation zeroed in on West Coast guitar manufacturers; my first column was about early Rickenbacker basses.

I loved being a columnist, though I'm neither a natural writer, nor a trained journalist. So it was hard work at times. I saw myself more as a researcher trying to find connections in the history of guitars. The chance to work with pro editors was an invaluable opportunity. Jon Sievert edited my column for years. Tom Wheeler took a special interest in what I was doing and gave me freedom to cover a lot of ground. I loved the subject and dove in. As I remember, the idea of rotating the column never really took hold, which was good thing for me.

I went on to write or collaborate on several books. That led to work in museums. I went back to school and earned an MA degree in exhibition design. Today, I'm the curator for the Fullerton Museum Center, in California, which includes the Leo Fender Gallery. With the help of Rare Bird, I was able to find a life after bar bands and stay close to what I love. A good ending. Thanks to everyone at *Guitar Player*!

June Millington

I don't remember ever *not* knowing about *Guitar Player* magazine, even though Fanny started playing electric in late '64, before its official launch. And actually, in 1967–1968, before we went down to L.A. with a record contract, we spent a lot of time in the Los Altos/San Jose Bay Area. It was our stomping grounds where we rocked out, all-girl style. There was a lot of amazing music going on right there, right then.

Being contacted by *Guitar Player* for an interview probably came through official channels, but I remember clearly where I was when we did the phone interview: at Al Brown's loft in NYC. It was a great vibe in which to speak, and I really enjoyed it. Al was a really good friend of Jimi Hendrix's who'd stayed there a lot, practicing and whatnot—I think it was a space away from everyone, where he could go into his own thoughts; and he produced Cris Williamson's very first album, so both those facets of my life were represented in real time. (Later, Al was the concertmaster on an album my sister and I did called *Ladies on the Stage*.)

People still talk about and share that *GP* interview even today! I've even had copies of the original issue sent to me as a sort of homage when people find them, which I love. "Michael Pierce" [Michael Brooks] was a pleasure to chat with and did a great job. I was very comfortable with the interview, which is saying something, because so often I felt challenged by men—as if they just couldn't help it. I'm talking from day one. But Michael put me right at ease, and just by the sound of his voice, I knew there was respect. I appreciated that. And the inter-

I don't remember ever *not* knowing about *Guitar Player* magazine.

June Millington in
Fanny (Bob Riegler)

view itself I believe gave me more respect in the industry. What, a girl/
young woman on electric guitar? Yup. For a while it pretty much felt
like just me and Bonnie Raitt and, by the way, Ellen McIlwaine. That
was about it, our event horizon for years.

I'm the cofounder of the Institute for the Musical Arts, a nonprofit for women and girls in music and music-related business. Among other things, we do Rock 'n' Roll Girls' Camps in the summer—up to five now! Preteen, Teen, and Recording Camp—and what makes this organization supremely important is that we are passing everything on down to future generations. That is, the property (house, barn with performance space/recording studios, twenty-five acres, equipment, archives), and we do all we can to support women in music: their entry, classes and workshops, hands-on experience, mentoring, loaning equipment out, even a place to stay if they're touring in the area. I'm big on the discussion of our foremothers, in fact teach that class at our camps, as a through line in which we can understand that we're going down a path that was actually paved by many others.

June Millington
(Per Brandin)

It doesn't have to be rock 'n' roll per se: the important thing is that we know we are part of a lineage. In my classes I talk about Bessie Smith, Big Mama Thornton, Sister Rosetta Tharpe, the Sweethearts of Rhythm, Ella Fitzgerald, Sarah Vaughan, Billie Holiday, Peggy Lee, Nina Simone, and so many others. Then we can begin to talk about Janis Joplin, Betty Wright, Mavis Staples, Bonnie Raitt, Miriam Makeba, and of course Fanny et al. The list is practically endless, which is the good news. (Bonnie, by the way, was first on our advisory board and is still on it today—a quietly steadfast supporter.)

I'm also finishing up an autobiography, which will most definitely set the record straight regarding our early (read: ukulele in Manila going into acoustic guitars, electric guitar/bass in high school) years, and straight through Fanny. As it turns out, I'll have to end it around 1975 and write book two, as so much has happened since! (That's when women's music started to overlap with the rock, funk, and emerging disco in our lives.)

Al Di Meola

I first came across *GP* when all of us young guys saw it on the newsstand and immediately signed up for a subscription. I heard about it through Jim Crockett. He and I had made contact and met several times, along with Don Menn, in the early days of the magazine. At the time, I was nineteen and playing with Return to Forever.

My interview experiences with *Guitar Player* were always great because they asked all the right questions, and although I hardly felt worthy at the time, they were so inquisitive about what the heck I was doing and how it was done.

As years went by and I had been offered several other covers, I had always thought of the magazine as the best of the ones that were out there. The best writers covering far more ground than the metal mags, etc.

The effect on my career from the covers, articles, and poll awards in the '70s and '80s was pretty darn huge, I'd say. Sure, it was the most important guitar magazine by far, and still is, so naturally the publicity coverage made awareness of whatever I was doing at the time more known in its importance.

Now I'm living more in Munich, Germany, where in Europe they gravitate more gracefully toward their appreciation of acoustic music, helping me save a little of what's left of my hearing; however, I still yearn for a U.S. comeback, even electronically.

February '78 (Cover photo by Len DeLessio)

February '86
(Cover photo
by Jon Sievert)

Al Di Meola
(KiFra)

Jorma Kaukonen

Guitar Player was the first national magazine that actually took our kind of music [Jefferson Airplane] seriously. We've all come to take for granted the fact that the guitar is probably the most popular musical instrument of all time. This wasn't always the case, and *Guitar Player* certainly helped our cause. It was a big deal to get respect from a national mag that was geared to serious guitarists.

The *GP* interviewers were knowledgeable about the guitar. Good questions, good conversations. The magazine certainly gave me a voice and a visibility that I would not have otherwise had.

And being on that June cover in 1976? How could it get any better than that? What an honor, and it still is, after all these years, when I see that cover. At the time, I was deeply in the throes of early Hot Tuna shenanigans. It was all about the guitar—all the time. Speaking of which, as I write this I'm at the Lebanon Opera House in New Hampshire with Hot Tuna, sharing a bill with Leon Russell.

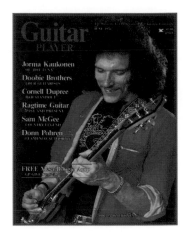

June '76 (Cover photo by Jon Sievert)

Jorma Kaukonen (Val Gorski)

Frank Gambale

Frank Gambale (Michael Hiller)

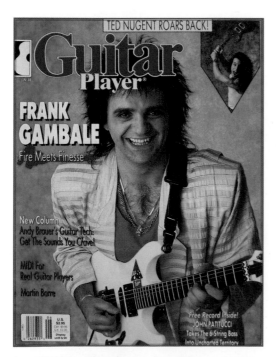

June '88 (Cover photo by Ann Summa)

I first heard about *GP* in the '70s. I grew up in Australia, and my older brothers were into guitar, too, and they used to buy copies and subscriptions, even though, at that time, we would receive the magazine three months later than the shelf date in the U.S.

We would read the interviews and see all the gear, and do the usual amount of salivating—mostly at the prices, which were way less than half what we would have to pay for the same stuff in Australia.

I believe it was Jim Ferguson in 1988 who contacted me and said the magazine wanted to have me on the cover. Naturally, I was honored. My experience with the writers was just great; everyone was very courteous. June 1988 it was, and I had been touring with my music and with the Chick Corea Elektric Band. I also had some pretty successful instructional books and videos such as *Chopbuilder*, *Monster Licks*, and *Speed Picking*, which revealed the secrets of my "sweep picking" technique, which, back then, was as shocking and new as Eddie Van Halen's tapping technique. Both techniques hit at roughly the same time.

The covers, articles, and poll awards really helped spread my name out there. Then other magazines around the world had me on their covers, too. I won the *Guitar Player* Readers Poll Fusion Guitar category for the only two years it existed as a category. After that, it was reduced to "Jazz"— the all-encompassing Jazz category—which I clearly don't belong in. Consequently, no further poll wins—ha ha.

When the *GP* cover hit, my career was well under way. I'd already been touring the whole world for over two years. In the subsequent years I went on to write monthly lessons and various articles for *GP*.

The magazine is more of a fanzine these days, with whoever is on the pop charts usually appearing on the cover. Gotta sell those magazines, right? Like a lot of things I'm nostalgic about, back in the day, *GP* really was about players of all types, not just who's the most popular. As we all know, just because something's popular, it doesn't mean that it's good.

I'm still touring a lot, and starting an online school. I have nearly two dozen solo albums now, and at least that many more as a contributor, producer, or major writer. Plus, there are books and DVDs. There's always more to do.

Joe Perry

I think I first heard about *Guitar Player* probably being on the road and getting out and opening for bands and getting on the circuit, moving to that next level and bumping into those magazines. That was the start of a kind of counterculture, and it was great to have a magazine that talked about guitar players. C'mon, that was fucking amazing!

You couldn't find out stuff like that. I can't remember the first time I read it, but I remember it was "Holy shit! This is great! There's actually a magazine out there for string benders."

I can picture that March '79 issue with me on the cover, but I can't remember the interview. I really can't. Every once in a while I see it because a fan will want me to sign it, and of course it brings back memories. I was with Aerosmith, and still trying to make my bones back then, you know what I mean. Trying to prove myself to myself.

Being on the cover definitely meant a lot to me. It was really an honor, and I was probably a foot off the ground for a month.

Joe Perry (Ross Halfin)

March '79 (Cover photo by Neil Zlozower)

Advertisers Remember

1960s C.F. Martin & Co. ad

THE CLASSIC

The 000-28C shown has a spruce top and rosewood body.
The 00-18C and 00-16C with spruce tops and mahogany bodies are also available.

C. F. MARTIN & CO., 201 NORTH MAIN STREET, NAZARETH, PENNSYLVANIA • WRITE FOR FREE ILLUSTRATED CATALOG

Our hardworking sales staff faced unusual challenges: Absolutely no non-music ads; no going on the road to possible clients (we did all our ad pitching via frequent mail, phone calls, and NAMM shows). Advertisers appreciated this because it meant substantially less expense on Guitar Player's *part, so lower rates for the ad space.*

And coupon ads could not back editorial on the reverse sides; full-page ads got right-page preference; similar products could not be displayed opposite each other. And the GP ads worked, as you'll see.—JC

C.F. Martin & Company

Dick Boak, Director of Artist and Public Relations

I didn't start at Martin until 1976, but when I came on board, *Guitar Player* was in full swing. You couldn't be in the guitar business and not advertise in this guitar-centric publication.

When the following article, "The Classic Martin OM—Fingerstylists'

1985 Martin
Guitar Co. ad

Choice," ran in *Guitar Player*'s March 1985 issue, it had a big impact upon the revitalization of the Orchestra Models that were to be recognized as the quintessential fingerstyle guitars, invented by Martin!

In general, all of the reviews and articles about Martin that appeared in *GP* had a huge impact upon the success of our business here in Nazareth, Pennsylvania.

1985 Dunlop ad

1979 Jim Dunlop ad

Dunlop
Jim Dunlop, Founder

Our company first heard about *Guitar Player* from Bud Eastman, who was the founder of the magazine. And he put me in the first issue. I was included in the It's New section.

I have every edition of *Guitar Player*, excluding perhaps three.

As a small company it was nice to find out what gear various artists used. We would get ahold of people like Stevie Ray Vaughan and read up on what they used for gear. And every time we found that they used our gear, we liked it. So we enjoyed that very much.

I also used the magazine when I designed the Jazz III pick. I went through the *GP* editions and selected all of the picks guitar players used; then I designed the Jazz III pick with the help of that information.

Initially, we couldn't afford to advertise in *Guitar Player*, because, at that point, it was quite expensive. As we grew up a little bit as a company, we managed to place full-page ads in the magazine.

It was also a fact that *Guitar Player* was read in many different countries, and we managed to follow that. We knew that if we advertised in it, or if we were mentioned in it, we knew that it was getting abroad.

Fender

Joe Phelps, Founder and CEO, Phelps Agency

By 1977, the Fender brand was suffering from neglect at the hands
of an increasingly dysfunctional CBS management. In 1981 when
Bill Schultz, Dan Smith, Eddie Rizzuto, and others came over from

1967 Fender ad

Guitar Player was the standard by which all others were measured.

Yamaha, things began to get back on track. *Guitar Player* was already well established. We knew Crockett, the writers, and the sales staff, and simply continued the relationship we'd built while at Yamaha. Fender hired me and my new agency, and our first ad campaign was "The Sound That Creates Legends," which celebrated the great guitarists who had played Fender instruments. Buddy Holly, Jimi Hendrix, Eric Clapton, Albert King, Stevie Ray Vaughan, Robben Ford, Buddy Guy, and James Burton were just a sampling of the artists featured.

Our job at Phelps was to contact the players and tell them that people who cared about quality were now in control of the company. We showed them the "Sound That Creates Legends" layouts and got their approval on photographs to use in the ads. We offered a "favored nations" agreement that said we were not paying anyone for their endorsement, but we'd love to have their support. I don't recall any artist ever turning us down. And we never paid a penny for their participation.

Guitar Player was the standard by which all others were measured. There was great editorial, great production quality, and comprehensive newsstand and subscription coverage. Multiple Fender guitar, amplifier, and accessories ads were in virtually all issues.

In 1985, CBS relinquished its ownership of Fender, and leadership was assumed by Bill Schultz in a leveraged buyout. Bill's first order of business was to reinvigorate Fender's U.S. manufacturing, resurrecting the quality and innovation that made the brand famous. With Dan Smith at the helm of guitar design, new and standard-setting instruments began to flow out of Southern California once again. (In 1998, a new manufacturing facility in Corona cemented Fender's comeback.)

In 1986, Fender created its first signature model guitar, the Eric Clapton Stratocaster. Our Phelps Group agency was commissioned to advertise the new instrument, and Fender's two-page ad, "There's Only One Eric Clapton . . . and There's Only One Fender," was a pivotal moment in the brand's resurgence.

But having the testimonials ads with no way to distribute them would be fruitless, of course. There was no Internet back then. Frankly, GPI's publications, along with *Musician* magazine and a few others, were well distributed, and were our main conduit for getting the word out about the "new" Fender.

Back then, one of the most exciting advertising events for us was when we produced 16-page catalogs for guitars and amps and inserted them into *Guitar Player*. The magazine loved it, for obvious reasons, and we loved it, because with our 16 pages preprinted on 100-pound paper, we "owned" the magazine.

1986 Fender
"Blues Power" ad

The company's breakfasts at the NAMM shows were often the highlight of the weekend.

We also designed ads for the newly created Fender Custom Shop the following year with endorsements from such rising stars as Stevie Ray Vaughan, Robert Cray, Robben Ford, Richie Sambora, and Yngwie Malmsteen. Our campaigns appeared in GPI's *Guitar Player*, *Frets*, and *Bass Player* along with *Guitar World*, *Guitar for the Practicing Musician*, and *Musician* magazines.

Thinking back to *Guitar Player*, in addition to the magazine being a standard, the company's breakfasts at the NAMM shows were often the highlight of the weekend. Crockett, along with the editors and sales staff, was on hand, along with lots of great players. One of my favorite NAMM show memories was when we sat on Crockett's hotel room floor listening to Robben Ford and B.B. King having a ball playing familiar tunes.

As Fender's agency, our function was to get the best deals we could on behalf of our clients with the media. When we first started buying space for Fender and other clients, it used to frustrate us that we couldn't get GPI Publications to discount their rates. Just about every other magazine would give us special positioning at no additional cost, or they'd discount their rate card. But not GPI.

That said, they were still our highest priority on our media schedule. Why? Because they had integrity. They had editorial integrity, quality production, solid distribution—and they verified their circulation numbers with independent audits. We always knew what we were getting for our money. And with the feedback we got from the retailers, the ads in *Guitar Player* and the other GPI publications were, by far, the most important in our media buy.

1970s Heil Sound ad

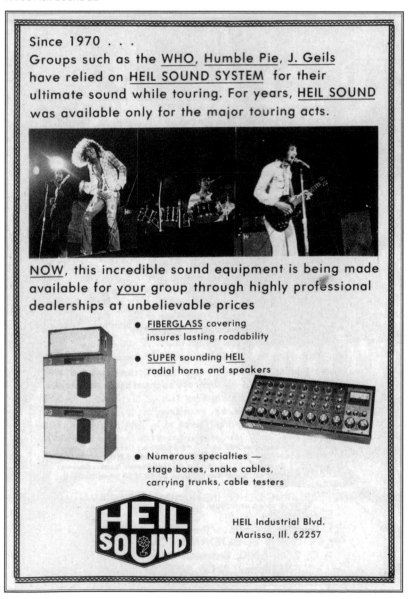

Heil Sound
Bob Heil, Founder and CEO

I first learned about *Guitar Player* when a kid showed it to me in my music shop in Marissa, Illinois. This was Ye Olde Music Shop, in the late '60s. I'd been teaching and selling Hammond organs, was also a ham radio operator since I was fourteen, and experimented and built these things, too, so kids started bringing me their amplifiers to fix. This one kid said he had a Fender and it was broken. I thought he meant the fender on his car! That's how stupid I was! He brought his Fender in, and I turned it upside down, and I recognized the circuit from my ham radios. I had the parts in the back and about fifteen minutes later, I had his amplifier going! The first thing you know, I was bombarded with kids coming in to get things fixed. I started renting Hammond organs to these kids, as well, which was really a new deal, because back in those days people bought Hammond organs to use like pretty flower pots in their houses, just to look nice. So here were these scraggly looking kids coming in with their broken amps and renting my organs for shows.

Now, I had no concept whatsoever about rock 'n' roll in those days. I hardly knew who the Beatles were when they came up. I didn't pay attention to any rock music; I was thoroughly into theater organs. But I started renting these things out for bands. Guys like REO Speedwagon and Michael McDonald, who were kids still in high school, were coming to Marissa, Illinois, because I had a soldering iron and knew what to do with it, and I'd rent them organs. This was a whole new world for me. Once I began putting together massive, 20,000-watt sound systems for these guys, promoters started renting them from me for the Kiel Auditorium in St. Louis, and then all hell broke loose! I realized I had to know what was going on. So one of these kids had a *Guitar Player* magazine with him, and I said, "What's that?" The kid showed it to me, and that's how I learned about *GP*. It became my education as to what the heck I was doing! I didn't play the guitar, never did. I was on the other end of the soldering iron!

I learned about Gibson distributors in *GP* magazine. Guitars were foreign to me so I found the address for this distributor in *Guitar Player* and this nicely dressed salesman came out to help me get guitars in my store. Another time, a kid came in saying he couldn't find left-handed guitars, so I got those in, too, and became a Fender and Martin dealer—selling really nice guitars with pearl in them.

I can't count the times people came in with *Guitar Player* magazine and asked if I could get this thing for them—some pedal or something—and I'd pick up the phone and call the company from the ads; they'd have the phone numbers in the ads! The Internet in those days was *Guitar Player* magazine. There'd be an article or an ad with phone numbers in it, and that was like Google! Customers started driving from Chicago, Nashville, Kansas City, Des Moines. . . . They'd sleep in their cars, and they'd bring their *Guitar Player* ads in with them, and I'd get the stuff for them right there. I'd be their dealer for it. And I'd use this information to learn what to have in my store so it was loaded. I became the largest Sunn Amplifier dealer in the world.

My business expanded, and we were on the road then. We started doing the sound for tours. The bands would hire me to do the sound

1975 Heil Sound ad

for their shows starting in '68 or '69, and Ye Olde Music Shop was growing like crazy. I built a PA that we could move, with connectors. It was historic, but we didn't know it then. I started going out on the road with the James Gang, Jerry Garcia, the Who, Humble Pie, Peter Frampton, to name just a few. This all started from *Guitar Player* and paying attention to things. *GP* helped me to learn about all of the things that were going on. Jim Crockett put me in focus, which led to the Rock and Roll Hall of Fame opening a display of the early Heil Sound innovations.

When I started Heil Sound, and built the first high-powered Heil Talk Box for Walsh and Frampton in 1973, I started advertising in *Guitar Player*. We were also building speakers and PA systems that people were using on the road. We started advertising these with dealers around the country. Heil Sound ads were in *GP*. What other magazine could you do that in to get dealers? Other magazines were trade publications for organs and pianos, but we wanted rock 'n' roll. JC had that in his back pocket! He was the guy! If you wanted to take your message to that market, you took it to Jim Crockett.

Today, Heil Sound is the only manufacturer invited to exhibit at the Rock and Roll Hall of Fame.

Randall Instruments
Gary Sunda, VP of Engineering

I joined Randall Instruments in 1970, as vice president of engineering. At that time, we were already advertising in *Guitar Player*.

Jim Crockett and Don Randall had a special rapport with one another. Mr. Randall used to say, "It's the only game in town." He didn't mean that in a negative way. *Guitar Player* really was the only thing going. If you were looking for gear or articles or any of that, there was only *Guitar Player*, and we knew it, so we advertised in it, and there was always a positive return from advertising in *Guitar Player*.

Every month we'd be called by someone at *Guitar Player* to put something new in, and I helped Mr. Randall come up with the ads, the musicians who were involved, etc. There were times we'd just run the same ad again if we didn't have anything new ready.

A funny story to share . . . I remember one time, in the mid- or late '80s, when the guys at *Guitar Player* would critique amplifiers. Someone would get the amplifier, play it, and review the good qualities about them. Well, we got the magazine and they were critiquing some new amplifier. This one was supposedly a big mystery to people, but I knew what was in it, and there wasn't anything particularly special about it. *GP* ends up critiquing this amplifier that was going for $5K or $10K, which was unheard of for an amplifier back then, and

There was always a positive return from advertising in *Guitar Player*.

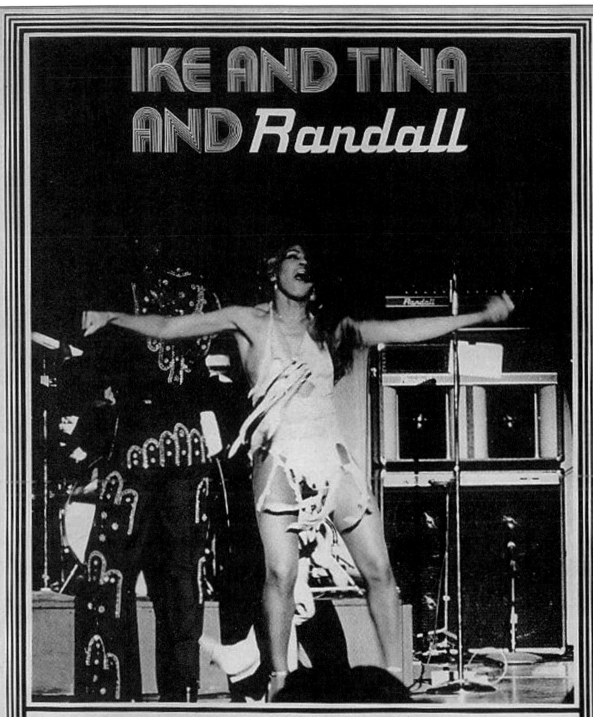

1976 Randall Instruments ad

1980s Randall Instruments ad

We advertised in *Guitar Player* every month for twenty years.

there was this big, glowing report on this amp in *Guitar Player*. I read it, and Mr. Randall read it, and he became unglued. By this time, all of the guys were advertising in the magazine—Peavey, Fender, everybody—but here this guy just built this one in his garage, and he was portrayed as the holy grail of amplifiers. Mr. Randall said, "Here is a guy who built one amplifier, and he gets reviewed! We've been advertising every month for X number of years, and we don't even get ours reviewed!" I've never seen Mr. Randall upset except for that one time. So Don called up Jim Crockett and said, "Hey, this guy hasn't spent a nickel in your magazine, and he gets a review?!" So someone at *Guitar Player* said, "Okay, send us something, and we'll look at it," and we sent an RG-80. They tested the thing, and it got a glowing report. The guy told me, "When I got your amp, and I pulled it out of the box and here was yet another single 12 amp. . . ." He started playing it, and it had great tones, and it got a glowing report and everyone was happy.

We advertised in *Guitar Player* every month for twenty years.

D'Addario

Jim D'Addario, CEO

I remember the early days of *Guitar Player* magazine vividly. I was just starting my career in the music business. I worked part time for my dad and for Martin Guitars throughout my college years (1968–1970) and began my career full-time in 1970. This was a year after my dad had sold our family business, Darco Music Strings, to C.F. Martin & Co., Inc. There was a wave of acquisition hysteria at that time, with CBS buying Fender and Steinway and many other companies thinking that the future of our industry was going to be a handful of conglomerates who would own portfolios of formerly family-owned businesses.

Obviously that model was not successful, and over time many companies like C.F. Martin, who acquired Darco, Fibes Drums, Vega Banjos, and Levin Guitars, returned to their roots and realized their strengths and weaknesses. For nearly five years the D'Addario family worked for C.F. Martin, and during that time I wore many hats. Working out of the Darco plant in Long Island City, I started an in-house printing facility to improve our string packaging and advertising. I was also the local sales rep for Martin products in the metro area and eventually was promoted to advertising coordinator, working closely with Schroeder Advertising in Philadelphia, Martin's ad agency at the time, and president Frank Martin.

In 1970 there were not very many media choices for us to pick from. Essentially we had *DownBeat, Sing Out!* (a small folk music magazine), two trade publications (*The Music Trades* and *Musical Merchandise Review*), and that was about it. *Guitar Player* came along and filled a monstrous void.

The guitar quickly became the most popular instrument in America and eventually the whole world. It was portable, you could play alone, you could sing along, you could collaborate, you could solo, you could amplify it, you could arrange multiple guitars in a recording to have different voicing and tonal characteristics; it became the essential component, on multiple levels, for all pop music.

Somewhere around the time *GP* was founded, Bud came up with the idea of inserting a small card into guitar string sets to attract subscribers. They created a nice little four-by-four-inch card on which were printed "String Tips," and we eagerly inserted them into all our Darco and Martin guitar string sets, as did just about every other string manufacturer. I believe this little campaign was a huge success for *Guitar Player*, and it helped them procure thousands of fans for the magazine.

Guitar Player quickly became my personal, and our company's, fa-

Guitar Player quickly became my personal, and our company's, favorite magazine to advertise in.

The brightest strings made the most intelligent way.

We designed a computer winding system to wind our XLS Stainless Steel round wound strings. Because it's the most intelligent way to guarantee their exceptional brightness, crisp harmonics and accurate intonation. It's also the most intelligent way to guarantee that you get what you pay for. Each and every time you use a set. D'Addario XLS computer-wound strings. For guitar and bass. The brightest strings made the most intelligent way.

D'Addario®
E. Farmingdale, NY 11735 USA

1982 D'Addario ad

vorite magazine to advertise in. When my family and I decided to move on from our relationship with Martin Guitars and start D'Addario Strings, *Guitar Player* became the cornerstone of our advertising campaign. My family had never had success marketing their own brand of guitar strings. My dad made private-label strings for the likes of Martin, Gretsch, Fender, Guild, D'Angelico, etc., but he did not understand marketing and how to build a brand.

We had never used our family name, D'Addario, on our strings at Darco or during our period with Martin. With the little bit of knowledge and on-the-job training I was fortunate to absorb working for Martin, I felt we could establish our own brand and become iconic in the string category. When we started our new company, J. D'Addario & Company, Inc., in February 1973, many of the private-label customers that my dad worked for came over to us as loyal and supportive customers.

My strategy was simple: Let's take the major portion of our profits making private-label strings and reinvest them in advertising for D'Addario Strings. Let's tell the world about all the innovation and quality improvements in strings that have been the result of the D'Addario family's work, and create a new brand. My brother John D'Addario Jr.; my father, John Sr.; and myself all worked on $150 a week salary for nearly three years. Any profit we made was put into advertising and machinery and technology.

And where did the lion's share of the advertising go? *Guitar Player* magazine. We began taking full-page color ads for strings each issue. Sometimes more than one. I don't know the exact chronology, but the full-page ads probably started toward the end of 1974 after the brand was launched. A month after the first ad hit, I received a telex (that

D'Addario

The Inside Story on Great Strings

If you had to make a better string for your guitar, how would you do it? Here's how the D'Addario family does it.

☐ The best way to give a string longer life and stronger tone is to use a hexagonal core wire. Not sometimes. Always. The edges of a hexagonal core grasp the wrap wire firmly, to keep it from slipping. This gives you a more uniform string, all along its length—for stronger response, better harmonics and overtones—longer life.

☐ That's just one quality that makes D'Addario strings better. Another factor is "strand annealing." Simply, that means we temper the wrap wire a foot at a time under precise control. It gives you more consistency and better dependability than treating wire in batches like others do.

☐ And where it matters, we guide the winding wire by hand.

☐ Not everybody makes strings this carefully. But the D'Addario family has been making strings for eight generations. With our name on the package, we can't afford anything less than the best quality.

☐ We even give you a choice of brass or bronze windings in four gauges for acoustic guitar…nine different gauges for electric guitar…strings from banjo to dulcimer.

☐ Ask for D'Addario—knowing how we make strings should change the way you buy them.

D'Addario
LINDENHURST, NEW YORK 11757 USA

Cross-section of string magnified 50x.

1976 D'Addario ad

was the era's equivalent of an e-mail) from a distributor in Australia. He had seen our ad and wanted an exclusive distributorship for our line. A $5,000 order followed. This is one example of an ad triggering a relationship that would last over forty years and would help us become the leading brand in the Australian market overnight. The same would happen in other English-speaking countries.

It was evident, after we positioned ourselves in *Guitar Player* as string experts, that people took notice, and our brand had instant credibility. To this day *Guitar Player* is a very important part of our media plans. Unfortunately, things are not as simple today as they were in 1974. We have to choose between multiple media channels and sometimes too many choices in each channel. But the bottom line is *Guitar Player,* and my friend Jim Crockett, played an integral role in the success we were able to achieve for our brand.

I recall passing through Cupertino one time and stopping by *GP* just after the art boards for the monthly issue had been submitted. This was long before desktop publishing. The whole staff was having a pizza-jam session party and I got to sit in on a few tunes. It is one of my fondest memories of the relationship we had with *GP* over the years.

1978 Seymour Duncan ad

Seymour Duncan Pickups
Cathy Duncan, Cofounder and CEO

Everyone knew about *GP*. It was, as I remember, *the* only source for serious musicians. Sure, *Circus* (remember them?) and others like that were around.

I have a wonderful copy of the original artwork. I still remember the days of writing out our very first 1/6-page ads, then laying out the type the old-fashioned way, with wax! It was hard work, but soooo enjoyable.

It was a very creative and fruitful time for so many of us. I still call it "the class of the mid-'70s." From Wayne Charvel to Dave Schecter to Grover Jackson, Paul Reed Smith, Floyd Rose . . . You name it.

We were only word of mouth, and here were our gross sales per year: 1976, $15,000; 1977, $35,000; 1978, $85,000 (we first advertised about then); then in 1979, $500,000 (that was also because we were able to borrow enough money from the future wife of Phil Kubicki, an heiress, for a humbucker mold. So now we were selling new humbuckers, and not just rewinds!). We more than doubled the next year with some award-winning full-page ads.

1980s Seymour Duncan ad

As I said, *GP* was the place where the editors, the writers, and the musicians themselves loved to talk about their craft. And as such, it was a fertile place for us as developers and providers of product.

Carvin Guitars

Mark Kiesel, VP

Carvin was founded by our dad, Lowell Kiesel, in 1946. My brother Carson started working full-time for Carvin in 1965 and I started full-time in 1970. Dad always told us that we had a big advantage to have a magazine like *Guitar Player* to advertise in because of its consistent high-quality guitar content. Prior to the startup of *GP*, the only magazines that he had available to advertise in were *Hit Parade*, *Popular Mechanics*, and a few other magazines that were not guitar oriented at all.

Once Carvin began to advertise in *GP*, sales started to climb. We bought very small, 2 1/4" x 1" column ads in the early '70s. We then switched to full-page ads by the mid-'70s, which allowed our sales to grow by a huge factor every year. In 1972 our sales really ramped up when we placed a full-page black-and-white ad showing a back line of PA gear, large amp stacks and several guitars and basses.

By the early '80s we ran as many as four ads in each *GP* issue. *Guitar Player* gradually became 50 percent of our magazine advertising budget.

I remember running full-page ads starting in 1982 featuring Craig Chaquico with our double-necks and X100B stacks. Then, in late 1983, Craig starting using our V220T guitar standing in front of several stacks of X100B amps. These ads with Craig really helped our V220T guitar and X100B amp stacks become our best-selling products throughout the '80s.

During this same era we ran several different ads featuring Frank Zappa using our M22 guitar pickups, our X100B amp stacks, and our PA gear, which he had equipped his mobile concert recording studio with. Frank gave Carvin a big boost of credibility throughout the '80s.

One of the biggest things that *GP* did to boost Carvin guitar sales was in the February 1984 issue, when they did a Carvin guitar factory tour featuring seven pages of photos with captions showing how Carvin guitars were made.

Once Carvin began advertising in *GP*, sales started to climb.

Carvin's first *GP* ad, from 1973

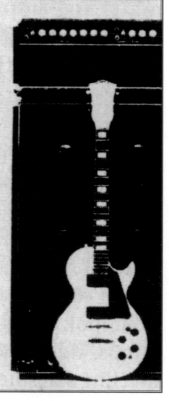

CARVIN

CARVIN now offers PROFESSIONAL 8 Channel PA Sound Systems, Monitors, Power Slaves, Horn Drivers, Altec Lansing Spks., Folded Horn Bass Amps, Guitar and Organ Amps up to 240 RMS (600 Watts Peak), High Powered Compact Amps, Professional Acoustic and Natural Maple Solid Body Bass, 6, and 12 String Guitars, Steel Guitars, Pickups, Parts, Etc. Low Prices include Factory Warranties. Send Postcard for

FREE 1973 CATALOG

CARVIN CO.
1112 Industrial, Dept. GP-4
Escondido, Calif. 92025

"My V220 is more serious than my other guitars because it feels more solid and better balanced. The Kahler is the only tremolo I have ever used that really works without going out of tune. The V220 is now my main guitar. I love it!"

"People keep asking me if my Carvin X100B's have been modified, and my answer is always the same, they're totally stock. I really can't say enough about Carvin amps. After 3 years of heavy touring and 2 albums, they keep delivering the sound I like, without failure."
— Craig Chaquico, Jefferson Starship

The V220 guitar and X100B amp stack are available "DIRECT" from our manufacturing plant in California. If you haven't tried Carvin products, you are missing an opportunity to improve your sound. If not convinced after trying them for 10 days, your money will be refunded.

Send for your FREE CARVIN 84 page color catalog, or send $2 to rush by 1st class mail.

Product Information
619-747-1710

V220T with Kahler locking tremolo $549
V220 with standard bridge $399
(Prices are for standard finishes, not curly)
X100B 100 watt tube head $499
X60B 60 watt tube head $419
4-12" celestion speaker box $399
Single stack (X100B and 1 bottom) $879
Double stack (X100B and 2 bottoms) $1259

FREE CATALOG
☐ Free Catalog   ☐ $2 for First Class Mail
Name
Street
City
State
Zip   GP53

CARVIN

Dept GP53, 1155 Industrial Ave.
Escondido, Calif. 92025

1984 Carvin ad

1986 Mel Bay ad

1960s Mel Bay ad

Mel Bay Publications

Bill Bay, Chairman of the Board

My father, Mel, was friends with Jim Crockett. The guitar community was much smaller then, and lots of the key players and industry people knew each other on a first-name basis. Dad liked the idea of *Guitar Player* and was pleased to help get it started by placing ads from Mel Bay Publications.

We published books by many members of the *GP* advisory board. People such as Johnny Smith and Chet Atkins had books with Mel Bay, so my guess is we advertised their material. In those early days people were starved for literature about the guitar world, so the ads got lots of attention. Also, in those days there was much respect among guitarists for players of differing styles. I also think there was an intense hunger for learning anything in relation to the instrument.

I just recall that it was a very close community and players had tremendous respect for each other.

Ibanez Guitars

William Reim, President, Hoshino
USA Inc.

Long before (and while) working for
Ibanez, I was a drummer. However, I *loved*
guitars . . . and *as* a drummer, spent most
of my time looking at them when playing.
Friends I played with in bands subscribed
to *Guitar Player*, so I would always pick it
up and read it at practices if there was one
around. It was at once enticing and intim-
idating—it painted a picture of a world
that was so far away, it barely seemed real.
Little did I realize that, less than ten years
later, I would not only be dealing directly
with those who created one of the coolest
magazines around, but I'd also have work
published there in the form of advertising.

I joined Hoshino USA Inc., the brand
holder of Ibanez, in May of 1981, which at
the time was called Elger Company. By the
time I came on board, Ibanez had already
established a firm relationship with *Guitar
Player* and, in fact, held the cover-two position in the book. Jeff Hasselberger, my pre-
decessor (and also the person who hired
me), was the first advertising and marketing person for Ibanez in the U.S., and a
longtime guitarist as well. He knew from
his own experience that *Guitar Player* was
the first *real* guitar magazine of its kind,
and if you wanted to reach and influence
players in the market for a guitar, this is
where you had to be. That was in the mid-
to late '70s. By the early '80s, *Guitar Player*
had clearly established itself as the guitarists' bible—the Holy Grail of both professional guitarists seeking respect and recognition through coverage, and aspiring
players looking to gain insights into legends, or those who would *become* legends.
So whenever we had to make a decision
about where our ad dollars were going—

Rocket Roll Sr.

The most
sought-after
oldie is back!
And just as it was
then.

Built-in neck, back-
loading strings,
Smooth-Tuner
machines, natural
finish korina body.

Under $400.00 at
your Ibanez dealer.

Ibanez

P.O. Box 469
Cornwells Heights, PA
19020

327 Broadway
Idaho Falls, ID
83401

1975 Ibanez ad

Less than

ten years

later, I would

be dealing

directly with

those who

created one

of the coolest

magazines

around.

Guitar Player was never a question. It was a given.

Gauging how well an ad pulled during that time (the early '80s) is difficult because—due to a number of factors—the company was in a serious state of decline, so nothing really seemed to be working. It wasn't until later in the '80s that Ibanez found its footing again and its identity, much of which came as the result of the ads we were running in *Guitar Player*. In 1987 we launched Steve Vai's Jem, the RG, the S, and SR bass, so there was a lot to talk about. Leading up to this time, we had done a lot of fun, conceptual ads with a some relatively unknown players at the time (Paul Gilbert, Vinny Moore, Richie Kotzen, etc.), but when it came to finally unveiling the Jem to the public, we knew we wanted to pull out all the stops. We also knew *Guitar Player* would be essential in achieving this. The first ad for the Jem series was leaked through a series of teasers that ran in the months preceding the guitar's official street date, and culminated with a sort of Sgt.-Pepper-meets-Dr.-Who spread that was quite unusual for the time. Everyone really responded to that ad, and even today, people still talk to me about it. Another ad we produced specifically for *Guitar Player* was for a special Jimi Hendrix tribute issue. For this issue, we worked with *Guitar Player* to have the cover-two position turned into a gatefold, and we did another cosmic kind of thing featuring Joe Satriani contemplating the wisdom of Hendrix.

After being with Ibanez for a while, I began to develop a love/hate relationship with the magazine. Why, you ask? Because it was the hottest guitar magazine on the streets, it was critical that the Ibanez brand received as much editorial coverage as could possibly be wrangled. Of course, every guitar, amp, effects, or accessory company had the same idea, and it grew to become a real crusade for coverage for everyone. Product release news was cool; artist product mentions were key; but product reviews were *critical*. A review in *Guitar Player* could make or break a product. So lobbying to have things reviewed, and then trying to ensure that everything would be reviewed *favorably* was the other part of the equation. When there was a positive review on something, *Guitar Player* could do no wrong. When there was a negative review, things would go sour for a time, but never for very long, and advertising was never cut as a result. Not being in *Guitar Player* wasn't an option if you wanted to remain alive.

Other guitar magazines surfaced, and as a result, *Guitar Player* had to up its game . . . something not easily achieved. The quality of the writing, the content, and *variety* of content, were all excellent: so where to go from here? Even though other books came into their own during the late '80s and early '90s, *Guitar Player* retained its status as the serious player's *go-to* when it came to in-depth product coverage, insightful artist information, and technique development.

1987 Steve Vai "Angel Landing" Ibanez ad

Dean Markley USA

Dean Markley, Partner of Dean Markley USA

Having been a musician and a salesman in a music store, then owning my own store and ending up in manufacturing and distribution, I learned early on that *Guitar Player* was *the* definitive guitar magazine to which to subscribe. When we (Dean Markley Strings) perfected the Voice Box and brought it to market, a good friend of mine who had been in the music industry for all his life told me the thing to do was take out a full-page ad in *Guitar Player* and *never* get out of the magazine. He said we needed to stay in it every month, even if we couldn't run in any other magazines. I took his advice (thank you, Scotty), and it worked out fantastically. We got well-known in a short amount of time and our business soared.

Our first ad was a hand-drawn picture of the acoustic strings "old man" under a weeping willow tree with the mountains in the background and text talking about how great Dean Markley acoustic strings were. But with the Voice Box coming out, we immediately created a black-and-white ad of my friend standing, playing electric guitar, and using the Voice Box, with text explaining the Voice Box and letting people know how to get in touch with us. We immediately started selling Voice Boxes. For about nine months, while Frampton's song was on the top, we sold Voice Boxes like they were going out of style. When the Voice Box attention waned, we went back to advertising the strings. We had a number of simple black-and-white ads touting Dean Markley strings.

Probably the most memorable ad, and the most ballsy ad, to run (especially in those times, where most ads always had so much to say in them) was when Jim Crockett called me and asked me what I was going to run in the next issue. I was so busy selling strings and such that I hadn't taken the time to create the next ad. He needed the ad right then. I didn't have an ad ready and had been kicking an idea around for what I thought would be a real eye-catcher and would make a solid statement. So I asked Jim if he could take the Dean Markley logo (the signature) out of the last ad and place it in the middle of a full-

1970s Dean Markley ad

1986 Dean Markley ad

page ad space. He said he could. He asked what else I wanted done. I said, "Nothing." I remember he kind of freaked out and said, "What about text and your address and phone number and all of that?" I said, "Nothing, just the signature in white with a black background. That's it. Nothing else." He said okay and we went on with life. In about three weeks the issue came out with that ad in it. It was so powerful looking and said it all. I received calls from all around the industry saying, "Well, Dean, you've made it, you've arrived." Everyone loved that ad. We ran the ad several more times in succession and then changed to some witty and entertaining ads like, "QUICK . . . Run down to your favorite music store and slap on a set of Dean Markley strings. You and your music will never be the same. Oh yeah! Don't forget to pay the man."

Or the "Anything Less Is Just Baling Wire" ad (by the way, Dennis, back in shipping, came up with that headline) was also one of the really great ads that showed our sense of humor while letting people know that Dean Markley strings were the best.

All of those ads were very cool. Everyone couldn't wait to see what we were going to do next. Very successful. Jim and I had some good talks about all of those ads. He was very supportive of what we were doing.

Guitar Player always did a great job with their editorial. They also covered existing, as well as new, products. Jim and his gang were easy to work with and were a real treat. I remember going down to Sunnyvale/Saratoga Road in Sunnyvale, California, for the Friday night jams they held. You never knew who might show up for the jam. People like B.B. King and other famous players would be right in the thick of it with all the *GP* worker/players having a great time.

Guitar Player has been a legend since it was started. Great job, you guys!!!!!!!!!!!!!

Homespun Tapes

Happy Traum, Founder and President

Homespun Tapes and *Guitar Player* started in the same year (1967), so it was a natural fit for us to advertise our newly recorded guitar lessons in the new publication. The fact that it was the first magazine geared specifically to guitar players of all kinds, and *GP*'s inclusion of acoustic instruments and styles in the mix, only added to the symbiosis of our two companies.

I don't specifically remember the first ads, but I can assume they were for my own twelve-tape series on fingerpicking based on my successful Oak Publications

> I learned early on that *Guitar Player* was *the* definitive guitar magazine to which to subscribe.

1975 Homespun Tapes ad

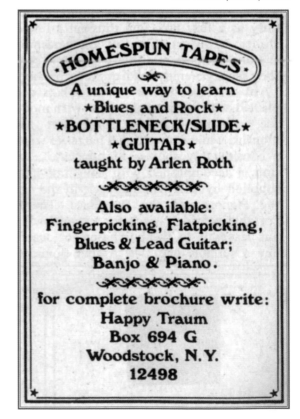

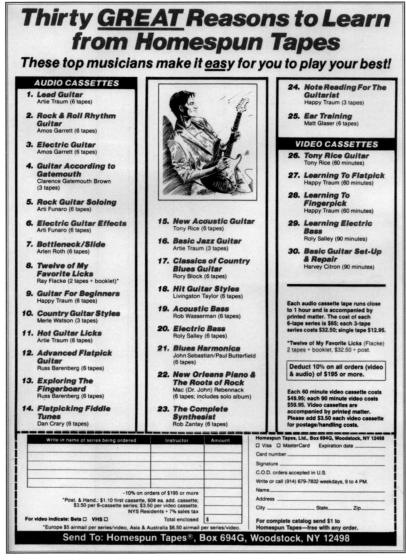

1986 Homespun Tapes ad

book, *Fingerpicking Styles for Guitar*. They took a beginner through a variety of songs, increasing in complexity until, hopefully, the student was fairly advanced by the end of the course. (By the way, these lessons are still available today on six CDs, and are unchanged except for the recording format.)

The magazine was of great importance for me, as a reader, as it brought to the public, for the first time, many of the players and products that were making the guitar a prominent part of American (and international) culture. I remember avidly reading the profiles and scouring the pages for the guitars and gear that were just becoming available. Since I was already a professional player myself, it was also fun to see many of my friends and colleagues brought to public attention in the pages of *GP*.

Of course, also as an advertiser and someone who was also promoting some of these same artists, having them appear in print was an extra bonus for us.

My wife, Jane, and I developed a strong relationship with Jim through our mutual desire to help professional guitarists reach a wider audience, and to teach learning and aspiring players to improve their skills. Aside from our regularly advertising Homespun products, I was proud to have contributed to the magazine through my Strictly Folk instructional columns for several years. I was always grateful to Jim for extending the scope of *GP* to us folk and traditional players along with all the other genres that were extant at the time.

Finally, the magazine that Jim Crockett headed was well edited, beautifully designed, and had on its staff some of the best young music writers of the day. All of these things made it a flagship publication and one that was the forerunner of others to come. Jim was a true pioneer in this field.

Bartolini Pickups and Electronics

Bill Bartolini, Founder

My first contact with *Guitar Player* was Jim Crockett's request that I interview flamenco guitarist Sabicas in 1970. That article was published in *GP* in the March 1970 issue. In September 1973 we placed our first ad in *GP* for hexaphonic and quadraphonic pickups.

Since then we advertised in GPI's *Guitar Player, Frets,* and *Bass Player,* always with very rewarding results. There were ads for our pickups, electronics, and distortion pedals over the years as our production capacity allowed.

Even the earliest and very amateurish ad in September of 1973 brought results from *GP*. Our distributors placed ads for our product from 1976 until 1978. After that we placed the ads directly.

I know the velox for the first ad exists somewhere in our vast and disorganized storage but I may not be able to put my hands on it for quite a while.

GP was always the most authoritative source of reviews and commentary about gear in particular, and the guitar and bass music scene in general. Always the most accurate information in the field.

1973 Bartolini Guitars ad

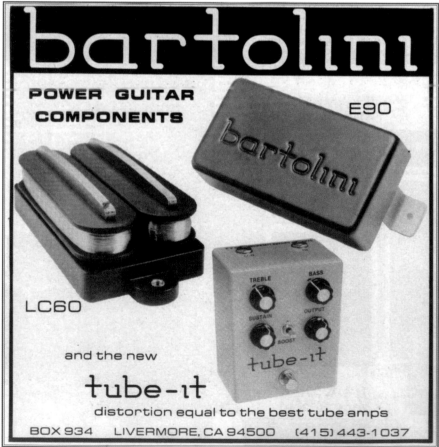

1985 Bartolini ad

Gretsch Guitars
Fred W. Gretsch, 4th Generation President

March 24, 2014

Jim Crockett
jim_crockett@hotmail.com

Dear Jim:

Thank you for asking the Gretsch Company to participate in your upcoming book. I wish I could answer your questions, but I left Gretsch shortly after my uncle, Fred Gretsch Jr., sold the family business to the D. H. Baldwin Company in 1967. Unfortunately, we have no advertising records from the 1970s and Baldwin ceased production of Gretsch guitars in 1978.

Fortunately, I was able to keep my 17-year promise of purchasing back the family business from Baldwin in late 1984. Being able to announce this news at the January 1985 NAMM Show was one of the highlights of my nearly 50 years in the music industry.

When Gretsch successfully launched our new line of electric guitars in 1990, the timing was right and the market was hungry for "That Great Gretsch Sound" again. I'd like to thank Guitar Player Magazine for your role in helping to keep the Gretsch flame alive—especially during the 1980s. Your magazine's covers and articles from that decade paid tribute to the Chet Atkins 6120 model, Brian Setzer's rockabilly revival, and legendary Gretsch artists and rock pioneers Eddie Cochran, Duane Eddy, and Bo Diddley.

Jim, thank you again for being a true pioneer, a brilliant writer, and contributing so much to the success and worldwide popularity of the guitar.

Best regards,

Fred W. Gretsch
4th Generation
President

THE GRETSCH COMPANY
GREAT MUSIC SINCE 1883
PO BOX 2468•SAVANNAH•GA•31402
TEL(912)748-7070•FAX(912)748-6005
WWW.GRETSCH.COM

Early Gretsch ad

1979 Gretsch ad

Norman's Rare Guitars

Norman Harris, Owner

My friend Robb Lawrence was writing his Rare Bird column, which spotlighted different vintage guitars for *Guitar Player*, and I had purchased copies pretty early on. I thought it would be a good vehicle to help get the word out about Norman's Rare Guitars.

At the time, I was playing in a band called the Angel City Rhythm Band with Rick Vito, who was our guitarist. Rick had written other stories for other magazines and told me he wanted to submit a piece about the store to *Guitar Player*. The article he wrote was in the December 1976 issue with Robbie Robertson on the cover, and I believe this was the first story about a vintage guitar store that was ever published in any magazine.

1978 Norman's Rare Guitars ad

OPEN 7 DAYS

HAVE YOU BEEN LOOKING FOR...
A 1959 Les Paul, a 1955 Stratocaster, a 1958 L-5, Martin D and 000 herringbones?

Occasionally, you may see one or two of these fine pieces, but there is a place where you can find all these and more.

The place is Norm's Rare Guitars, in Reseda, California. We have, *in stock*, the largest selection of rare guitars, basses, and mandolins in the world. Old instruments are not a hobby at Norm's, it is our only business. Norm's has a buying network that extends throughout the country, and new finds are happening constantly. If you have a guitar you think is of value, call Norm or Scott at (213) 344-8300. Tell us the model, year, and asking price. We can arrange shipping from just about anywhere in the country.

So if you have an old guitar you'd like to sell, or if you would like to buy that one of a kind piece, call Norm's. Expert repairs also.

6753 Tampa Ave.
Reseda, CA 91335

We had just supplied all the instruments for the movie *The Last Waltz*, which was about the Band's final concert. Appearing in the movie were Bob Dylan, Van Morrison, Joni Mitchell, Muddy Waters, Eric Clapton, and many others.

In the Robbie Robertson article he talked about the store and the numerous instruments he acquired from Norman's Rare Guitars. Following this edition of *Guitar Player* we began advertising in the magazine, and we feel this put us on the map. We had numerous different ads throughout the years. One was "Buy Your Dream Guitar," and there were many variations on this theme. We felt the magazine really brought our store to the attention of the guitar-playing public.

I always enjoyed reading the articles about the musicians and their choices of gear, as well as the Rare Bird column. *Guitar Player* was the first magazine to really let people know about the quality and construction of older instruments. I feel it was a catalyst in exposing people to differ-

1980 Norman's
Rare Guitars ad

ent models and the exceptional build and woods of the old guitars.

I still have an almost complete set of back issues of *Guitar Player* that I like to thumb through and reread from time to time.

PRS Guitars

Paul Reed Smith, Founder and Owner

Are you kidding me?! People waited with anticipation for *Guitar Player*. It was before *Guitar for the Practicing Musician*, it was before *Guitar World*, it was before all that. . . . *Guitar Player* magazine was the only magazine available for guitarists. There wasn't any Internet. *Guitar Player* was our only solid source of good information about what guitarists thought. I read every word of *Guitar Player*. We all did! We read it cover to cover! The early *Guitar Player* had a crack group of people that Jim Crockett put together, including Tom Wheeler, Jas Obrecht, Tom Mulhern, and others. I'm not saying anything bad about *Guitar Player*'s current team. It was just that at that time, it was the bible, because that's where we got our information.

The writing quality was great and the content had impact in the marketplace. For example, there was an interview where Carlos Santana was quoted saying, "I've got these amps that really boogie," while in another issue, John McLaughlin told readers what gear he was using, and those companies started getting orders! That was it! It was the real deal! It wasn't even a question. It was not a crowded market. It was a very limited market with highly skilled people reporting. *Guitar Player* invented a new way of distributing information about music, and we read every word of it!

Paul Reed Smith, from March '82 issue (John W. Wright)

When *GP* did the first article in 1982 about my shop, it carried great

March '82 (Cover photo courtesy Frank Driggs Collection)

weight, although that was not immediately apparent. The article was in the 1982 Charlie Christian issue. I got five pages in the magazine, with three of my guitars in the corner, but we didn't get any orders. The phone didn't ring and it didn't make any sense! But later, when I went on the road in 1985 to get orders for the company, it was that article that helped me secure my appointments. The music stores had read and remembered the article.

For PRS Guitars, there was no question that we would advertise in *Guitar Player*. You didn't have a guitar company unless you advertised in *Guitar Player*, and later, in *Guitar World* and a few other magazines. The first ad we ran in *Guitar Player* (1985) did really well. The ads had impact. Now, how much it cost per issue took my breath away! But I paid it, and I paid for full-page ads because I didn't want to look small. Quarter-page ads, although functional, were going to say we're a quarter-page company, and that is not how we wanted to be thought of.

It's a crowded market now, and everyone has a website. Back then, if you put out an ad featuring black guitars, you'd get orders for black guitars. Now, folks see an ad for a particular model and head to the Internet to research the product. I don't miss those days, but they were powerful days.

PRS Guitars ad

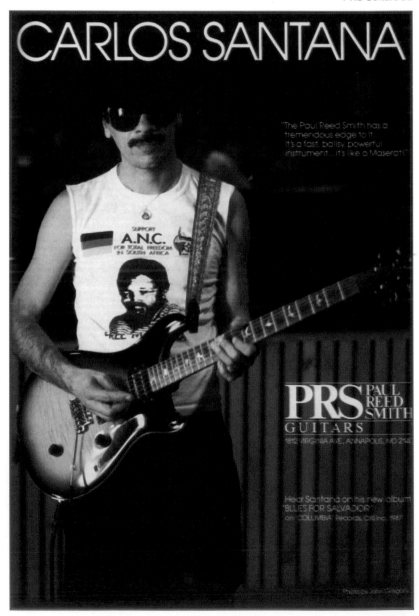

In Conclusion...

What a terrific ride it was. Something we all have never forgotten.

It was an exciting time in so many ways, with us having to create systems and methods for things that didn't exist yet—computers, for instance. There weren't all the programs that we have today, and Lord knows the hardware is ever so more advanced; in our case, we went from the Basic 4 in 1981, moved on to Kaypros and then a massive Sperry Univac system that never worked right for publishing (I remember asking the technician the difference between a byte and a bit—and he had no idea). Whatever system we ultimately settled with, we first took on subscriber fulfillment, then music stores, then accounting, then editorial uses. And ran out of memory for our PR list of 150 names.

I digress.

We all hope you enjoyed this colorful little history. We certainly did.

Bud and I decided, back in '85, it was time to move on in our lives. I spent the next five years meeting with magazine companies here and in Europe, searching for the right type of company for our baby, settling on Dalton Communications in New York. Peter Betuel was the founder of this publishing firm that produced *Penny Stock Journal* for small-level investors. The key, though, was that Peter was a guitar player and longtime reader of *GP*. Not only that, he assured me everything would remain as it was—people, products, systems. About a year later, maybe less, Peter sold GPI to a San Francisco publishing company that was very successful, but in the business trade magazine field. Not a musician in sight. They wanted to get into the "consumer" field and thought buying a successful music mag was the way to do it. Oops. They began by chopping the higher salaries and folding everything but *Guitar Player*—in retrospect, dreadfully shortsighted. For them and for GPI.

After losing respect and many millions, they bailed out, and GPI's magazines were acquired by NewBay Media with home offices in New York City. *Guitar Player* was their seventh music publication.

The staffers are as serious about the guitar as we were, though

What a terrific ride it was.

the office and business environment are substantially different. But, then, so are the times.

Jim Crockett

1976 *GP* staff photo—front row: Jim Crockett, Patricia Brody, Jon Sievert, Steve Caraway, Claudia Bennett; second row: Carolyn Antolin, Jerry Martin, Susan Owen, Frank Fletcher, Marcia Hartman, Carole Hagner, Chris Ledgerwood; back row: Linda Evola, Don Menn, Bill Koshelnyk, Dorothy Douglas, Dan Forte, Susan Johnson (Jon Sievert)

Acknowledgments

Thanks a lot . . .

. . . to my daughter Dara, who cajoled, pleaded, begged, and then virtually threatened if I didn't sit myself down and get to organizing and contacting folks to re-create what many have called the "glory years" of *Guitar Player* magazine. Without Dara's help and diligence, this book would have just been a paragraph somewhere.

. . . to John Cerullo, who is not only a longtime *GP* reader and guitar lover, but also the group publisher for the Hal Leonard Performing Arts Publishing Group. When I cautiously approached John about this book idea, he didn't break out in hysterical laughter, but enthusiastically embraced it and encouraged it at every step along the way.

. . . to designer Damien Castaneda, whose visual creativity and endless problem-solving has made the book a delight to see and a pleasure to read.

. . . to our staff photographer and assistant editor for so many years, Jon Sievert, for maintaining our photo archives and searching day after day for just the right shots.

. . . to my wife Roberta/Bobby and my adult children Chenoa, Dara, Cordell, Kessel, Adelaide, and Devon, who furnish constant inspiration.

. . . and to all those members of the early *Guitar Player* magazine family who I simply overlooked or was not able to locate, but who were just as important to our success as the rest of us. At *Guitar Player*, and GPI in general, no one was more important than anyone else. There was no hierarchy. We all contributed as best we could toward making the company an enjoyable place to work, producing publications we could respect. From 1967 through 1988 we had more than 350 employees, and obviously not everyone could be referenced for this history. We simply know we could not have done it without each of them, and I give them all my complete thanks.

Jim Crockett

I give them all my complete thanks.

Thank you . . .

First, let me thank my father for not only allowing me to persuade him to take on this project, and to provide his archives, memories, and contacts, but for also believing in me, as a collaborator in putting this legacy together. I'm honored, and I love you.

Also, a huge thank-you to John Cerullo, our publisher, whose immediate enthusiasm for this project lit a fire that continues to burn brightly. And a special note of appreciation to our editor at Backbeat Books, Jessica Burr, and our copy editor, Polly Watson, who were tremendously hardworking and dedicated partners in helping us to polish the finished product.

Jon Sievert, Steven Rosen, and Jessica Anne Baron also deserve an extra special thank-you for giving so much time and support for this project above and beyond what would ever have been hoped for. They really made a difference.

Next, there was no way this could all have come together without the interest, commitment, and generosity of so many people who were equally as passionate as we were about seeing this book come to fruition. Aside from those individuals whose voices were heard in these pages, there were many more assisting behind the scenes to help us gather the stories and the images, to provide contact information for folks who were more difficult to find, and who just offered emotional support along the way. I'm so grateful to each and every one of you who not only helped to make this book possible, but who also made the process such a pleasure! I enjoyed meeting and working with all of you . . . thank you.

Here are just a few of those angels that I would like to personally acknowledge, but please know that it is not a complete list (that would take another volume!): Jeff Albright, Ina Behrend, Anita Boone, Clyde Clark, Chenoa Crockett, Susie Dougherty, Jasmin Dunlop Powell, Cash Edwards, Jordan Fritz, Stephanie Gonzalez, Glenn Gottlieb, Diane Hadley, Jason Henke, John Lappen, Vanessa Menkes, Heidi Meyer, Janine Morse, Jeanne Nooney, Omar Ojeda, Rodney O'Quinn, Pauline Powell, Judy Roberts, David Sholemson, Jennifer Troia, Jean Weston, and Mary Young.

Oh, and let me not forget the current guard at *Guitar Player*, who've also shown support and enthusiasm for this project and for the history of *GP*. Cheers and all the best to your team as you continue to shine a bright light on the music and musicians we all love!

Dara Crockett

Let me not forget the current guard at *Guitar Player*.

Index

OTHER GREAT TITLES FROM NEWBAY MEDIA

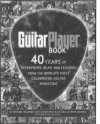